# Shortridge High School
## 1864–1981

*In Retrospect*

# Alma Mater

Words by
E. T. Forsyth

German Folk Tune
Arr. by Edythe Dale

SHS song "In the Land of Milk and Honey"

# Shortridge High School 1864–1981

## In Retrospect

"A Disciplined Mind and a
Cultivated Heart are
Elements of Power"
—CALEB MILLS

Laura Sheerin Gaus

Indianapolis: Indiana Historical Society 1985

© 1985 Indiana Historical Society

*Library of Congress Cataloging in Publication Data*

Gaus, Laura Sheerin, 1919–
    Shortridge High School, 1864–1981, In Retrospect.

    Includes index.
    1. Shortridge High School—History,   I. Indiana
Historical Society.   II. Title.
LD7501.I4647G38   1985      373.772'52      85–21968
ISBN 0–87195–003–0

# Contents

# Preface

As soon as the project for a history of Shortridge High School was presented to me, I knew I would like to be the author. Over the years I have been involved with many schools—as a student, as a parent, and as a teacher. I have found much of value in all of them, but I have never seen another school that generated the kind of enthusiasm that was present at Shortridge, both when I was a student there and when my children were. I have always wanted to find out how that Shortridge mystique was established. This was my chance.

One hundred and seventeen years is a lot of history. I do not pretend to have covered it all. I have tried to create a narrative that would convey the flavor of the school and underscore its commitment to excellence. Limiting the cast of characters has proved to be an absolute necessity. Sketches of distinguished Shortridge alumni would make a book in itself. So would a description of the school's outstanding teachers or an account of all its varied activities. Many of the people and events that have been left out of this history were just as important to Shortridge life as some that have been included. I could not manage to fit them all into a single volume, but I have done my best, and I finish the project even more impressed with the importance of the subject than when I began.

The endeavors of many people have made this history possible, but first and foremost is Frank Snyder, class of 1932, who conceived the idea of the Shortridge History Project.

As a result of his efforts in collecting memorabilia for his class's fiftieth reunion, which came just one year after the school had closed, Frank developed a strong conviction that Shortridge deserved a full-length history. He was able to convey his enthusiasm to the Indiana Historical Society and the Lilly Endowment, both of whom provided generous support for this project. He also enlisted the help of many alumni and teachers, who responded to his idea with enthusiasm and agreed to serve as part of the organization to support the history.

Major credit also goes to Elizabeth S. Creveling, Harriet C. Cassell, Jean M. Jackson, Carol E. Smith, and all the members of the Advisory Committee on Relocation of Historic Shortridge, who saw to the preservation and proper distribution of Shortridge memorabilia after the school was closed in 1981. Because of their efforts, copies of all the Shortridge *Annuals* going back to 1894 and almost all the Shortridge *Daily Echos* dating back to 1898 reached the Indiana Historical Society and have been available for research. Other Shortridge artifacts, including pictures from the Roda Selleck Gallery, are at the Indiana State Museum and the Indianapolis Museum of Art. The Hufford collection of books by Shortridge authors is at the Indiana State Library.

I wish to give particular thanks to Alex M. Clark, general chairman of the project, and members of the editorial committee: Robert J. Shultz, chairman, Jean Grubb, Gene McCormick, Dorothy Otto, Gayle Thornbrough, and Jean Whitcraft.

The staff of the Indiana Historical Society has been endlessly helpful. I would especially like to acknowledge the assistance of executive secretary Gayle Thornbrough, who retired in September, 1984, and her successor Peter T. Harstad; members of the Society's library staff, particularly Carolyn Autry, library assistant, and Timothy Peterson, head of the photographic services. Special thanks also to Paula Corpuz and Kent Calder, editors.

Finally, I wish to express my sincere gratitude to all those alumni who have taken time to talk with me or have written to me, recalling their Shortridge experiences. For the most part, they are identified throughout the text, as are most of my other sources of information.

Research by Ernestine Rose provided the data on the Underhill mansion in Chapter 2, and the Indianapolis Community Service Council supplied the population data in Chapter 13. Works by Emma Lou Thornbrough, professor emeritus of history at Butler University, and Stanley Warren, director of black studies at DePauw University, were the principal sources of information regarding school segregation for Chapter 8. Finally, a wealth of Shortridge material relating to the 1960s and 1970s was lent to me by Shortridge teacher and parent Dorothy Otto and by Shortridge parents Rachael Beck, Patricia Read, and Patricia Wood.

My thanks to all!

May, 1985                                          LAURA S. GAUS

# Shortridge High School
## 1864–1981

*In Retrospect*

# The Land of Milk and Honey

IN TERMS OF PUBLIC EDUCATION, Indianapolis before 1864 could more accurately be described as a wilderness than as a honeyed land. Although the Indiana Constitution of 1816 stated that "knowledge and learning generally diffused, through a community," are "essential to the preservation of a free Government," and called upon the General Assembly to pass laws "calculated to encourage . . . improvement of the arts, sciences, commerce, manufactures and natural history," it did not provide for funding and neither did the legislature. (The grant by Congress of the sixteenth section of each township in new states for school purposes did not provide much in funds, for land was cheap.)

From its establishment as the capital city in 1824 until 1853, Indianapolis had no free primary schools and no thought of a high school. The city's illiteracy rate was among the highest of cities in the free states.

The transformation into the Land of Milk and Honey came primarily as a result of the efforts of two remarkable men, each imbued with a strong sense of mission. They were Caleb Mills and Abram C. Shortridge.

Caleb Mills, born in 1806, grew up on a New Hampshire farm, was graduated from Dartmouth in 1828 and from Andover Theological Seminary in 1833. While still a student, he had traveled southern Indiana and Kentucky for a Sunday school agency and developed a lifelong objective, which was to establish common schools in the western country. During his last year at Andover, he read an article in the *Home Missionary* written by the Reverend James Thomson of Crawfordsville, Indiana, stating his intent to start a classical school for the education and training of teachers. Mills not only opened correspondence with the author, but immediately declared his purpose for coming west. "I hope

*Bass Photo*

Caleb Mills

to reach the Wabash country the last of October," he wrote. "Can you find me a good parish and a log house to dwell in when I arrive?" He went on to explain his reasons:

> My thoughts have been directed of late to the subject of common schools, and the best means of awakening a more lively interest in their establishment in the western country. Public sentiment must be changed in regard to free schools, prejudice must be overcome, and the public mind awakened to the importance of carrying the means of education to every door. Though it is the work of years, it must and can be done. The sooner we embark in this enterprise the better. It can only be effected by convincing the common people that the scheme we propose is practicable; that it is the best and most economical way of giving their children an education. Introductory to, and in connection with these efforts, we must furnish them with teachers of a higher order of intellectual culture than the present race of pedagogues.

The correspondence continued and resulted, not in an appointment to "a good parish," but in the appointment of Caleb Mills to the English Department of the new institution at Crawfordsville, the Wabash Manual Labor College and Teachers Seminary. He was married on the 13th of September, 1833, to Miss Sarah Marshall of Vermont, and shortly thereafter they started for Indiana, accompanied by four other teachers. Upon his arrival in December, Mills organized the first classes in the school, and he also served as principal. The school became Wabash College, and he stayed on as a professor until his death forty-six years later. Still, he never lost sight of his original objective: the establishment and maintenance of free schools to promote popular education in Indiana.

In addition to his duties as a teacher in Crawfordsville, Mills traveled the state as a preacher and Sunday-school agent. This gave him many opportunities to observe the wretched state of education and the degree of official apathy in regard to it, which for many years he found impossible to affect. Finally, in 1846, after previous attempts to arouse the governor and the General Assembly had failed, he went public in a dramatic way. He wrote the first of six messages addressed to "Gentlemen of the Senate and House of Representatives" and signed "One of the People." This message, which filled five wide columns of the December 8, 1846, *Indianapolis Indiana State Journal*, appeared on the desk of every legislator on opening day of the session, December 7, 1846, marked prominently "Read and Discuss." The tone of the message was more of sorrow than of anger, but "One of the People" was not going to be ignored.

Mills began by alluding to Governor James Whitcomb, "who will in his annual message shed the light of executive wisdom upon the path of your legislative duties," and then said in part:

> I have examined the proceedings of the Legislature for the last twelve years in the earnest expectation of seeing the subject of Education discussed and disposed of in some good degree as it deserves at the hands of the appointed guardians of the commonwealth. . . . And I am not alone in my disappointment, for I often hear my fellow-citizens expressing their deep regret at the inefficient character of our schools and the wretched condition of our county seminaries. . . . Only one in three of the children of school age attends any school. . . . We have *borrowed* millions for physical improvements of our state, but we have not *raised* a dollar by ad valorem taxation to cultivate the minds of our children.

So effective was the message that eight days after it appeared Governor Whitcomb, for the first time, included the subject of education in his annual address to the legislature. He spoke in favor of free public schools.

A second address from "One of the People" followed immediately. This one contained specific recommendations for legislation, and it was debated with some heat. After all, it involved taxes. Opponents not only said that taxes should never be levied except for building roads and supporting the government, but that "schooling led to extravagance and folly, law and ruin." According to their argument, "A man could keep store, chop wood, physic, plow, plead, and preach without an education and what more was needed?" The legislature sidestepped the problem by providing for a statewide referendum on the question of tax-supported schools. This vote took place in the fall of 1848, and Indiana voters endorsed free schools by a majority of fifty-five percent.

Indianapolis had already held its own referendum under its charter of 1847, and the urban vote in favor of free schools was an overwhelming ninety-three percent. Each of the seven wards of the city was provided with a school as promptly as possible, but building expenses consumed all the local tax levy, and tuition had to be charged.

Meanwhile, "One of the People" sent messages three and four to the 1848–49 legislature, bombarding it with increasingly specific proposals for school legislation, including a statewide tax. No action was taken. The 1848–49 session ended with a call for a constitutional convention, which was approved by the voters, and when framers of the new constitution met in October, 1851, they were greeted by message number five. In addition, all the leading Indiana newspapers printed dozens of letters to the editor supporting public education. Most of these were probably written by Caleb Mills. He got his constitutional provision for the establishment of free schools without unnecessary delay. He then needed only to write his sixth and final message to the legislature of 1852, calling for implementation of the constitutional requirement. That legislature did provide some tuition money. It also gave the townships power to tax themselves to maintain schools after the state funds were exhausted.

Soon after that the identity of "One of the People" was revealed, and, as a result, Caleb Mills was elected the first superintendent of public instruction for the state of Indiana. He took a leave of absence from Wabash and gave full time to his dearly loved common schools from November, 1854, until February, 1857. He visited every county, promoting the construction of well-furnished and well-ventilated schoolhouses (the question of ventilation came up often in relation to nineteenth-century schools). He encouraged better education of teachers, adequate courses of instruction for the students, and graded schools wherever possible. He frequently expressed his firm belief that "a disciplined mind and a cultivated heart are elements of power."

Caleb Mills labored mightily for public education in Indiana. His biographer says that a school, or at least a hall, should have been named for him in every county in the state. A hall was named for him in Indianapolis with his statement of educational philosophy inscribed above the proscenium arch. As a result, thousands upon thousands of students have contemplated the power of "a disciplined mind and a cultivated heart" in a high school named for another man who labored mightily for public education.

. . . . .

Abram C. Shortridge was born in 1833, the year that Caleb Mills came to Indiana. He lived and worked on his family's farm in Henry County, Indiana, until he was eighteen, and he managed to attend a

*Purdue University*

Abram C. Shortridge

country school for an average of about three months a year for six years. His only personal property was a horse which he had raised. He valued the horse, but he did not want to spend his life as a farmer. He wanted to learn, and he wanted to teach. So, when he turned eighteen, he sold his horse and used the money to go to what he considered to be a real school. The proceeds from the sale of the horse were enough to pay for a five-month term at the Fairview Academy in Rush County. He later described the experience:

> At the head of this school was one of the clearest headed and best instructors that it has ever been my pleasure to recite to. My first lessons assigned me were found immediately after the preface in *Ray's Arithmetic*, *Well's Grammar*, *Olney's Geography* and *McGuffey's Fifth Reader*. At the close of a five-months' term, in addition to the above-named studies, I had partially mastered elementary books in physiology and natural philosophy and a few pages in the first lessons in algebra. In April, following this term of school, I was engaged to teach school for the first time.

Shortridge served as an assistant in a school in Dublin, Indiana, for three months, at the princely salary of $10 per month. After that he got a teaching job in his hometown of Milton. He taught there for three years and saved enough money to pay for a few months study at Greenmount College near Richmond. Just as his money ran out, he was asked to teach for a couple of weeks at Whitewater College in Centerville. He said of this:

> This service was to last but a few days. And I was to take the place of the regular instructor of mathematics who was ill with an attack of typhoid fever. The regular instructor, however, while I suppose he finally recovered, never appeared to take his place and I never heard of him afterward. . . . I remained at the institution for six years and it was here that I made most rapid progress in my studies. I could select from a long list of subjects taught in the schools and studies I desired to pursue and in hundreds of instances between 9 and 12 o'clock at night I mastered the subjects I was to teach the following day.

At the end of six years, when Shortridge had learned enough to teach every subject the school had to offer, he was asked by his old teacher from Fairview Academy, Dr. Allen R. Benton, to come to Indianapolis. This "clearest headed and best instructor" was now president of Northwest Christian (later Butler) University, and he wanted Shortridge as principal of its preparatory department. Shortridge came. He

served two years in the principalship and was then elected superintendent of schools for Indianapolis.

The time was the summer of 1863 and Abram Shortridge was thirty
years old. He was also a married man and a father. He had married
Sarah Evans at New Lisbon in 1858, and they had two small sons,
Walter and Willard.

.   .   .   .   .

The school system Shortridge took charge of had had a difficult
ten-year history. In April, 1853, the first free public schools in Indianapolis opened for a two-month session under a code of rules drawn up
by Indianapolis lawyer and banker Calvin Fletcher. There were fourteen teachers for an average attendance of seven hundred pupils. By
1857, there were thirty-five teachers, a nine-month school year, and an
average attendance of eighteen hundred. This caused some difficulty as
the total seating capacity of the schools was 1,210. During this period a
high school was organized. It opened in 1853 and closed in 1858, but it
did not graduate anyone.

Progress in public education in Indiana came to an abrupt halt in
1858, when the state Supreme Court declared the local school tax unconstitutional. State funds were only sufficient to keep the Indianapolis
grade schools open for one free quarter, and in 1859 they closed altogether. No attempt was made to reopen the high school, but in 1860–61
and 1861–62 grade schools were open for free terms of eighteen weeks
each and in 1862–63 for twenty-two weeks. Twenty-nine teachers were
employed that year, and 2,734 pupils enrolled, 82 pupils for each
teacher. Seven of those teachers had to teach in halls and cloakrooms
because there were only twenty-two classrooms.

.   .   .   .   .

Abram Shortridge had a great deal to do. Still, he was in a community that was filled with determination and optimism much like his
own. Indianapolis was now clearly the major city in the state. It had
become a railroad center. Business, which had previously been confined
to Washington Street, was spreading out all over the mile square:
wholesale houses, machine shops, retail stores, manufacturing. The war
years were boom years. The Indianapolis arsenal provided ammunition
for the Union army and employed seven hundred people. There was a
large prisoner-of-war camp, Camp Morton, located in the town, the
local hospital grew to meet wartime needs, and industries expanded.

The street railway system was begun. New buildings went up in all directions. So did prices and wages.

When Shortridge took charge of the Indianapolis schools, the city was prosperous and almost out of debt or, as he said, "we began to have a little money." It was September 1, 1863. The battle of Gettysburg had been won and the siege of Vicksburg had succeeded. Along with the rest of the Union, Indianapolis was looking forward to victory and to the postwar years. Its leading citizens were determined that those years should include a first-class system of free public education. The judge who had declared the school tax unconstitutional was no longer on the bench. The general belief was that nobody would dare to challenge school taxes again, and that if anyone did, he would lose. This proved entirely correct—there was no challenge for eighteen years, and when one did come it failed.

Shortridge had the enormous advantage of a hard-working, dedicated school board that had complete confidence in him. He also labored under an enormous disadvantage. Jacob P. Dunn in his *Greater Indianapolis* describes it this way:

> Superintendent Shortridge's first execution was in the line of grading the schools and organizing and drilling his teaching force. In this he was sadly handicapped by the fact that one week after he entered his office he was stricken with blindness, and weeks passed before he recovered partial sight. But he went right on with the work, and its effects were soon manifest in more efficient instruction.

Dunn exaggerated only slightly. Shortridge himself seldom alluded to his vision problems, but he did tell one interviewer that when he took office he was so nearly blind that he appeared to live in perpetual moonlight. He really did go right on with the work. This work included supervising the building of new schoolhouses, hiring and examining teachers and somehow providing for their improvement, devising a course of graded instruction, deciding on textbooks to be used, ruling on matters of discipline, and, dear to his heart, providing the city with a high school.

·  ·  ·  ·  ·

The school board minutes for the years when Shortridge was superintendent (1863–74) reflect both his own decisiveness and the extent of his support. They are full of statements that "Superintendent Shortridge recommended . . . the Board so ordered."

He went to Boston to look at schoolhouses and recommended that the John Hancock School be used as a model for the new schools to be constructed in Indianapolis. The board so ordered.

He recommended that, in view of the shortage of funds and the small salaries paid, female teachers be employed. The board agreed, and the male teachers were dropped, except for William A. Bell, who was soon to become principal of the high school.

He recommended a complete revision of the state system of school government to provide for more responsible administration and better funding. The board and other prominent citizens concurred. Austin Brown drew up the bill, and it was passed by the General Assembly without much difficulty.

Shortridge proposed a training school for teachers. He devised a plan whereby as many as twelve young women could be trained at one time with no extra expense to the school board. He proposed to put the sixth ward school under the supervision of two experienced teachers, one of whom, Miss Junnelle, was a normal school graduate, and to provide both practice teaching and class instruction for those in training. Under his plan, six were to teach in the morning under supervision. They would then take classes in the afternoon. The other six were to receive their instruction in the morning and to teach the children in the afternoon. The teachers-in-training would not be paid, but neither would they pay for their instruction. The board approved his plan.

Graduates of the Teachers Training School
Among those pictured is Charity Dye, second row, second from left.

He said that, in view of his constantly expanding duties, he needed somebody to take charge of the primary grades. This was the area of education in which he felt least competent. His suggestion was "to select a bright, strong young woman and send her to the Normal School at Oswego, New York with instructions to begin at the lowest grade and learn as much as she could." The board accepted the plan.

The young woman selected went to school in Oswego for three months at the expense of the city, and after she came back she first taught in the training school for teachers and then became supervisor of primary education in the Indianapolis schools, a post she held for over forty years. Her name was Nebraska Cropsey. She had a hall named after her, too: Cropsey Auditorium in the Indianapolis-Marion County Central Library.

In 1864 Shortridge proposed the organization of a high school for Indianapolis, but he reported to the board that it would take a year to bring even the most advanced pupils up to the level of high school work. Twenty-eight students, selected by examination, spent a year in preparation and then started actual high school work in the fall of 1865. They were taught by William A. Bell, principal, and one assistant, first in two rooms of a ward school and then in the old Second Presbyterian Church on the northwest corner of Market Street and the Circle. Five of them graduated in 1869. Their diplomas read "Ad Astra per Aspera"—to the stars through difficulties. One difficulty they had to go through was a twice-yearly examination by the school board. Their families and friends and interested members of the public were invited.

Shortridge believed in examination. William A. Bell examined all applicants for teaching positions, including those in the high school, as well as all prospective students for the training school. Shortridge himself examined individual schools and settled any disputes that arose. Nothing went to court. Grievances were presented to the superintendent or to the school board.

A boy in the sixth ward was discovered to have drawn dirty pictures in his geography book. He was suspended. A boy in the fourth ward struck his teacher and bloodied her nose. He was suspended, too, and only allowed back in school after apologizing to the teacher and to the whole school. In the fifth ward some boys vandalized a schoolhouse. They were turned over to the police.

A mother complained that her daughter was punished too severely. The matter was investigated, and the teacher was counseled to avoid punishing in anger. Another teacher complained that the children in her class refused to sweep the room. With the approval of the board, Shortridge told her that children could not be *required* to perform such ser-

Indianapolis High School on the Circle

vices. When a teacher was unable to obtain service pleasantly, she should perform the task herself.

When the superintendent found that the instruction in arithmetic and grammar in the intermediate grades was unsatisfactory, he ordered those teachers to be called together once a week for drill until they came up to standard.

. . . . .

Both Shortridge and his school board believed that education should not only be of as high a quality as possible, but that it should also be available to everybody. This concept had to be fought for over a period of years because the state of Indiana was strikingly inhospitable to Negroes. The Constitution of 1851 that provided for the common schools also provided that "no negro or mulatto shall come into, or settle in the State, after adoption of this Constitution."

Even after the end of the Civil War, Indiana school law provided that "school taxes shall not be levied and collected from negroes nor mulattos, nor shall their children be included in any enumeration required by this act, nor entitled to the benefits thereof." Black children could not attend a public school even by paying tuition, if one white parent objected. By 1866 there were more than sixteen hundred black inhabitants of Indianapolis, many of whom were trying to educate their children through private pay schools, as Thomas B. Elliott, president of the school board, reported in 1866:

> Without the generous sympathy of the public generally, with very moderate funds, with buildings unsuited to school purposes, with limited or no school apparatus, with uncomfortable school furniture, with insufficient textbooks, without classification, and with teachers unskilled in the art of imparting information.

The passage of the Fourteenth Amendment by Congress in 1866 encouraged Shortridge to lead a move for a change in the state law. Although the amendment did not become part of the supreme law of the land until 1868, when it had been ratified by a sufficient number of states, it did state clearly that:

> All persons born or naturalized in the United States and subject to the jurisdiction thereof, are citizens of the United States and of the State wherein they reside. No state shall . . . deny to any person within its jurisdiction the equal protection of the laws.

The effort to change the state law failed in 1867, and it failed again on the last night of the regular session of 1869, although Indiana was now in clear violation of the federal constitution. Shortridge remarked about this, "A truthful description of what took place on this particular night would not look well in print." Then in May, 1869, at a special session of the Indiana legislature, an act was passed providing for separate public schools for Negro children.

Shortridge threw himself into preparation. He had old buildings repaired. He rented additional rooms to provide space. He held meetings during the summer for the instruction of parents. He hired teachers. Shortridge was able to assemble what he described as "a strong teaching force in number about equally divided between the races." He said further, "Five years after they were first admitted to the schools there were in attendance at both day and night schools over 800 colored pupils."

In 1872 a committee of Negroes met with Shortridge and asked that Negro pupils be admitted to the high school. In spite of the fact that the law gave him no authority to do so, Shortridge agreed to admit one black student as a test. One member of the school board had grave doubts about this, but he expressed them to Shortridge privately. The board presented a united front to the public.

The student was Mary Ann Rann. Superintendent Shortridge took her to school on the first day, led her by the hand to the office of the principal, George P. Brown, and said, "Mr. Brown, here is a girl that wishes to enter the high school." There was no trouble of any kind, and Mary Ann graduated with a full diploma in 1876. The high school record book for that year shows a senior class of thirty-four pupils, only twenty of whom received diplomas. Ten were given certificates, and four students failed. Mary Ann's senior record was: Literature–89, Mental Philosophy–85, Latin–81, Trigonometry–86, Astronomy–82, Natural Philosophy–65, Chemistry–90, and Geology–75. Her overall average was 84, which placed her about in the middle of the group receiving diplomas.

The school act of 1877 clarified the matter of high school attendance by providing that when a child attending a Negro school showed that he was prepared to be placed in a higher grade than that afforded by the school, he was to be admitted to a white school. There was no high school for Negroes, and a sizable number of black students attended Indianapolis, later Shortridge, High School with almost no problems until the 1920s.

·   ·   ·   ·   ·

Shortridge was a man of extraordinary determination. He worked night and day for the schools of Indianapolis in spite of health and vision problems that would have disabled most men. By 1874 his difficulties had worsened, and his doctors warned him that it would probably be fatal for him to remain longer in the public schools. So, said Shortridge, "In conformity with their wishes and in response to the wishes of Governor Hendricks, I retired for a time upon the work of organizing the new school of agriculture, now Purdue University."

He was the second president of Purdue, succeeding Colonel Richard Owen, who served only a year and a half. The *Purdue Alumnus*, September, 1943, describes his tenure:

> It was left to President Shortridge to get the university actually under way. This he did with the first regular classes starting September 17, 1874 on a course of study he had largely planned . . . the general organization of the University today stands as a tribute to his ability in this field.

Shortridge himself said of this:

> The task was only partially complete, when, in view of complications not needed to be mentioned and, in view of my continued bad health, I was induced to give up, January 1876.

The same *Purdue Alumnus* article sheds additional light on the "complications":

> President Shortridge, a strong character, did not meet the fancy of John Purdue and there was more or less friction between them during the Shortridge reign, which ended abruptly on December 31, 1875 with his resignation.

This time he really did retire from education and went back to farming. He was not quite forty-three years old, and his life was only half over. He settled on a farm a mile and a half south of Irvington, an eastern suburb of Indianapolis, and was a justice of the peace for Warren Township, but for the last twenty years of his life he was totally blind. He was still determined, however, and managed to get around independently until 1906, when he attempted to take the interurban into town and evidently stepped in front of the car before it had stopped. One of his legs was badly injured and had to be amputated below the knee. After that he lived with his son, Walter, in Irvington until his death in 1919.

At the time of his accident, good wishes and offers of material assistance came from all directions. The Indianapolis schools held a benefit concert for him in Caleb Mills Hall. The *Indianapolis News* reported that the most enthusiastic support of all "came from the colored people of the city, especially in educational circles." The hospital reported that he was a cheerful patient, and he spoke graciously of his care there. However, as has been mentioned, he was a strong character, and he discharged himself saying, "This is a fine place for a sick man, but it isn't any place for a man who is trying to get well, and so I'm going home."

Abram C. Shortridge certainly had a difficult life. Still, he was able to see the educational system for which he had worked so hard grow both in size and in quality. He was honored during his lifetime by having the first Indianapolis high school named for him, and he had the enormous satisfaction of seeing that high school carried forward by administrators and teachers who shared his vision and dedication. This book is a story of that school.

William A. Bell

# CHAPTER 2

# Indianapolis High School

ALTHOUGH INDIANAPOLIS HIGH SCHOOL started in 1864 in two rooms of a grade school, with only a principal, one assistant, and twenty-eight students, none of whom were judged ready for high school work, it always had both aspirations to excellence and clear-cut academic standards. It was also directed by a strong school board and a principal who was only the first of a long line of exceptionably able educators.

William A. Bell, like Abram C. Shortridge, was born in 1833, grew up on a farm in Indiana, and had to struggle for his education. He managed a few months a year at a country school until he was eighteen. He was then judged ready to teach, and he did so for three winters. His first term was for sixty-five days at a dollar a day. When he was twenty-one, he entered Antioch College, which had just been opened by the distinguished American educator, Horace Mann, in Yellow Springs, Ohio. He spent seven years there, the first three in the preparatory division.

By the time he graduated in 1860, Bell was not only well educated, he was totally imbued with Horace Mann's enthusiasm for teaching. He went first to Mississippi to open a school of his own, but when the Civil War broke out he returned to Indiana. He was made principal of an Indianapolis ward school in 1863 and principal of the high school the following year.

Indianapolis High School not only started small, it faltered in its second year when Bell left to go to Richmond, Indiana, as superintendent of schools. Two principals came and went rapidly that year, at the end of which Bell was called back with an increase in salary. He was also given an additional assistant, Eliza Cannell, whom he later married. From then on the school grew rapidly. By the fall of 1868, Bell had five assistants, and Indianapolis High School had moved to the old Second Presbyterian Church on the northwest corner of Market Street and the Circle. The course of study included English composition, literature, algebra, geometry, Latin or German, and natural philosophy (science). These were referred to as "severe subjects." At first there were no others, and many more people attended high school than managed to graduate.

Bell immediately demonstrated his administrative ability. He was principal of the night school, which served the black adult population of the city, and examiner for the schools, as well as principal of the high school. He is described as an enormously busy man who never seemed to be in a hurry—a man who took time to listen and to think before he gave an answer. One of his colleagues described him as having "a rare hospitality of mind."

By the time he resigned from the principalship in 1871 to become editor of the *Indiana School Journal*, he had established high standards for Indianapolis High School, and he continued to support them. So did his most valued assistant, Eliza Cannell. A glimpse of her appears in a history of the Indianapolis Woman's Club:

> In the '70s, when "Hattie" Noble and "Libbie" Vinton were at Vassar College, its English department inquired, "who is it, at the Indianapolis High School, who 'prepares' so well in English?" That was Miss Eliza Cannell. Personally modest, dainty in frame, she graced this club in literature and ladyhood for many years. . . . [She also served twice as its president.]

Miss Cannell became Mrs. William A. Bell in 1871, immediately after her husband had resigned as principal. She continued to teach for another year before she, too, resigned and joined him as associate editor of the *Indiana School Journal*. The Bells made their home in Indianapolis, and after he resigned as principal, Bell served on the school board for twelve years, seven of them as president. Later in life he spent three years as president of Antioch College, but then returned to Indianapolis where he died in 1906.

The Bells always maintained a close relationship with Abram Shortridge. After his accident Mrs. Bell was made treasurer of the fund which had been raised for him, and she helped to care for him during the last years of his life.

·   ·   ·   ·   ·

Indianapolis schools benefited from continuity in high-quality leadership. Bell was succeeded as principal of the high school by another

George P. Brown

energetic, able educator, George P. Brown, who reached out coun-
trywide for the best available faculty for his high school. In the summer
of 1873, he sent a telegram to David Starr Jordan, a young scientist who
had just completed his studies at Harvard under famed scientist Louis
Agassiz, inviting him to come to Indianapolis to teach "natural philosophy" at the high school. Jordan accepted. He taught only one year at
Indianapolis High School before moving up to college teaching and a
remarkably distinguished career, but he left his mark on the school.

In the fall of 1874 the school board agreed to spend one hundred
dollars to acquire "Professor Jordan's collection of fishes" for the high
school's science department—its first such acquisition. Jordan was only
twenty-three years old, but his "collection of fishes" displayed both his
skill as a taxidermist and his ability to gather interesting and significant
specimens. The shark from that 1873 collection is still in excellent condition and still in Indianapolis in the possession of longtime Shortridge
science teacher Mildred Campbell.

Jordan's remarkable career began with his distinction as an ichthy-
ologist, already apparent when he was at Indianapolis High School. He
taught at Butler University for four years, and then went to Indiana
University, where he headed the Department of Natural Science before
becoming university president in 1885. In 1891 he left Indiana to be-

come the first president (1891–1913), then chancellor (1913–19) of Stanford University. He is credited with establishing Stanford as an educational institution of the highest rank. A major public figure, he was also a prolific writer, a noted speaker, and a crusader for peace. He died in 1931.

George P. Brown served as principal of the high school only from 1871 until 1874, when he succeeded Shortridge as superintendent of schools. He served in that capacity until 1879, and then became president of the State Normal School at Terre Haute. Brown was the author of several books: *Elements of English Grammar*, *The Story of Our English Grandfathers*, and *The King and His Wonderful Castle*, a children's book. He also spent twenty-three years as editor of *Public School Journal*, later called *Home and School Education*. The first three principals of the high school all wrote books or edited journals, and they all belonged to the Indianapolis Literary Club (male). Their wives belonged to the Indianapolis Woman's Club.

Brown was succeeded as principal by Junius B. Roberts, who served during difficult times (1874–81) in a school that was expanding rapidly and in an economy that was in trouble. After Roberts resigned, he did not, like his predecessors, go on to become a college president, but instead, after a few years, he returned to Indianapolis High School to become a much-loved professor of history. All these men were given the title of professor and, along with it, the respect of the community for their scholarship and for their service. Education was valued highly.

Indianapolis had not only able administrators and teachers, but some remarkably dedicated school board members as well. Clemens Vonnegut held the record, both for longevity and for variety of assignments. He served on the board for twenty-seven years, and during all that time he was a member of five committees: Finance and Auditing; Building and Grounds; Appointment of Teachers and Salaries; German, Music, and Drawing, of which he was chairman; and Heating, Ventilation, and Janitors.

Austin H. Brown was another board member who gave yeoman service. He was a member of four committees: Building and Grounds; Furniture and Supplies; Textbooks and Course of Instruction; and Appointment of Teachers and Salaries. George Merritt, Hugh Carey, and John Bingham served on three committees apiece. These were all working committees, and the board itself met twice a month, so the commitment of time and effort was prodigious.

Vonnegut was the voice of the German community, which was

extremely influential in early Indianapolis. In the spring of 1867, he and Shortridge were sent to Cincinnati to find German teachers. They came back with four, and from that time on until World War I German was taught, not only in the high school, but in any grammar school where as many as twenty-five parents requested it. One of the black schools requested it, and the request was honored.

German, music, and drawing were included in one school board committee because they reflected interests of the German community in general and of Clemens Vonnegut in particular. The principal musical organization in Indianapolis was the Maennerchor, of which Vonnegut was president. He wanted the youth of the community to enjoy singing, so in 1867 he promoted an entertainment benefit for the schools, proceeds of which went first to buy a piano for the high school and second to begin a teachers' reference and school library.

At first what music instruction was available came from volunteers and was not part of the curriculum. This was also true of drawing and physical education. There was not even a school board committee on physical fitness, but the minutes for November 15, 1880, record that a committee on hygiene from the State Medical Society had protested to the board that the high school students had no opportunity for exercise and only a few minutes to eat lunch, and that this situation was dangerous and unhealthy.

In response, the board shortened the high school day so that it ended at one o'clock instead of three. Also volunteers from the Turnverein, later the Athenaeum Turners, offered to provide optional physical fitness classes in the afternoon, and their offer was accepted.

Although physical education did not come until later, by 1875, along with the "severe subjects," the students were spending a period each day on morals, drawing, music, and elocution—not all at once—one period a week each for morals, drawing, and elocution, two for music. By that time it was also possible to lessen the academic severity by taking a business course, which did not include foreign language or literature, but did include commercial arithmetic, bookkeeping, mechanical drawing, and telegraphy.

The tone of the board minutes, while not always severe, reflected strictness and care. Not only was the average attendance recorded each month (ninety-two to ninety-five percent), but the time lost throughout the school system by tardiness was also reported. In December, 1878, for instance, it was 116 hours and 40 minutes. That year, the board even noted the occupations of all the parents of children in the Indianapolis schools:

| | | | |
|---|---|---|---|
| Agents | 572 | Manufacturers | 658 |
| Artists | 77 | Mechanics | 2,383 |
| Boarding House | | | |
| Keepers | 144 | Merchants | 1,316 |
| Butchers | 110 | Professionals | 632 |
| Clerks | 501 | Public Officers | 265 |
| Confectioners | 89 | Railroaders | 559 |
| Draymen and | | | |
| Teamsters | 289 | Saloon Keepers | 131 |
| Gardeners | 487 | Seamstresses | 278 |
| Laborers | 2,954 | Unclassified | 736 |

In the 1870s Indianapolis needed its strong school board members. The country was in the grip of a severe depression, which began in 1873, but did not cause panic in Indianapolis's education circles until 1876. That year all teachers took major cuts in salary, $400 down to $300 a year for some of them. There is no record of any protest.

The next suggestion for economy was submitted to the school board to dispense with foreign language instruction in the high school. The board compromised by making German or Latin optional subjects, no longer required for graduation, but available for those whose parents requested them. As the financial situation worsened, several board members suggested closing down the high school altogether. This decision was postponed. The record of the following school board session provides a response in the strong voice of Austin Brown, speaking for the High School Committee and the Committee on Textbooks and Course of Instruction.

The High School should be continued.

First—The High School is the "poor man's college." In it many fit themselves for teachers and for other employments requiring a more thorough education than the District Schools can give, who would not be able, because of their limited means, to obtain such an education if the High School were discontinued.

Second—The High School is a powerful incentive to pupils in the lower grades. From their first entrance into these they look forward to the time when they shall be declared fitted for admission to the High School and many are induced to complete the course in the District Schools who would, otherwise, leave school at an earlier period.

Third—The existence of a first class High School affords facilities for the more wealthy of our citizens to give their children an excellent education in the Public Schools, who would otherwise patronize private schools to secure that end. The establishment and encouragement of private schools would have a tendency to bring the public schools into disrepute by creating a public sentiment in the community that the latter are exclusively schools for the poor. Such a public sentiment would be greatly injurious to the cause of education and directly in conflict with the spirit of our State Constitution. . . . We believe that our school system should be so organized and maintained that no encouragement should be given to the false anti-Republican idea, that the better class of schools should be for the wealthy—This can be done by so conducting our public schools that they will be, in fact, the best that can be had.

Fourth—Pupils should be prepared in the Public Schools to pursue, intelligently and successfully, the different industries incident to our present civilization. In these there are two classes of laborers; one consisting of those who labor under the direction of others, and the other of those who direct the labor of the first class. These directors of labor require a greater knowledge of the sciences of mathematics and of other branches of learning than it is possible for them to receive in the Primary and Grammar Schools.

This being so, it is better that we should educate our own people to carry on successfully our various industries than to look to other states and countries for our skilled laborers and supervisors. . . .

After this argument was presented there was no further question of closing the high school for approximately a hundred years. While times got better, severe financial difficulties continued to plague the school board. Enrollment increased. By 1878 the high school had 502 students and 11 teachers. Suddenly, without any recorded discussion, the women teachers began to be paid as much as the men.

.    .    .    .    .

Indianapolis High School flourished during its first forty years in spite of continuously unsatisfactory housing. From its first home in the ward schoolhouse at Vermont and New Jersey streets, it moved the following year to the old Second Presbyterian Church on the Circle, which had once provided a pulpit for Henry Ward Beecher. From there it progressed, in 1871, to a larger building on the northeast corner of Michigan and Pennsylvania streets. This building had originally been the spacious home of the Robert Underhill family.

Underhill at one time was said to own more property than any other man in Indianapolis. He had established an iron foundry at Vermont and Pennsylvania streets where he manufactured steam engines, stoves, and plows. He also owned a flour mill. He purchased the ground for his mansion in 1834. When the house was completed, it had two large parlors, a large dining room, and an impressive center hall. It also had an ample kitchen with a large chimney and a great fireplace.

The upstairs had a number of spacious bedrooms. But Underhill was caught in the bank panic of 1855. He sold his home in 1858 to the Baptist church, which remodeled it for use as the Baptist Young Ladies Institute and subsequently enlarged it. The school flourished for a few years but could not compete with the Indianapolis public schools after they were reorganized, and so it closed its doors.

Indianapolis High School 1872–84

In 1871 the Board of School Commissioners bought the Institute and the land surrounding it for $41,000. They erected another building and remodeled the original house at an additional cost of $53,000. The new building housed the classrooms, and the old house provided offices for the Board of School Commissioners, Principal William A. Bell, Superintendent Abram C. Shortridge, and Assistant Principal of Elementary Education, Miss Nebraska Cropsey. It was also the first home of the Indianapolis Public Library, which was dedicated with great enthusiasm on the night of April 8, 1873. Governor Thomas A. Hendricks was the principal speaker. On the opening day five hundred people registered as library borrowers, and the shelves held more than twelve thousand volumes. The library occupied the double parlors and the dining room, with a reading room and work room upstairs.

Both the high school and the library outgrew their quarters with alarming speed. The library and the school board offices moved to the Sentinel Building on the Circle in 1875, releasing their space for high school classrooms. But enrollment was growing by seventy or eighty students every year, and the buildings could not accommodate them all. Moreover, they were in an increasingly bad state of disrepair. Willard W. Grant, the principal during the 1880s, was an able educator who greatly expanded the science offerings of the high school. He was also a very large man, weighing well over two hundred pounds. Every time he walked down the hall the building shook.

The school board was, as usual, pressed for funds and extremely reluctant to finance another high school building, especially as it was required to continue building grade schools. The grade school population was increasing by seven or eight hundred students a year.

Indianapolis was forbidden by state law from taxing more than twenty cents per one hundred dollars of property valuation for schools, although other communities in the state were allowed a higher rate. Tax revenue was increasing with the population increase, of course, but it was not enough to keep up with construction needs.

Financial stringency was reflected in the school board minutes. On July 21, 1882, the Committee on Building and Grounds reported that no money had been spent for repairs at the high school for the past six years. The committee hoped that the board would replace the old building with a new one, but admitted that "the state of the finances is not very flattering for such a move in the near future." The committee also reported that the building and fence were becoming unsightly. The board voted to spend two hundred dollars to paint the fences.

On January 5, 1883, the city's superintendent of schools recommended construction of a new high school building as "the present building is entirely unequal to the demand, either in capacity or suitableness for the work." On January 19, the board voted that no new buildings or additions be built due to the "financial embarrassment of the board." In August two architects were hired to ascertain the safety of the high school building. They determined that it was indeed unsafe and strongly recommended that it be replaced. In January, 1884, it was resolved "that it is the sense of this Board that there should be erected a High School Building on the present High School grounds (cost not to exceed $50,000) and a building on school 8 grounds of 8 rooms to accommodate the high grades of the district schools and the first and second years of the High School." School 8 was on Virginia Avenue, serving the south side of the city and the German community.

This plan was strongly debated. John P. Frenzel, treasurer of the school board, said funds were not available. President Austin Brown ordered a count of dollars in the treasury. A surplus of $61,545 was found. The board resolved and adopted "that a High School building be built for no more than $50,000 and a building on the south side for High School and grammar school purposes for $18,000." A minority report signed by John P. Frenzel, Joseph J. Bingham, and Robert L. Browning registered their continued opposition on the grounds that "several classes have graduated without undue detriment and accident" and that "the Board is going beyond its legal responsibilities in this, with doubtful and unlawful revenue expedients."

Nonetheless, in April of 1884 the high school building was condemned and torn down. Several teachers recalled years later that they returned from their spring vacation in 1884 to find an excavation beside a wall of the building and a door boarded up, bearing a sign reading, "This building unsafe. Pupils not allowed to enter. Teachers will bring out books of pupils and their own belongings." A new building was built on the site, and during construction classes were held in the Meridian Street Methodist Church at Meridian and New York streets, and in Roberts Park Methodist Church at Delaware and Vermont. The new school building, which opened in April, 1885, was described as "imposing and spacious," but it was inadequate almost from the beginning.

The board realized that they were going to have to provide a high school on the south side of town, but until they could manage this they used the new building on Virginia Avenue as a kind of annex to the high school. It was known as "High School #2" and provided instruction for only the first three years of the regular course, at the end of which the pupils would go up to High School #1 for their senior year. This arrangement lasted until Indianapolis Training High School opened in 1895.

In spite of all this, high school education prospered. The aspirations to excellence remained, and the school began to acquire some of the teachers and establish some of the institutions for which it became famous.

# A School of Many Virtues

A GROUP OF NEW TEACHERS came to Indianapolis High School in the early 1880s. They were remarkably well educated, they devoted their lives to the school—several of them taught there for more than forty years—and they expanded the idea of excellence in high school education. Among them were the following: Charity Dye, English teacher and author; George Hufford, Greek and Latin teacher, and later principal; his wife, Lois Grosvenor Hufford, for many years head of the English Department; Angeline P. Carey, English teacher and author; Amelia Platter, teacher of mathematics; Eugene Mueller, teacher of German; Roda Selleck, head of the Art Department; and, perhaps most remarkable of all, Laura Donnan.

Miss Donnan, born in 1854, grew up in Indianapolis and lived almost her entire life at 229 North Capitol. She graduated from Indianapolis Normal School, taught in grade schools for a few years, and then went to the University of Michigan. She stayed there until she had earned both an A.B. and an M.A. degree and then returned to Indianapolis to begin her career at the high school, teaching, at various times, history, civil government, political economy, Latin, and geometry. Founder of the Senate, she was also the first sponsor of the *Echo* and, in fact, at one time or another, sponsor of nearly every school activity.

The Indianapolis High School Senate was Miss Donnan's invention. It lasted for nearly a hundred years and was copied by a number of other schools around the country. Students took names of United States senators and debated the issues of the day, following the strict parliamentary procedure that Miss Donnan insisted on. As senators graduated, their names became available to underclassmen who were eager to assume their roles. Membership was by permission of Miss Donnan. She also sponsored another important extracurricular activity,

Laura Donnan

the Oratorical Society. Whenever the students went any place as a group, Miss Donnan was there, chaperoning the girls. She was, along with her other interests, a feminist and a pioneer for woman's suffrage; she did not want the girls to miss out on anything. Still, the greatest testimonial to her came from a male student.

The boy was Claude G. Bowers, and his is the first student voice that comes to us across the years. He kept a journal from 1894 until 1898, when he graduated from Indianapolis High School. This journal, edited by Holman Hamilton and Gayle Thornbrough, was published in 1964 by the Indiana Historical Society under the title, *Indianapolis in the "Gay Nineties."* Bowers paints a picture of a high school life that was stimulating but not for him "severe." He and his friends were particularly interested in politics and public speaking and so, of course, Miss Donnan was his favorite teacher. In his autobiography he says of her:

> In one member of the faculty, Laura Donnan, I found one of the greatest women I have ever known, who had a decisive effect on my life. . . . Her specialty was civil government, and everyone but the

dullest emerged from her classroom with the keenest and most lasting understanding of the meaning and obligations of citizenship. She did more to make citizens, and to make them fundamentally American, with a reverence for American institutions and the American way of life, than anyone else I have ever known. . . .

She was vigorous and vivid in her teaching, and her voice, though ordinarily warm and pleasant, had at times a booming quality which made her somewhat formidable. . . . She was not only a teacher, she was a Personality.

Bowers speaks well of many of his other teachers, too. He refers to Junius B. Roberts, history teacher and former principal, as "the patron saint of the school," and later says, "I am sorry that in history I must part from 'that grand old man,' Professor Roberts." He mentions Charity Dye often—speaks of getting a letter from her, of visiting at her house, of meeting her on the street when "in her usually kind and enthusiastic manner she urged me to begin at once upon my graduating essay." In another place he says, "Miss Charity Dye, my English teacher, is a graduate of Harvard and the University of Chicago." Obvi-

Amelia Platter

Eugene Mueller

Junius B. Roberts

ously, he was proud of her. Charity Dye had actually taken courses at Hartford University, not Harvard, but she had acquired a Bachelor of Philosophy degree from the University of Chicago. She did it by a combination of correspondence and summer school courses, without ever taking time off from her teaching.

On September 8, 1895, the journal entry begins, "Hip, hurrah! School once more!" Claude Bowers was an eager sophomore. He and his friend, George Langsdale, a brother-in-law of Senator Albert Beveridge, pursued their interest in public speaking by going to listen to both preachers and politicians. They were entirely ecumenical. They particularly admired the rhetorical styles of Father Denis O'Donaghue of St. Patrick's Roman Catholic Church and of the Reverend Joseph A. Milburn of the Second Presbyterian Church. They were equally broadminded in politics. Bowers says of Indiana's then junior Republican senator:

> Beveridge can put grand concentrated thought into fiery, and flowery language thus appealing at once to the emotion and the intellect. Of all the orators of whom I know anything, he can cram the

most into least space. He couches it in short, sharp, and impressive sentences. His diction is always elegant. . . . He is the orator complete.

Then there was William Jennings Bryan and his Cross of Gold speech at the Democratic convention of 1896:

> His speech was gloriously grand and fairly set the convention on fire. He is a statesman, orator and a born leader. . . . He may be named for President. Would to heaven he was. I love him.

and again the next day:

> About 3 p.m. the break came and Wm. J. Bryan of Nebraska was nominated for President. His superb oration of yesterday was sublime. He reads like a cavalry charge. It inspires and moves and enthuses. I am perfectly happy.

Bowers and Langsdale did not just go to listen to orators; they read and studied them. The entry for November 1, 1895, reads, "all afternoon studying Adams (John Quincy). We practiced jumping, wrestling and boxing after our work." Frequently they studied Edmund Burke. They also argued with each other about the issues of the day at all hours of the day. They both delivered the morning *Sentinel*. The entry for July 31, 1896, reports, "This morning as Langsdale and I were out with our papers at about 4 A.M. we got into an earnest discussion of the money question—so exceeding warm did we wax, that we brought the neighbors to front windows, and one lady asked us if we were not ashamed of ourselves."

In addition to settling the problems of the world on street corners at four o'clock in the morning, Bowers managed to see and evaluate all the greatest actors of his day. They all came to the English's Opera House, located on the Circle, and, although he was a poor boy, he had enough from his earnings to make his way into the peanut gallery. He devotes pages to a description of Henry Irving and Ellen Terry in the *Merchant of Venice*. He says of Irving's Shylock:

> Our hearts are actually melted with pity for the avaricious wretch. We behold him without a friend in the world surrounded by sneering enemies, who threaten him with violence both physical and financial. For a moment he stands as if stunned. Then as the full import of his terrible situation dawns upon him, the effect is sickening. . . .

and of Portia:

> Ellen Terry! what shall I say of the stage's sweetest, grandest woman? . . . She is beautiful personally. . . . I shall never forget the

manner in which she gave that part pertaining to mercy. She holds out her hands in a pleading attitude, and seems to put her whole soul into the lines. . . . She is the noblest, sweetest and most brilliant woman I have ever seen.

Only a month later:

I saw the grandest actress that has ever lived, the sweetest, the greatest, the best—Sarah Bernhardt, the renowned Parisian, the "Divine Sarah," the "incomparable," the warm friend of Hugo, of Dumas, of Gladstone, and the beloved and adored of all true lovers of real art.

Later, he expressed comparable admiration for Helen Modjeska, Julia Marlowe, and Mrs. Leslie Carter.

There were also girls to be admired off the stage. Bowers was not a gentleman who preferred blondes. All the beautiful girls who dot the pages of his journal had dark hair and flashing eyes, and he was wonderfully relaxed about them.

I am just now captive to Mary Stubbs, who reminds me very much of Mary Vajen of two years ago. In feature and form she is absolutely perfect. She has a pale complexion with now and then a rosy glow. Her heavy jet black hair is silky. Her brows are clear cut. Her eyes are always beautiful, now dreamy, now calm and thoughtful and now brightening and dancing with laughter. . . . When she smiles she lights up the entire room. She seems to me now as Pearle Moody did when I was seven years old; as Ruby Cross did when I was fourteen; as Mary Sayles does still.

Bowers's closest friend among the high school girls and the one who continued a friend for life was Myla Jo Closser. Beginning in September, 1897, she appears frequently in the diary.

September 27:

This evening I met Myla Jo Closser who is even more brilliant and promising than Mary Sayles. Her sister is a great actress and Myla is an accomplished elocutionist. She is beautiful too—dark eyes, dark hair—with the stamp of southern Europe whence her family came. She is a charming conversationalist—eloquent, poetic, witty, humorous—and she acts her words. She will write for our paper—"The Comet"—expecting to enter literature.

From then on Myla Jo's name appears often. She did write for the *Comet*, which was the forerunner of the *Echo*, the high school's newspaper, and she did enter literature with short stories, poetry, and plays. She also saw to it that the previously masculine Reader's Club should include girls.

Bowers's comment:

> This evening met with the Reader's Club, which is now composed
> of several very beautiful and bright girls, who are not at all adverse to
> discussing very delicate bits of literature such as illegitimate children
> and so on. Myla Jo Closser simply would not let us escape from the
> subject, bringing it ever before us.

The Clossers lived in a big, tree-shaded house on Delaware Street,
and one entry after another reads, "We went to call on Myla Jo Closser.
. . ." Myla's opinions and literary preferences are noted: novelists,
Dickens and Meredith; poets, Keats and Lowell; and almost always her
appearance is described:

> This evening Jones and I went to Myla Jo Clossers and passed an
> evening of Bohemian abandon. Myla was dressed in black—the silk
> she had made especially for Richmond. Her hair was curled and I
> never saw her look more beautiful.

Not long after the evening of Bohemian abandon Bowers reported
that Jones attempted to kiss Myla and failed.

.  .  .  .  .

Claude Bowers's high school years were filled with working and
studying, arguing with friends, presiding over the Senate, trying to
start a magazine, going to the theater, and calling on girls, but his
principal ambition continued to be to make his mark as an orator.

Indianapolis High School still had no gym, no physical education,
and only a little, loosely organized athletic competition. It did, however, have its full share of competitive spirit. The principal outlet for
that was the State High School Oratorical Contest, and the principal
rival was Richmond. In 1898 Bowers won the right to represent his
school at this all important event. A whole trainload of students, four
hundred strong, took off from Indianapolis to support their contestant.
The girls were chaperoned by Miss Donnan; the boys were entirely on
their own. They went prepared to cheer. They had cheerleaders and
some cheers which they practiced on the way over. They came home
with a new yell which the school would use ever after.

When the enthusiastic students from Indianapolis arrived, they
were met at the station by an equally exuberant Richmond contingent
shouting:

> Give 'em the ax, the ax, the ax.
> Give 'em the ax, the ax, the ax.
> Give 'em the ax, give 'em the ax, give 'em the ax—
>   where?

> Right in the neck, the neck, the neck.
> Right in the neck, the neck, the neck.
> Right in the neck, right in the neck, right in the
>    neck—there!

Indianapolis responded with, "We've come to make the Quakers shake—we've come to make the Shakers quake," and "Indianapolis, rah, rah, rah." When they were all assembled in the auditorium packed with fifteen hundred students, Indianapolis burst forth with a tremendous "Injun, Injun, Injunap!" that fairly shook the building, but Richmond was always ready with the same reply, "Give 'em the ax. . . ."

The schools participating in the contest were Portland, Madison, Plainfield, Indianapolis, South Bend, and Richmond. All the screaming and cheering came in response to these rhetorical efforts: first, Sherlocke of Madison on "Cuban Independence," next Bowers of Indianapolis on "Hamilton, the Constructionist," then Miss Green of Plainfield on "Death, a Punishment for Crime," then Miss Hollingsworth of Richmond, whose speech was praised but not named, followed by Jellison of Portland and Locke of South Bend who spoke on "The Dangers of Vast Fortunes" and "The Worship of Mammon."

When the judges announced the victory of Claude Bowers of Indianapolis, the Indianapolis contingent leaped to their feet and began yelling, "We gave 'em the ax, the ax, the ax. . . ."

They continued yelling in the streets of Richmond and all the way home on the train. The 1898 *Annual* says, "Few are the persons along the road from Richmond to Indianapolis who did not know that I.H.S. was out on a holiday lark that day." When they got back to Indianapolis, they marched around the Circle and then up Pennsylvania to Michigan Street and around their high school, proclaiming to the whole city,

> We gave 'em the ax. . . .
> Right in the neck. . . .

From that time on this was the favorite Shortridge yell.

Claude Bowers not only left us a picture of the life of a high school boy in Indianapolis in the nineties and captured for Shortridge its most popular cheer, he is the strongest possible example of what Austin Brown meant when he said, "The high school is the poor man's college." Bowers was a poor boy. His father died when he was quite young, and his mother worked as a seamstress to keep the family going. He never went to college. There were no scholarships available in those days, although Bowers did have one opportunity. A prominent Indianapolis lawyer, Addison C. Harris, offered to send him to Princeton and pay all his expenses, but, since Harris was a staunch Republican and Bowers had decided that he was philosophically a Jeffersonian Democrat, the offer was conditioned on Bowers's promising not to enter politics until he was at least forty. Bowers refused.

In spite of that, with only his education at Indianapolis High School and his own self-education, much of which had been inspired by his high school teachers, he became a highly successful newspaperman, an eminent historian, a sought-after public speaker, and a distinguished diplomat. He wrote first for the *Indianapolis Sentinel*, then for the *Terre Haute Star* and the *Fort Wayne Journal-Gazette*, and finally for the *New York Evening World*, where his editorials attracted national attention. He authored more than a dozen historical works beginning with *The Irish Orators* and including *Jefferson and Hamilton*, which went through twenty-seven printings. Two other works, *The Tragic Era* and *Beveridge and the Progressive Era*, continue to be influential.

Bowers achieved his ambition to be an outstanding public speaker. He was known in his young manhood as "the Gatling-Gun Orator of the Wabash." He made the first political speech to go out to the whole country over the radio. It was the keynote address to the Democratic National Convention in 1928 when Al Smith was nominated for president.

Bowers served as ambassador to Spain from 1933 to 1939 and then as ambassador to Chile until 1953. After his "retirement," he continued to be extremely active as both a writer and a speaker until his death in 1958. He always gave major credit for his success to Shortridge High School.

# The Birth of the *Echo*

ONE STRIKING CHARACTERISTIC of Indianapolis High School almost from the beginning was the general interest in writing. All of the early principals and many of the teachers were published authors, and a considerable sprinkling of students were also anxious to break into print. Their first chance came under the leadership of Miss Charity Dye who sponsored the *Dawn*, a collection of the best works of her English II classes, published first in 1892 and for a number of years thereafter. The Indianapolis Public Library has a bound volume of these. The motto for the publication was "Earnest Work for the Day, Bright Hope for the Morrow," and it succeeded in being both earnest and hopeful. Although most of the material was literary in tone, the issue of December 25, 1892, contained two short political essays which cast an interesting light on the questions of the day as seen by the youth of Indianapolis.

### Why We Are Republicans

We think that the three great principles of the Republican party, Protection for American Industries, an Honest Dollar, and Reciprocity, are the grandest principles ever laid out. . . . Therefore we are Republicans.

What we call protection, Democrats style "war tariff"; but we think that if an article *can* be manufactured in this country, it should be protected as a thriving industry. . . . A heavy duty upon an import would prevent it from entering our ports and this would necessitate our manufacturing the same article here. This would give employment to just so many more men, and we could buy home goods instead of foreign. . . . The greatest evidence that protection benefits this country is the attitude of foreigners toward the Republican party, and especially of foreign newspapers.

What is meant by an honest dollar is a dollar worth one hundred cents everywhere. At present such is the case, but the Democratic party favors wild-cat currency. . . .

Reciprocity, according to Jas. G. Blaine, is, in substance, an agreement with countries which produce some useful article, which our country cannot possibly make, wherein we agree to admit this article free of duty, provided our exports are allowed to enter its ports free.

On these principles we base our belief that the Republican party is the party for the people, and although now in defeat, it will triumph again and bring with it prosperity.

Sam Adams
Morris Townley

### Why We Are Democrats

In reply we presume to say: Because the issues of our party are favorable to the masses; because we believe in that great principle, Tariff Reform,—tariff for revenue only; and because the Democracy opposes Protection, which tends to fill the coffers of the rich and empty those of the poor.

Then the question may arise: And how does protection do this? Why because (1st) it increases the prices of the necessities of life without correspondingly increasing the wages; (2nd) by fostering monopolies; (3rd) because it often decreases the wages. . . . The Carnegie Steel monopoly, the Standard Oil Co., and others, charging what they choose for their productions, are apt illustrations of the nature of protection. These men, with protection put down the wages despite all their promises to the contrary.

Now, with tariff reform, European manufacturers being put on the same footing with these monopolists, and competition being established, the said monopolists would be forced to lower their enormous prices.

These facts being evident, we are at a loss to conceive how any one, with the average human reasoning power and the good of the nation at heart, can conscientiously be an upholder of the Republican principles.

Alexander Holiday
Thomas McGee

One issue of the *Dawn* featured Sir Walter Scott, another Alfred Lord Tennyson, and another James Russell Lowell. One issue, published on April 19, 1893 (Patriots' Day), featured patriotic literature, particularly poetry. An issue devoted to Indiana writers appeared in two sections, one devoted to Maurice Thompson (*Alice of Old Vincennes*),

Charity Dye

Lew Wallace (*Ben Hur*), and Susan Wallace (*The Storied Sea*); the other, entirely to James Whitcomb Riley.

Riley was among a large group of authors who wrote encouraging testimonials to the young publishers of the *Dawn*, which were included in the May, 1893, issue. Some of the other authors were Edward Eggleston, Meredith Nicholson, Julia Ward Howe, and Oliver Wendell Holmes. The Autocrat of the Breakfast Table, then eighty-four, penned this note to the *Dawn* sponsor, Charity Dye:

My dear Madam,

It gives me great pleasure to send my best regards to you and your pupils and my best wishes for you all.

I have a great many letters to dictate, and some like this that I must write with my own hand. I cannot therefor say all that I should like to, if less occupied. Add as many kind expressions from the dictionary as this sheet will hold and I will be responsible for every one among them.

Very truly yours,

Oliver Wendell Holmes

Riley seems to have thought that the students were forming a James Whitcomb Riley Literary Club rather than writing a James Whitcomb

Riley issue of their literary magazine, for he wrote the following poem of appreciation:

### To "The J.W.R. Literary Club"

Well, it's enough to turn his head to have a feller's name
Swiped with a *Literary* Club—But *you're* the ones to blame!—
I call the World to witness that I never *egged* ye to it
By ever writing *Classic*-like—because I couldn't do it.
I never ran to "Hellicon," nor went about "Per-nassus,"
Nor ever tried to rack er ride around on old "P-*gass*us!"
When "Tuneful Nines" has cross'd my lines, the ink 'ud blot and blur it,
And pen 'ud jest putt back fer home, and take the short way fer it!
And so, as I'm a-sayin',—when you name your LITERARY
In honor o' this name o' mine, it's railly necessary—
Whiles I'm *A'thankin* you and all—to *warn* you, if you do it,
I'll haf to jine the thing myse'f 'fore I can live up to it!

More formal approbation came from the United States government:

Department of the Interior
BUREAU OF EDUCATION
*Washington, D.C.*

March 7, 1893

A stream of influence comes from the Indianapolis schools which must surely exert a wider and wider influence for the benefit of the whole country.

Very respectfully,

WILLIAM HARRIS
Commissioner

Beginning in 1894 the high school also published a yearbook, the first *Annual*, which included the best poems, short stories, and plays written by students in all classes in the school, as well as an account of the major events of each school year.

The first student newspaper appeared in September of 1896. A four-page paper entitled the *Silent Spectator*, it announced on the editorial page, "Published fortnightly in the interests of the Indianapolis High School, by S. W. Mansfield and L. B. Davis." Mansfield and Davis were both seniors, but they attracted to their enterprise juniors Paxton Hibben and Claude Bowers and sophomore Fletcher Wagner. The boys wrote the paper entirely themselves, with no faculty sponsorship, although they did have the permission of the principal, George Hufford. They managed to publish seven numbers, the last a fourteen-page Christmas edition. Then they were bankrupt. They turned their enterprise over to two students from Indianapolis Training High School, whose ownership was kept secret and who, rather mysteriously, managed to publish three more issues before they, too, ran out of funds.

Mansfield and Davis were graduated in June, 1897, but they left behind two assistants who were still determined to put out a school paper. Pax Hibben and Fletcher Wagner decided to try again, this time with a little more organization. In the fall of 1897 a board of twelve student directors was formed and a student business manager appointed for the publication of a weekly paper, the *Comet*. Hibben and Wagner planned to do much of the writing and all of the editing themselves. Then Wagner fell ill, and Hibben was sole editor during the fall months. He successfully edited twelve regular numbers and a sixteen-page Christmas edition.

Wagner had recovered sufficiently to help with this last project, and when it came out, Hibben resigned. The board of directors was disbanded, but Wagner and Charles Pettijohn obtained permission to continue the *Comet*. They published six weekly issues, an Easter number, and a June number. They had no faculty sponsor, but the principal, George Hufford, exercised general supervision and read proof for them.

George Hufford

At the end of that year Mr. Hufford decided that in view of the annoyance of his having to read proof and the disturbance caused by the weekly appearance of the *Comet*, it would be best to discontinue publication.

.   .   .   .   .

George Hufford was managing an extremely overcrowded school. Indianapolis Training High School had opened two years before, but it had failed to relieve the pressure on Indianapolis High School as expected. Indianapolis had more than doubled in population since it had built a new home for its first high school in 1884, and a much larger percentage of young people were continuing a high school education. Besides that, a compulsory school attendance law, passed in 1897, greatly increased the grade school population and put a strain on school funding.

High School No. 1, as it was frequently called, still had no gymnasium and no assembly hall of adequate size for the whole student body. The building was described as "utterly inadequate for its purpose." It was so crowded that the students had to be divided into two groups. They either attended school in the morning, 8:30 to 11:45, or the afternoon, 1:00 to 4:15. Extracurricular activities had to take place between the morning and afternoon sessions or at night. The teachers put in a very long day. So did the principal. It is understandable that he felt the need to hold down school activities.

Still, Mr. Hufford had underestimated the desire of the students to have a publication. After he discontinued the weekly *Comet*, in June, the former editor, Fletcher Wagner, appeared in his office in August begging permission to publish a *daily* paper the coming year, insisting that he and his two assistants could do it, that he was asking nothing from the school or the principal except permission. Perhaps Mr. Hufford was bemused by the progression from a fortnightly paper, produced with great effort and abandoned after seven issues, to a weekly paper that had managed to keep going, in spite of a change of editors, for twenty-one issues, to a daily paper, proposed as almost a one-man show and projected to run forever. At any rate, the young man was so persuasive that the principal agreed to let him try. The *Daily Echo* was born.

The first issue appeared on September 27, 1898. It was only one page, but the back of that page was solid with advertisements. The boys had secured at least some financial base. They also had a chance to describe some exciting events. On October 24, 1898, the *Echo* published an account of the visit to Indianapolis of President McKinley and the role that Indianapolis High School played in his reception:

When the President of the United States descended the State House steps, on his way to making his address to the citizens of Indianapolis, there fluttered from the lapel of his coat, two ribbons, blue and white. In his inner pocket was a copy of the daily ECHO.

After the second hour, the morning school formed in line and started out from the Michigan street entrance. Everyone was delighted at the prospect for a holiday and at the opportunity to see McKinley. The school started in a body until University Park was reached, and then the boys started off under Cohen's leadership to do some yelling. . . . Then it was rumored that the I.T.S. had arrived, and the two schools soon met in the north-west corner of the park. Jeers and "dares" were soon flying back and forth. . . .

Finally a half dozen H.S. boys led the rush, and started headlong for the "enemies." "Swift to the breach their comrades flew," and the whole mass rushed, whooping and yelling into the T.S. crowd.

Nobody knows who got the best of it. . . .

In order to string out the crowd Cohen started a run around the park and this ended at the corner of New York and Pennsylvania. . . .

When the President's carriage arrived the yelling began in earnest, and the President noticed the group of High School boys. The carriage halted just a moment, and in this interval Bernie Cohen sprang forward and handed the President a copy of the ECHO, tied in blue and white ribbons. The President accepted them and bowed his thanks. . . .

After the principal carriages had again passed, the boys broke through the lines and followed the President's carriage down Meridian street and around the Circle. At Pennsylvania, an officer attempted to drive them out, but he soon realized that we were an orderly and irresistible crowd, so he stepped aside, and we continued on our way. At the State House we heard the President's address from an excellent position, and at noon the I.H.S. crowd separated, some going to the depot, and others hastening (?) back to school.

Fletcher Wagner and his two assistants wrote the copy for the *Echo* every day and then rushed it to the printer. They picked up the papers the next morning and rushed them to school. They rushed all the time, but they did manage to keep the paper going for seven weeks, and it might have lasted a little longer if their parents had not finally said "no more." November 3, 1898, contains the farewell editorial:

The announcement that the ECHO will be discontinued, will probably be a surprise to many people. This is the twenty-ninth number, and tomorrow will be the thirtieth, and last, of the only High School daily ever published.

A month and a half is not a short existence. It is a long and creditable life for such a paper as this. The Echo has not failed; it merely stops. The Echo has been a grand success, if we do say it. We have proved that a daily paper is possible: and we have given you a suggestion of the things which such a paper can accomplish in this school. We have succeeded if, in the future, other classes with better organization, greater ability and more energy, will continue such a paper. Nobody can say that the Echo failed—and none can say that the Echo defrauded the public. We have completed half of the month, and any subscriber who has paid for the whole month may receive half of his money back by informing the room agent. If many should fail to ask for "their money back," and thereby leave a balance of profit the profit will be turned over to the Athletic Association, which we consider to be most in need of and most deserving of funds at present.

When we started this daily, we claimed that the boys would have time to manage it; but when room-agents complain that they have no time to distribute the papers, it seems that we were mistaken.

The editorial staff has had no difficulty in getting out the paper everyday: we have all gone without our breakfasts for thirty days, and we have eaten cold dinners at half past two. We have even kept off unsatisfactory notices, so far, and all of the staff are taking four subjects.

But the parents of the "editorial staff" object to late hours, and Mr. Hufford, also, has just about come to the conclusion that a daily is too big an undertaking.

We can't quite believe that yet, but knowledge is stronger than faith, and with one last flourish of the editorial pencil we bid our subscribers farewell.

This certainly did not prove to be the last flourish of Wagner's pencil. He was, for instance, editor of the 1899 *Annual*. Although he felt he had not had full support from the school, it turned out that both students and faculty hated to see the *Echo* stop. An all-school meeting was called and from that came the suggestions that what Indianapolis High School most needed were its own printing press and joint faculty and student management for the publication of its paper.

In spite of limited school funds and limited faculty time, a committee of three teachers was appointed to manage the press and the paper and to persuade the school board of the need for the project. They were: George Benton, chemistry teacher; Arthur J. Taylor, teacher of stenography and bookkeeping; and Miss Donnan. They appeared before the school board and came away with the promise of the money, perhaps because it was easier to provide funds for a printing press than

George W. Benton

Arthur J. Taylor

to build a gymnasium and an auditorium and additional classroom space, which everyone knew they needed.

In any case, on January 16, 1899, the *Daily Echo* reappeared, organized, as all Shortridgers remember it, with an editorial staff for each day of the week:

Monday

Fletcher B. Wagner

Assistants

Harvey Crossland, Paul Edwards

Tuesday

Alfred Ogle

Assistants

Fred Wallick, Edith Curtis

Wednesday

John Reagan

Assistants

Tillie Holle, Ruth Woodsmall

Thursday

Myla Jo Closser

Assistants

Jessie Gibson, Mary Pratt

Friday

H. Waite Colgan

Assistants

Theodore Schmidt, Fred Hirszch

It was a Monday, and Wagner flourished his editorial pencil thus:

This is the new ECHO. It is a reECHO. Strange to say it is larger than the original ECHO. Just twice as large. And it will grow. The press is here. The business end is established; the editorial staff is organized. The ECHO is now a school institution. When the present staff leave school other classes will take their places, simply as a matter of fact. . . .

Since the last ECHO was published, a great change has taken place. The students met and resolved to have a press. The faculty encouraged the plan, and showed how the scheme might be successfully carried out. The School Board was petitioned for money and on December 16 the High School was given two hundred and fifty dollars for the purpose. Then the faculty appointed a committee of three to manage the press and the paper.

Mr. Benton, who is well acquainted with the mysteries of the printer's art, and who was most active in securing the concession from

Old *Echo* press

the School Board, was put in charge of the office, and was commissioned to buy the press and outfit. Mr. Taylor was given charge of the financial end of the ECHO. In his energy and business ability both students and teachers have unlimited confidence. He has already reduced the financial management to a scientific basis, both in the subscription department, and in the advertisements. Finally, to control the editorial board, the faculty has appointed Miss Donnan. And about this choice, no comments need be made. When tenacity, enthusiasm and common sense are required to push any enterprise, everybody turns to Miss Donnan.

The press and the type and the ECHO are now, as we believe they should be, under the control of that calm, conservative body, the faculty. . . . But it still is, as it always has been, and always shall be, the students' paper. It is of the students, by the students, and for the students.

Fletcher Wagner left a tremendous legacy to his high school. The *Daily Echo* lasted for seventy-two years, but Wagner's own life was brief. A footnote in *Indianapolis in the "Gay Nineties"* reads:

An unusually gifted and promising young man, Wagner attended Leland Stanford University and then went to Harvard University. He was nominated for a Rhodes Scholarship, but did not receive it. Shortly thereafter he left his room in Cambridge and did not return and was never heard from thereafter.

· · · · ·

As noted earlier, the first *Annuals* are filled with literary and philosophical works and commentary, such as "Life Lessons as Taught by The Merchant of Venice" and "The High Heritage of Humanity," but they also show the development of other student interests and traditions. There were lots of school clubs. There was a Nature Club, which spent spring and fall Saturdays "in the dim mysterious tangle of Crows Nest, on the ferny banks of Big Eagle or along the sands of White River." In the winter its members met to discuss such widely recognized naturalists as John Burroughs and Henry David Thoreau, and the Indiana historian and nature writer George S. Cottman. The 1894 *Annual* reports that both Burroughs and Cottman wrote the club "pleasant encouraging letters."

Complementary to the Nature Club was the Agassiz Association, named for famous scientist, Louis Agassiz. This group was under the sponsorship of Mr. Benton, and it studied subjects chiefly relating to Indiana's physical features—its soil, mines, quarries, caves, and gas fields. It also created what is described as "a creditable exhibit," which was displayed at the Chicago World's Fair in 1893. The recording secretary for this group was Rousseau McClellan, who also appears as an editor of, and contributor to, the *Dawn*. As a sophomore in 1892 she wrote an appreciative piece about James Whitcomb Riley's most recent book, *Afterwhiles*.

Two organizations encouraged student interest in art. The Pen-and-Ink Club met once a week to study leading illustrators and illustrations, and the Sketching Club also met weekly, for art study and practice in

The Pen-and-Ink Club

technique. Still, the general student involvement with art was much greater than this.

Roda Selleck appeared on the faculty list as a drawing teacher, but she was much more. All by herself she was a Department of Fine Arts. Her classes worked with charcoal and watercolors. They also received a grounding in art history and art appreciation. Interest in art seems to have carried over into the whole student body, because, by 1895, the graduating seniors were putting on a money-raising event each year to make gifts to the school, and the gifts were nearly always art objects. For instance, in 1895, the February class put on Milton's *Masque of Comus* and applied the proceeds to the purchase of three pictures: "two etchings, one of Canterbury Cathedral and one of the Canterbury pilgrimage, and a rare copper-plate engraving of Chaucer imprinted in London in 1754."

The class of 1896 presented excerpts from Shakespeare's *Henry VIII* in English's Opera House with what they modestly described as "a superb cast." They made over one hundred and fifty dollars and presented their school with a larger-than-life-size statue of the Apollo Belvedere which was placed in the high school hall.

The class of 1897 staged a production of the *Merchant of Venice*, also in English's Opera House, which they described with the same diffidence shown by their predecessors as "the greatest and most successful show ever presented in Indianapolis."

The 1897 *Annual* has an article entitled "A Walk Through the Corridor," which says in part:

> I can not look upon these works of art without thinking how they came here. We owe these pleasures to the generosity and public spirit of pupils and teachers of our own school.
>
> There is the gift of the June class of '97, Millet's beautiful picture "The Shepherdess," that meets our eye immediately on entering. We next come upon a gift of the class of '96, a bust of Ralph Waldo Emerson. . . . The faces of Agassiz and Darwin are as yet slightly familiar to me, but their presence has awakened . . . a desire to become acquainted with the works of men so highly honored. The portrait of Hamilton and the busts of Franklin, Webster and Lincoln, gifts of the civil government classes, are also here. . . . The memory of their noble, active lives gives us a feeling of patriotism and pride, pride in our country that produced these great men, and pride in our high school that gives so much attention to their memory.

In spite of the presentation of the *Merchant of Venice* having been "the most successful show ever presented in Indianapolis," something must have gone wrong somewhere, because the next year's senior class was denied the privilege of putting on a senior play. They did, however, put on a Puritan Supper. The 1898 *Annual* reports:

> The idea of a Puritan Supper as a substitute for a class play, which had been forbidden by the faculty, was suggested by the generous sympathy of Miss Donnan, and was the method adopted by the Senior classes of '98 to raise a fund for the traditional purpose of presenting the school with a work of art to serve as a memento of their existence as a class, and as an emblem of appreciation for a life's education well founded, and a life's endeavor auspiciously begun.

The girls dressed in Puritan costumes and waited table and presided over the booths—including an ice-cream booth, a candy booth, a flower booth, and an art booth, and booths "where one could purchase anything from a sweater to a prayer book." Almost twelve hundred people came at some time during the evening, and the class took in over two hundred dollars. After that each succeeding class presented a money-raising entertainment in the school to provide their class gift. In 1899 it was a minstrel show; in 1900 a Festival of Hearts. Each project was more financially successful than its predecessor.

A somewhat different insight into the place of art in the high school is provided by an article in the *Echo*, March 8, 1900:

> Tuesday Miss Selleck gave the most interesting lecture of the year. It was the second of a series on vases. She told how Favrille glass is made, and showed two very valuable vases. One vase was an heirloom, made in France three hundred years ago. The other was from the ruins of Pompeii. At the end of the third hour a very valuable vase was broken.

The record is silent as to what was done about the broken vase, but it had evidently been lent by "Charlie Mayer's." The following week the *Echo* reported that the Charles Mayer & Company had again lent some vases to the art classes.

There was no teacher of music on the Indianapolis High School faculty in the 1890s, but there were, nonetheless, musical teachers and many students with musical interests. Chemistry teacher George Benton, one of the later champions of the *Echo*, organized a chorus. The 1894 *Annual* reports: "Good work was done at the weekly rehearsals, but owing to the scarcity of tenor voices, the compositions studied had to be selected with great care. There was a large attendance, and the drill was productive of fine results."

Arthur J. Taylor, teacher of stenography and bookkeeping and another of the *Echo*'s champions, organized and led an orchestra consisting of two first violins, two second violins, two cornets, one trombone, one bass, one flute, one clarinet, and a piano. Mrs. Hufford was yet another faculty member who encouraged musicians. She was the head of the English Department and taught literature, but she also presided over a session room in which she managed to include musical exercises. The 1894 *Annual* reports: "The musical numbers on these morning programs were . . . excellent. Early in the fall, four pupils from each division of the Senior Class, that is, from the February and June divisions, were elected; each of whom prepared a programme for, and presided at a series of such exercises. Mrs. Hufford's informal talks on such occasions were both profitable and of interest."

Then there was the Mandolin Club. First organized in 1896, it began with only four members, all male, but soon added three girls, one of whom was the accompanist. They operated without a director, but rehearsed every Wednesday and modestly reported that "the technique and ensemble are excellent and the precision and accuracy of the tempo are especially noticeable in the marches and waltzes."

The 1895 *Annual* also contained a tribute to music which said in part:

> It inspires, elevates, cheers, saddens and soothes the soul as no other one of the arts can. It gives voice to love, lends glory to every art, and performs its loftiest task as the "handmaiden of religion." So in our public schools to-day, music is one of the most important branches taught. This study seems to be such an aid to boys and girls that even in our high schools it is practiced. In our own I.H.S. for forty five minutes in each week (alas! how quickly they speed past) our school is flooded with a melody of music. This is to many of us a happy respite from the daily routine of our school work and an encouragement for more zeal in our studies. Then, too, in nearly all our session rooms are seen pianos, and many pleasant moments are spent in listening to the talent of outsiders, as well as to that of members of the school. . . .

The Mandolin Club was reorganized each year, with a varying membership which depended mostly on who was able to play what, but in the 1899 *Annual* a full page is devoted to its glories:

> The Mandolin Club of '99 has probably lived through a greater era of brilliant success than any of the clubs of former years. It was organized early last September by John Craig, its present leader, and made its first appearance before the school La Fayette day, when it was received amid showers of applause.
>
> The club intended at first to play only in the hall, but by urgent request, made a tour of most of the session rooms. It has since been in

constant demand, and has starred at church socials and many other entertainments.

It was decided that it would be best for the general welfare of the club if no girls were admitted, as several of the best performers have great aptitude for losing their places when in the presence of ladies.

The club is directed by Mr. Frank Z. Maffey, with whom it meets every Monday evening for rehearsal. After the rehearsal, it usually serenades Miss Donnan's night school and everybody else along the homeward route. The club never declines to play; it will perform at any place where a sufficient quantity of "eats" is guaranteed. . . .

The repertoire of the club is as varied as the eighteen different members. It plays everything from "A Hot Time" to Chopin's Funeral March. This last piece was learned as a serenade to the football team after its second brilliant victory (?) over the Training School. The club made its greatest hit at the oratorical contest, when it rendered a variation of the good old "Midway," known as "Kaya Kaya." This selection was pronounced by some of the musical members of the school to be the "real thing."

The school year will soon be over, and its close will mark the end of the '99 Mandolin Club. May its music echo forever within the High School walls, and be an inspiration to the clubs of future years.

The club at present consists of:

| | |
|---|---|
| John Craig, leader | First Mandolin |
| Walter Bond | ''        '' |
| Frank Kissell | ''        '' |
| Oatley Cockrun | ''        '' |
| Ralph Peck | ''        '' |
| William Sullivan | ''        '' |
| Fred Wallick | First Violin |
| Blaine Miller | ''        '' |
| Alexander Taggart | Second Mandolin |
| Noble Dean | ''        '' |
| Winfield Miller | ''        '' |
| Claude McGinnis | Guitar |
| Fred Day | '' |
| Charles Wilson | '' |
| Russell Sullivan | '' |
| Claire Peck | '' |
| William Craig | '' |
| Alfred Ogle | Banjo |

"Miss Donnan's night school," which the Mandolin Club customarily serenaded, had been formed in spite of the school board's decision that no funds could be spared to educate night school pupils beyond the grade school level. The board had been persuaded, however, to grant permission for interested high school teachers to use high school class-rooms for a night school, provided they served without pay. The January 31, 1899, *Echo* carried this article:

> Every Monday since the 5th of December night school has been held at this building. The purpose of this new departure is to open the High School course to busy people free of charge. There are now fifty-seven persons who have taken advantage of this opportunity, more than half of whom are colored, and who range from fifteen to fifty-three years of age. They are taught by Miss Van Dyke, Miss Rankin, Miss O'Hair, Mr. Talbert, Miss McClellan, Miss Marthens and Miss Donnan. . . . The list of subjects includes 9B Latin, Ovid, Penmanship, Arithmetic, Algebra, Geometry, Ancient History, Civil Government, 9B English, 11B English and Reading. As soon as a subject is completed, an examination is given, and all those who succeed in passing are given credit in the regular High School course. . . .

· · · · ·

Athletics were organized at least as informally as any of the other school activities. In January, 1894, for the first time, an athletic association was formed in Indianapolis High School. It had approximately the same status as the other clubs. The students' first decision was to have a field meet in the spring and to make it the "event of the year." In addition to the field meet, the 1894 *Annual* reported a cycling club, which was quite active, and a football team, which never quite got going. The *Annual* describes only one football game, which the high school lost to OMI (Ohio Military Institute?). (The article says that I.H.S. would probably have won if the opposing team had not had a professional coach who played with them.) The next year, however, football was a huge success. According to the 1895 *Annual*: "I.H.S. now claims the interscholastic championship of the State." They played six games and lost only one, but more than that, they scored a total of 116 points against their opponents and gave up only 4.

Whether because nobody cared to play against them the next year or because all the enthusiastic players had graduated, the high school was back down to only one football game in the fall of 1896. It was a triumph, however. I.H.S. played against Dean Brothers Pump Works and won thirty to nothing. That year baseball provided a longer season. The team played nine games and won six of them, including one against Butler.

Indianapolis High School 1893 football team

SHS 1899 football team

The year 1897–98 was a discouraging one for team sports: only three football games—one victory over Lebanon and two defeats by the Training High School, which had become the team to beat. (Indianapolis High School made a complaint that the Training School had someone on its team who was a professional athlete and did not actually attend school. This was just a complaint, however; no football league existed, so there were not any eligibility rules.) The baseball team had a victorious but extremely brief season. They defeated Franklin College in the only game they played.

The following year, the last of the nineteenth century, was the first year that faculty coaches were appointed for the athletic teams. John Lamay, a physics teacher, coached the football team. It played just three games and was able to hold its principal rival, the Training School, to a scoreless tie. According to the *Echo*:

> The High School came near scoring in the second half, and the ball was kept in T.S. territory most of the time, but time was called before a score was made.
>
> So our first game has turned out "nothing to nothing," but it is considered by both sides to be a victory for the High School. We played against a team which is ten or twenty pounds heavier, and we easily held down the star players (professional) of the South Side school.

The other two games were clearer victories. Indianapolis High School defeated Richmond 40–6 and Walnut Hills of Cincinnati 20–0.

John C. Trent, an algebra and geometry teacher, coached the baseball team to a winning season. The Field Day continued to be the athletic "event of the year" through 1899. It was held jointly with the Training High School from 1895 on. Both high schools entered the twentieth century ready for a full program of organized sports.

Both high schools also changed their names at the turn of the century. The school board had voted in 1897 to name its first high school after Abram C. Shortridge, the first superintendent of schools, but nobody paid any attention to this decision. In 1898 a plaque was affixed to the building declaring it to be Shortridge High School, but the school was still popularly called Indianapolis High School. It was not until the board decided in late 1899 that its second high school was henceforth to be known as Manual Training High School that both schools dropped Indianapolis from their names and became Shortridge and Manual to themselves and the whole community.

# Shortridge Is Her Title

I N THE FIRST FIVE YEARS of the twentieth century Shortridge High School experienced the supervision of an entirely new, reorganized school board, two changes of principal, the addition of new activities, and, finally, the move into a new building.

As the Indianapolis schools trebled and quadrupled in student population, the old school board and its committees became unwieldy. Gone were the unanimous resolutions that characterized the administrations of Superintendent Abram Shortridge and his successor, George Brown. All through the eighties and nineties, minority reports and majority reports were filed, and considerable wrangling took place among the eleven board members. Most of this disagreement was because they needed to do more things than their funding would provide for. But there were other problems about money.

Jacob Piatt Dunn in his *Greater Indianapolis* said:

> The school law of 1871 was effective for taking the schools out of ordinary party politics, but as the system developed, and the school funds became large, there grew up a system of public school politics, which was at bottom a contest of banks for the custody of the school funds, and which was as objectionable as party politics. It became a prominent feature of controversy in the nineties, and the *Sentinel* [Dunn was the editor of the *Sentinel*] made a protracted fight for the payment of all interest on the school funds into the school treasury as a remedy.

The matter of school law reform was brought before the Indianapolis Commercial Club in 1897 and a committee appointed to look into it. Both J. P. Frenzel and Austin H. Brown were members of the committee. It recommended no change. The *Indianapolis Sentinel*, however, continued to campaign for reform. Its editor, Jacob Piatt Dunn, believing that there would be no change in the school law so long as the influential longtime members were still on the school board, campaigned for their defeat and wrote a series of fiery editorials in June of 1898, declaring over and over that the principal issue in the upcoming school board election was "Frenzelism."

"Frenzelism" was not defined. By implication it was mixed up with high taxes and possible extravagance, which were clearly unjust accusations, since Frenzel had voted against every proposed major expenditure that came before the school board. In any case, "Frenzelism" was a ringing cry and the voters responded to it. The entire school board was voted out of office in June of 1898.

Another factor in school affairs was the organization, in 1897, of the Citizens' Education Society. This group reflected the strong community interest in the public schools. Its executive committee included, among others, Thomas C. Day, chairman, Hermann Lieber, Nebraska Cropsey, Benjamin Harrison, J. K. Lilly, Austin H. Brown, Gustav A. Schnull, and David K. Goss, superintendent of schools.

The society first campaigned for the compulsory attendance law, which was passed in 1897. This provided that parents of children between the ages of eight and fourteen must send them for at least twelve consecutive weeks to a public, private, or parochial school, and that children whose parents were unable to supply them with the necessary books and clothing should be supplied by the school trustees or commissioners. It also provided for the appointment of truant officers.

In 1899 the Citizens' Education Society investigated the local school law and called for amendment. Those appointed to prepare the bill were Thomas Day, Judge John E. Scott, Judge L. C. Walker, and William A. Bell. They were joined by representatives from both the Commercial Club and the Board of Trade.

Their bill, which became law on March 4, 1899, established a school board of five members elected by a general vote and not representing particular districts. The city controller was made auditor of the board, and the city treasurer its treasurer. The law now provided for a superintendent of schools, who had charge of all the school work proper, and a business director, who had control of all business and financial administration. It also provided for a librarian and a secretary.

Jacob P. Dunn, writing ten years later as an historian rather than as a crusading editor, described the changeover:

> Anyone ought to see the absurdity of carrying on such a business [involving millions of dollars] through a board of unsalaried trustees, with no business manager, who could give only their surplus time to

the business. The only wonder is that the school affairs were managed so well under the old system, for the business was large even then. . . . The explanation of it is the generous service given by some of the best business men of the city, several of whom served on the board for years. . . . As to Mr. Frenzel it is only just to say that notwithstanding the criticism in the heated period of the nineties . . . no one can fairly study the school conditions of the long period of his service from 1882 up, and not be impressed that his service was of very great value to the public in the financial management.

The truth is, that in the development of Indianapolis from a town to a city, and the development of public demand for the latest and best school accommodations, the school expenditures have grown out of proportion to mere population. . . . But teachers are getting fairer pay, and children are getting better school accommodations. It would be impossible to get competent teachers now for the salaries that were paid in 1871–72; and the public would revolt against a return to the kind of school houses in use then, just as they would against a return to the kind of streets we had then.

The new board took office January 1, 1900. Just like its predecessor, it was confronted with the fact that Shortridge High School was bulging—with more than eleven hundred students in a building designed for less than six hundred, that it had had to sacrifice its assembly hall for additional classroom space, and that it still had no gym. Manual had a larger building, which did include an auditorium and a gymnasium, but its enrollment was growing even faster than Shortridge's and space was becoming cramped there, too.

The board's first decision was to build a small annex to Shortridge. The building fund contained enough money to do this. The annex provided eight additional classrooms, but did not solve the space problem. It only gave the board additional time before they had to embark on a major building program. The pressure mounted steadily. Every *Annual* from 1894 on had contained an article lamenting the lack of facilities, particularly a gym, and hoping for better things in the coming year. Pressure was also coming from the long-suffering faculty.

This was the schedule of teachers and subjects offered for the year 1901–02:

## MORNING

| Session Rooms 8:00–8:45 | 1st Per. 8:45–9:30 | 2nd Per. 9:30–10:15 | 3rd Per. 10:15–11:00 | 4th Per. 11:00–11:45 |
|---|---|---|---|---|

5th Per.
11:45–12:30

## AFTERNOON

Session
Rooms          6th Per.          7th Per.          8th Per.          9th Per.
12:30–1:15     1:15–2:00         2:00–2:45         2:45–3:30         3:30–4:15

### Teachers and Course Offerings

Angeline Carey—Session Room C, 11A English, (1,2,3,4,5)

Charity Dye—Session Room D, 11B English, (1,2,3,4,5)

Charles S. Thomas—Session Room B, English 12B, (1,2,4), English 12A, (3), Senior Themes, (5)

Junius B. Roberts—English History, (1,3 and 5), Medieval History, (2 and 4)

Laura Donnan—Session Room A, Civil Government, (1,2,3,6,7,8)

George W. Benton—Chemistry II–IV, (Session and 1), Chemistry I, (2 and 3, 4 and 5)

Amelia Platter—Geometry I, (1,3 and 7), Algebra II, (6,7 and 9)

Agnes Rankin—Session Room C (aft.), Algebra II, (1,3,6,8), Algebra I, (7 and 9)

Roda E. Selleck—Drawing, (2 and 3, 4 and 5, 6 and 7)

John C. Trent—Session Room B (aft.), Geom. II, (1,4), Solid Geom., (3), Algebra I, (5,6), Algebra II, (7)

John E. Higdon—Session Room J, Trigonometry, (1), Geom. II, (2), Arithmetic, (3), Geom. I, (7)

Eugene Mueller—Session Room F, German VII, (1), German V, (2), German IV, (3), German III, (4), German II, (5,7)

Arthur J. Taylor—Bookkeeping I, (1), Bookkeeping II, (2), Stenography I, (3,7), Stenography II, (4)

Ella G. Marthens—Session Room N, Caesar II, (1,4), Caesar I, (7,8), Cicero, (5), Latin I, (9)

Rousseau McClellan—Physiology, (2), Physiography, (3), Botany, (4,5), Elementary Science, (7)

Flora Love—Session Room E (aft.), English 10B, (4,6,7,8,9)

Neil H. Williams—Physics II, (Session and 1, 4 and 5), Physics I, (2 and 3)

Lynn B. McMullen—Physics I, (Session and 1, 2 and 3), Physics II, (4 and 5)

Arthur W. Dunn—Session F (aft.), American History, (4,5), Ancient History, (6,7,8,9)

Josephine Cox—Session A (aft.), Ancient History, (1,3,9), Medieval History, (2,7,8)

Elizabeth Hall—Session D (aft.), English 10B, (2,6), English 9A, (7,8,9)

Janet Shaw—Session J (aft.), English 9A, (2,6,9), English 9B, (7,8)

Arthur Ferguson—Greek III, (1), Greek I, (2), Latin I, (6,7,9)
H. Fletcher Scott—Vergil I, (1), Vergil II, (2), Caesar I, (3), Latin II,
  (4,8,9)
Virginia Claybaugh—Algebra I, (1,2,3,4), Latin I, (7,8)
Anna Locke—English 10A, (1,2,3,4,5)
Zella O'Hair—English 9B, (1,2,9), English 9A, (7,8)
J. F. Millis—Session E, Geometry I, (1,5,6,7), Geometry II, (3,4),
  Algebra III, (2)
Peter Scherer—German I, (1,3,4,6,7,9)

School opened in September, 1901, with twelve hundred students and twenty-nine teachers. Most of the faculty were teaching six classes a day. Eleven of them also taught from 7:30 to 9:30 in the Monday evening night school, still without additional pay. Many of them were also sponsoring all sorts of student activities. Actually, they were not called sponsors in this period. They were critics or censors, severe terms for an appreciated service. Appreciation may have helped supply some of the necessary energy and stamina.

The most extreme example, Laura Donnan, taught six classes, presided over the Senate, read proof for the *Echo*, taught in, and served as principal of the night school, and managed the girls' basketball team. Chaperoning the girls was an extra. Miss Marthens and Miss McClellan not only taught six classes apiece, they each had four separate preparations, and Miss Marthens had a session room besides. They both taught in the night school. Miss McClellan spent many of her Saturdays on field trips and, like Miss Donnan, they pitched in for every occasion.

George Benton was another extremely dedicated teacher and sponsor. He taught six periods a day, all the chemistry classes, acted as censor of the Agassiz Club and of the Chorus, helped with the *Echo*, and constantly promoted the interests of the school.

The *Echo* of September 25, 1901, carried an article about Mr. Benton's report on his summer vacation. He had spent it visiting high schools in other midwestern cities and taking notes on how those cities provided for their high school students. He reported that they all had both gymnasiums and auditoriums.

Particular mention was made of Cleveland High School, which had two gyms, one for boys and one for girls, plus a room for the athletic association, and of Detroit High School, which had an auditorium with a seating capacity of well over one thousand and was as large as one whole floor of Shortridge High School. The *Echo* reported:

> Mr. Benton told of a number of respects in which we were surpassed by the aristocratic schools in other states, all of which tempted

us to break one of the Commandments. Still we can comfort ourselves greatly by reflecting a little on the pleasant relations between the faculty and pupils which exist here. It is a common thing to hear of regular feuds springing up between the authorities and students in High Schools, which bespeak an unhappy condition of affairs. . . .

Shortridge has been happy in a great freedom from these dissensions, a fact which more vitally concerns the life of pupils and school than anything else. As long as this state of amity continues, the poor, downtrodden members of Shortridge High School can still survive even if they are not consoled with a gilt edged building, desirable though that may be.

Changes for the better are sure to come in time, so for the present we will endure our misfortunes comforted by the knowledge that a better faculty can hardly be found in the United States.

Along with appreciation from students, another source of strength for the overworked teachers was the success of the graduates of their high school. The September 25, 1901, *Echo* gave a sampling of where some of the recent graduates were:

| | |
|---|---|
| Princeton | Alfred Ogle, Alex Taggart |
| Cornell | Bert Coffin, Dick Tolin |
| Yale | Russell Sullivan, Harris Walcott |
| Purdue | Edward Mayo, Burt Mitchell, Herbert Johnson |
| Vassar | Mary Pratt, Cerene Ohr |
| DePauw | Irene Berryhill, Louise Tutewiler |
| Berlin | Marie Jungclaus |
| Smith | Sarah Lauter |
| University of Chicago | Julia Hobbs, Martha Allerdice, Ernest Sims |
| Wellesley | Edith Beck, Elsie Appel, Edna Franck |

The night school was also experiencing success. On June 6, 1902, Miss Donnan invited all the senior boys to her home to meet Clifton Hendryx, the first graduate of the Shortridge Night School.

One name missing from the 1901–02 teachers' list is that of Lois Hufford. She had been one of the original incorporators of the Free Kindergarten Association and also of the Children's Aid Society, which had grown into the Teachers College. She left Shortridge in June, 1901, in order to teach English literature at that college to a new generation of aspiring teachers. She was replaced by Charles S. Thomas, another outstanding teacher, who took over as head of the English Department and taught all the senior English classes.

At the end of the year 1901–02, George Hufford also left Short-ridge. He was in frail health and had to retire from his demanding job. Both Huffords, however, continued to maintain close ties with the school.

The new school board, faced with the need to appoint a principal for Shortridge, chose to look for one outside of Indianapolis. They picked a man with impressive credentials. Lawrence C. Hull had been principal of Detroit High School, then chairman of the Latin Department at Law-renceville (New Jersey) School and, at the time of his selection as prin-cipal of Shortridge, was head of the Academic Department at Brooklyn Polytechnic Institute.

Hull does not appear to have been a fortunate choice. The *Indianapo-lis News* ran a large picture of the new principal of Shortridge and an enthusiastic welcoming article, but he was not featured in that paper again. He was seldom mentioned in the *Echo*, in contrast to Mr. Hufford, who had been spoken of almost every day. Hull's picture appeared in the 1903 *Annual* with his name underneath it, but that was all. He stayed for only one year. From 1903 to 1909 he served as headmaster, then presi-dent, of Michigan Military Academy and then became a representative of the Massachusetts Mutual Life Insurance Company.

When school resumed in the fall of 1903, George Benton, who had taken a year's leave of absence, was back at Shortridge, this time as principal of the school. The new chemistry teacher was Frank B. Wade.

Arthur J. Taylor resigned from the Shortridge faculty in 1902, when the school board chose an outsider as principal. He moved to Chicago and went into business, but he did not go away mad. He wrote a letter addressed to "My dear Echo," which was featured on the front page of the issue of October 17, 1902. It clearly illustrated the "pleasant re-lations" and "the state of amity between faculty and students" which has been mentioned previously.

Mr. Taylor began by saying that on the preceding Monday his *Echos* had not arrived and that this had thrown him into a panic; he could not get along without them. He wanted all of Shortridge to know that "teachers of school here hold the Indianapolis schools in very high es-teem," and he went on to say:

> The ECHO furnishes much that is interesting, all that it furnishes is interesting, but once in a while I would be delighted to get those bits of gossip that fail to get past the censor. Send me your canned articles.

Our friend Marie the "Town Pump"
   worked,
  And also many others.
She worked the parents, teachers, girls,
  But chiefly the girls' brothers.

Up the stern steep, toiling slow,
  The President toward fame doth steer;
While we, applauding from below,
  His short, loud pants do hear.

The booth was Art: the maids within
  Were artless, one might think;
Alas, one's think did quickly change
  When he dropped there all his chink.

Drawings from 1902 *Annual*

Here's friendly Sernest Eton,
  With illustrated " spiel ";
If he had felt like catin',
  His beasts had made a meal.

There was a Farce once on a time
With jokes and roasts and songs and
  rhyme ;
But in the future we'll recall
The leading lady first of all.

We'll drop the point of morals,
  For those were dulcet tones,—
Forgive the erring choir boys,
  And not disturb the " bones."

With nothing but the fondest recollections of more than seven years spent at the finest, most progressive high school in the world, I beg to remain,

Loyally yours<br>
Arthur J. Taylor

P.S. Come and see me.

.     .     .     .     .

After 1900 the popularity of the new sport of basketball with both boys and girls increased the pressure for a gym. The first year that the girls had any sort of athletic team was 1901. They organized themselves, rented the YWCA gymnasium one afternoon a week for practice, and found themselves a coach. Miss Donnan agreed to act as their manager. Several of the girls had played at the YWCA previously and at least knew the rules of the game. Girls played six to a team. Their first game was played against the Girls Classical School, a private Indianapolis institution, and resulted in an 18–9 victory for Shortridge. The team went on to defeat the YWCA 19–4 and to tie the German House team at 12–12. (Two of the members of that first team were Anna Ray Herzch, later Mrs. Lee Burns, and Sybil McCaslin, later Mrs. Claude Bowers.) The next year the Shortridge girls secured the use of the German House gym for weekly practice. Miss Donnan continued as their manager for the next five years, and they had a winning season every year. In 1904 they won the championship of the state with ten victories and no losses. They played Kokomo, Columbus, and Veedersburg and, best of all, they defeated Manual twice.

The boys' basketball team practiced at the YMCA gym whenever they could. There was a local basketball league, which consisted of Shortridge, Manual, Butler, and the YMCA. They played six games, all teams playing each other twice. The YMCA was the big victor in 1901, the first year of the league, winning all its games. Shortridge came in second with three victories and took home a runner-up cup, but in the crucial confrontations with Manual they lost one 9–12 and won the other 23–20.

The question of who should be allowed to play on the high school basketball teams caused friction between the two high schools, just as it had in football. There were still no clearcut rules. It was not strictly a high school league, but all that either school really cared about was beating the other. In 1903 it was Manual who challenged Shortridge's use of a basketball player who was not attending classes. Both schools made sanctimonious statements. The captain of the Manual team announced on the sports page of the *News* that he would not be playing in the final

Girls 1905 championship basketball team

game, because he was a January graduate and no longer a high school student. He could, he said, pretend to be taking a postgraduate class, but he did not want Manual to be like Shortridge in putting in a ringer for an important game. A few days later, Manual threatened to refuse to play the final game unless Shortridge also dropped its ineligible player.

A reply came in the *Echo* on January 23, 1903:

> The question is too small to cause MTHS and Shortridge to come to a parting of the ways, in which they have run so long with hearty rivalry prevailing. . . . We do not believe that any school has a right to determine the eligibility rules of her opponent. Nor do we believe that any school has a right to demand the withdrawal of any member of an opposing team. . . . But we do believe that any school has a right to refuse to play any school whose rules she may question. . . . In conclusion, the right of MTHS to play whom she pleases has met our right to play any man that we deem eligible. Tact and courtesy alone can solve the difficulty. Masters himself possesses both of these and has proposed the happy solution—that of withdrawing himself from the game.

After all that Shortridge defeated Manual 19–16.

·  ·  ·  ·  ·  ·

Shortridge won the State Oratorical Contest again in 1901. The successful orator was Jim Gipe, speaking on "Wendell Phillips, the Abolitionist." The school was proud of him, but the celebration of his victory did not compare with the enormous triumph scored by Claude Bowers just three years earlier. The oratorical contest was still a major event, but it was now only one of many. Not only had sports become much more important, so had debating. There were even some editorials in the *Echo* questioning the continuance of the oratorical contest and suggesting that many were attending only to yell. Spirited rebuttal followed. Shortridge continued its interest in oratory and oratorical contests, and Coburn Allen produced another victory in 1902. But many students were more interested in debating.

Miss Donnan's classes held a debate every Monday, and the Debating Club, for which Mr. Fletcher Scott was the faculty critic, was very popular. Club members argued the pros and cons of such controversial issues as the annexation of Cuba, the installation of gas meters, and Sunday baseball. In the Senate there was spirited debate about proposals for an appropriation to enlarge the U.S. Navy, as well as woman's suffrage and the popular election of senators. In the spring of 1902 the Senate held a trial for high treason. The charge against the accused persons was that they had been too intimate with the Russian government. They were acquitted.

In 1902 the sponsorship of the *Echo* was reorganized so that there was a different faculty sponsor for each day of the week, as well as a different editorial staff: Monday—Miss Donnan; Tuesday—Mr. Ferguson; Wednesday—Miss Love; Thursday—Mrs. Carey; Friday—Mr. Thomas. The classes continued to give fairs every year to raise money for their class gift: a Street Fair, a Book Fair, a Chinese Fair, and, finally, an Arabian Fair. Each one raised substantially more than its predecessor. The class of 1902 broke the tradition of always giving a work of art. They left their money, some eight hundred dollars, to buy equipment for the gym in the new building, which they now believed would soon be a reality.

The class of 1903 left its money to the *Echo*. That class also established another popular Shortridge tradition, the spring vacation trip. Mr. Trent of the Math Department was the organizer and sponsor for this enterprise. The first year he took his adventurous students to Washington, Mount Vernon, and Monticello. The next year the group went to New Orleans, and the next, to Knoxville, Tennessee; Savannah, Georgia; and Birmingham, Alabama.

After 1900 the musical groups not only continued to flourish, they received professional attention. Although no teacher of music appears on the faculty list, Edward Bailey Birge, director of music for the Indianapolis public schools, took over the direction of the Shortridge orchestra and the girls' and boys' glee clubs. In May, 1903, the groups combined to give their first annual concert, which was pronounced "unqualifiedly successful, both financially and artistically" and included "A Shortridge March" written by Mr. Birge.

The first years of the twentieth century also saw the rise of social clubs. These were frowned on by many parents and educators, but their members loved them. The two principal objections were that they were exclusive and cliquish and that they usually were secret organizations. Officially the school discouraged them, but they flourished anyway. The 1902 *Annual* lists ten such clubs, eight for girls and two for boys. The largest of the boys' clubs was Gamma Epsilon, with Garvin Brown as president and sophomore Eli Lilly as one of the twelve members. The other boys' club was WHIST. The girls took all sorts of names: O.T.Q., DO DO, Sigma Delta Rho, G.G.G.G. The initials had a secret meaning, which made these clubs much more dashing and tended to upset parents.

Eli Lilly served as president of the 1903 junior class and was a member of the football team in both his junior and senior years. He is listed as 5 feet, 9 inches, weighing 135 pounds, but was by no means the smallest of the football players. Eli enjoyed football, but his favorite sport was track. He ran the hurdles and won for Shortridge against Manual in the 1904 track meet. He also had a favorite teacher—Charity Dye.

.    .    .    .    .

Indianapolis in the early part of the twentieth century was a bustling, expanding community, but it was still compact and the Circle was its center. On the Circle were Christ Church, already a landmark, and English's Opera House and the English Hotel, the Columbia Club, which opened formally on December 31, 1900, and the Soldiers' and Sailors' Monument, which was finally completed and dedicated on May 15, 1902. Few automobiles roamed the streets. There were horses and carriages and horse-drawn wagons, of course, but it was possible to get almost any place in town either on foot, by bicycle, or by streetcar. A sizable contingent of students came from Irvington to Shortridge by streetcar every day. Students and teachers could walk from school to the downtown stores in a few minutes.

The downtown merchants and businesses supported the high school in many ways. L.S. Ayres, Wm. H. Block, and H.P. Wasson department stores all advertised regularly in both the *Echo* and the *Annual*. So did H. Lieber & Co., Bowen-Merrill, Vonnegut Hardware, Parrot-Taggart Bakery, Gregory & Appel, and many others. Strauss advertised

"Swell Suits $10—$25." The Turnverein at the German House advertised "Physical Education, $2.00 per term (special classes available for pupils of the H.S.)." Carlin and Lennox Music Store offered "Talking Machines" plus "Music Boxes, Mandolins, Guitars and Pianos." A number of stores offered prizes for school events, such as tennis tournaments or field days. ·

The year 1904 provided the only racial incident on record during the years that Shortridge was an integrated school prior to the segregation established in 1927. A white student appealed to the school board for reinstatement after his dismissal on the grounds of refusing to occupy the seat designated by his teacher. On February 16, in Miss Donnan's civil government class, he was assigned a seat "adjacent to a seat occupied by a colored girl." The student flatly refused to obey in the presence of the entire class. Miss Donnan dismissed him from her class. He then appealed to the principal, Mr. Benton, who sustained Miss Donnan and suspended the boy until he was ready to obey school rules. The next appeal was to the superintendent of schools, Calvin N. Kendall, who looked into the matter and then upheld the principal and the teacher.

The recalcitrant student, accompanied by his lawyer, made a final appeal to the school board. The reason given by the lawyer for his client's refusing to sit where he was assigned was that "the seat next adjacent was occupied by a young woman who was personally objectionable to him." The board adjourned to executive session to consider the matter. Since they had received a letter from the young woman asking to be transferred to another class "in order to relieve her from the embarrassment which the acts of the suspended pupil was causing her," they settled it that way and allowed the boy to return to class. He did not graduate.

Few people besides the school administration and the students in that particular class were concerned about this incident. The focus of school interest was on expansion of the school's physical facilities. By the end of 1903 enrollment was up to 1,495, and bids had been received for clearing the area just north of Shortridge in preparation for the new Shortridge High School building. In 1904 construction actually began on the southeast corner of North and Pennsylvania. The new structure was going to be much larger than the building to which it was an addition. It was going to have a gymnasium and an auditorium and even a lunchroom. The students and the whole community watched its progress with great interest.

Finally, on January 30, 1905, the new building opened and with it a new era for Shortridge High School.

CHAPTER
6

# Across the Bridge of Sighs

S HORTRIDGE HIGH SCHOOL'S NEW BUILDING brought the student body together. No longer were there morning students and afternoon students. The schedule of classes was from 8:30 to 2:30, Monday through Friday, with everyone able to attend school at the same time. The additional space also provided greatly improved facilities for the science classes and the Art Department. The two main buildings were connected by a corridor at the second story level, which was promptly named "the Bridge of Sighs." Theodore Roosevelt had just been elected president in his own right. The class of 1906 took as its motto "Don't Foul, Don't Shirk, But Hit the Line Hard." The 1905 *Annual* had been dedicated to a person who approved of that motto, Laura Donnan—"One of the best friends Shortridge students ever had. . . ." As their class gift, they commissioned a portrait of Abram C. Shortridge to hang in the new building.

For the class of 1905, however, there was something of a disappointment. The long-awaited gymnasium did not come into full use until the following school year. Blanche Stillson, class of '06, described the situation in the 1906 *Annual*:

> The well-equipped, well-organized gymnasium which is now one of the features of Shortridge, is quite different from the large, bare, embryonic gymnasium of a year ago. During the summer, one hundred and ninety-six lockers, and six shower baths, with twelve dressing rooms were put in. A new floor was laid to take the place of the old warped one which had been the cause of so much trouble.
>
> About the first of November, the gymnasium work began in earnest, for Miss Wilhelmina Morlock of the Boston Normal School of Gymnastics, who was secured as instructor for the girls, organized the classes . . . about two hundred and fifty girls entered them. The work

The "New Shortridge" at Michigan and Pennsylvania streets

had been going on, however, for some time before the arrival of the first
shipment of apparatus. It was during the Thanksgiving vacation that
four large ladders, a number of booms, several horizontal bars and some
bar-stalls were placed in position. Later came the ropes, poles, rings,
Indian clubs, dumb-bells, jumping standards, poles for pole-vaulting,
jumping boards, and half a dozen mats. Most of this apparatus was
bought with the money left by the '02 class and by the Athletic Association of '02. . . .

About this time, Mr. Benton announced that gymnasium classes
for boys would be formed the next term if enough boys would signify
their intention of joining them. When the time came, many boys
flocked to the "gym," and now Mr. Hugo Fischer has two classes daily
in physical training.

The gymnasium has not been used entirely, however, by these
classes. In the basket-ball season, it was used by the teams. . . . Last
season, our track athletes developed speed and endurance by using the
large floor space to its best advantage. . . . The gymnasium was used,
moreover, by the girls' basket-ball squad, and many spirited contests
were held there. . . .

Shortridge now had a program of physical education and it had a
schedule of high school football. In the fall of 1905 the team played the
high schools of Lafayette, Union City, Rensselaer, Anderson, and
Bloomington, Indiana; Dayton, Ohio; and Louisville, Kentucky;
finishing with MTHS of Indianapolis. The only college team they
played was Rose Polytechnic Institute at Terre Haute.

Blanche Stillson made another point about the gym:

> We must not, however, forget, in speaking of the uses of our gym-
> nasium, the numerous social functions which have been held in it; when
> the gloomy rafters in the ceiling were illuminated by many bright
> lights; and when the floor was covered by a throng of dancers. . . .

In addition to the wonderful new gym, there was the wonderful new
auditorium, described as "large and excellently lighted by a circular sky-
light," and with seating for about sixteen hundred. The whole school
could now assemble at one time, and they did this on a regular basis.
Every Wednesday morning included an auditorium program with a special speaker, a musical program, or, quite frequently, both.

The first year of Wednesday programs, 1905–06, included speeches
by six Indiana college presidents: Edwin Holt Hughes of DePauw;
Windred E. Garrison of Butler; Robert L. Kelly of Earlham; Winthrop
E. Stone of Purdue; William P. Kane of Wabash; and William Lowe
Bryan of Indiana. The students also heard from their school's first prin-
cipal, William A. Bell, speaking on the question, "Where Does Life Be-

gin?", and the man who might well be considered their founder, Abram C. Shortridge, speaking on "Growth of the Public Schools."

The regular auditorium programs offered great opportunities to the musical organizations. The Chorus, the Glee Club, the Orchestra, and the Mandolin Club all performed. The musicians no longer had to scout around for someone to direct them. Edward Bailey Birge continued to direct the orchestra and the choruses, and Lynn McMullen, the physics teacher, directed the Glee Club and the Mandolin Club. The SHS History Department, under the guidance of Junius Roberts, also put on two programs. One was a "Celebration of the 200th Anniversary of the Birth of Benjamin Franklin" and the other was simply entitled "Historical Exercises."

The Senate continued to be the largest of the extracurricular organizations, but the Debating Club with twenty members was equally active. The club met once a week under the direction of Charles Thomas of the English Department and Arthur Dunn of the History Department. In their first important debate they were pitted against Laura Donnan's senators on the question: "Resolved, that the free elective system is the best available plan for the high school course of study." Julian (Jake) Kiser, writing in the *Annual*, said, "Both teams engaged in what has been generally agreed to be the closest and best debate Shortridge has ever held. By a vote of two to one the judges . . . gave the decision to the Senate."

The Debating Club team soon faced another contest. They accepted a challenge from East High School of Cleveland to debate the question, "Resolved, that it should be the policy of the United States not to hold territory permanently unless with the view of ultimately conferring the right of statehood." Shortridge took the affirmative. Shortridge had only two weeks to prepare to face a school that had defeated them the year before. The Indianapolis team, consisting of Louis Segar, Julian Kiser, and Melville Cohn, with Sam Trotcky as alternate, went to Cleveland accompanied by Mr. Dunn. They were apprehensive, but they had worked hard and they won by a unanimous decision of the judges. According to the report in the *Annual*, "In Shortridge's rebuttal, Louis Segar was at his best, and won a storm of applause."

Two new organizations were formed in 1905–06, the French Club and the William Morris Society. French was a recent addition to the curriculum, and it had been received enthusiastically. The club was formed "in order that those studying French may the better appreciate the language, and the nation by which it is spoken." At each meeting the French teacher, Miss Brooks, translated a French story, and members reported on French items of interest. French music was featured in an open meeting each semester.

The William Morris Society displayed the power of Charity Dye (William Morris was a nineteenth-century poet and artist, well known in his own day. He was also the inventor of the Morris chair.) According to the 1906 *Annual*:

> The William Morris Society was founded early in 1905, as a supplement to the English V classes taught by Miss Dye. Its main purpose, briefly expressed, is the study of William Morris's life and writings. The roll of membership has been steadily increasing and the meetings are always well attended. . . . By the study of "Sigurd," (Morris's epic poem, *Sigurd the Volsung*) much interest has been excited in the Norse legends, and these were accordingly selected for treatment. . . . The stories were told in conversational form and afterward discussed by the members. . . . As has been said, the William Morris Society was originally established for the benefit of the English V pupils exclusively, but its scope has proved to be so extensive that the rights of membership have been opened to all students of the high school, and even to outsiders. . . .

Another highlight of the year 1906–07 was the selection of a design by a Shortridge art student, Marie H. Stewart, for a tablet commemorating the spot in Indianapolis where Abraham Lincoln spoke in February, 1861, on his way to Washington and his inauguration. The speech was delivered from a second-floor balcony of the Bates House on the northwest corner of Illinois and Washington streets. The selection was made from among nineteen designs submitted to a committee appointed by the Indianapolis Commercial Club. The judges then commissioned Rudolph Schwarz, a well-known sculptor, to model and cast the tablet. It was unveiled publicly with suitable ceremony on the afternoon of February 12, Lincoln's birthday. That evening the Commercial Club sponsored a program with Governor J. Frank Hanly serving as chairman. Bishop J. H. Vincent was the featured speaker, but, according to the 1907 *Annual*, "Probably the most pleasing feature of the evening was that the two schools [Shortridge and Manual] came together harmoniously and played no small part in the exercises. The combined orchestras of the two schools rendered several excellent selections, and a general spirit of good feeling prevailed."

Unfortunately, the spirit of good feeling did not last. In the fall of 1906 the Shortridge football team had a rather unsuccessful season. This made the whole school even more eager than usual to win the big Thanksgiving day game against Manual. For the previous two years they had gone into that game as underdogs and come out as winners. They were determined to do it again, and Manual was equally determined that they should not. This time Manual prevailed. Then the victors and large numbers of their supporters staged a march around the Circle, wearing costumes and displaying signs taunting their defeated rival. Shortridge supporters were on the Circle, too, and the result was a rough fight which went on for hours. Several boys were dunked in White River, and at least one boy was seriously injured. Many people, including the Board of School Commissioners, were outraged at the behavior of Indianapolis's high school students.

As a result the board decided that after the 1907–08 sports season was over there would be no more games between schools and that all athletic contests would be intramural. Shortridge did not resume football again for twelve years.

. . . . .

One who remembers Shortridge in the first years of the century is Margaret Noble Johnston, who entered the school in the fall of 1905 at the age of twelve. She lived at 19th and Meridian. She had tickets for the streetcar, which ran regularly up and down Pennsylvania Street, but she walked to school because Stokes Pharmacy would furnish a chocolate sundae in exchange for two streetcar tickets. The sundae was called a SHS special. There was another one with pink ice cream that was a MTHS special, but since she was entirely loyal she never tasted it.

She remembers her school days warmly, although she thinks now that she would have participated in more activities if she had not been quite so young. Her favorite teacher was Wilbert L. Carr, who had just come to Shortridge as head of the Latin Department. She says, "No one who had Mr. Carr could ever fail to have a sense of the structure of language or could take grammar lightly." She liked all her teachers except for her math teacher, who regularly told her that she was stupid—a new experience for a girl who had skipped two full grades in grade school. She still winces when she recalls his saying, "You are even more stupid than usual today, Miss Noble," but she did not tell her parents anything about it until the report cards came out and there was a big *D* in algebra. Her father, Dr. Thomas Noble, took her by the hand, and they went to call on the principal, Mr. Benton. As a result of that call, she got a tutor—the former principal, George Hufford. "He was the kindest, friendliest old man I ever met," is her recollection, "and he really knew how to explain things. After I had been with him a few times I had no more trouble with math. My teacher stopped picking on me, too. I don't know whether somebody told him to stop or whether it was just because I got better."

When she thinks about Shortridge, she particularly remembers the lockers, which were large enough to be shared by ten to twelve students, and opened and closed like rolltop desks. She says they were never locked, but her recollection may be faulty. Those who went to school a few years later say they were unlocked when the students arrived in the morning and then locked until it was time for them to go home. In any case, the school had a relaxed atmosphere. Students could eat in the cafeteria or they were free to go out for lunch at the YWCA, or Thompson's, or either Crawford's or Stokes's drugstore. They did not need a

···◄◉◄···          **1907**          ···◄◉◄···

# Shortridge High School
# LUNCH ROOM

### Open from 12:25 to 1:00 P. M.

**CHANGE OF MENU EACH DAY FROM THE FOLLOWING:**

### HOT DISHES

SOUP with Crackers - - - - - 5c
Vegetable
  Tomato
   Celery
    Bean
     Chicken and Noodles
      Creamed Corn

### MEATS

Roast Beef and Gravy - - - - - 7c
Roast Pork and Gravy - - - - 6c
Veal Loaf and Gravy - - - - - 5c
Creamed Dried Beef - - - - - 5c
Creamed Salmon - - - - - - 5c
Baked Beef Hash - - - - - - - 5c
Hot Wienerwurst (2) - - - - - 3c

### VEGETABLES 3c

Potatoes (mashed, fried, baked)
Baked Beans
Peas   Corn   Rice   Hominy

Hot Roast Beef Sandwich with Gravy 7c

### DRINKS 3c

Coffee    Cocoa    Tea    Milk

### COLD DISHES

Sandwiches - - - - - - - - 3c
  Minced Ham    Peanut    Cheese
   Lettuce with Mayonaise
    Date and Nut
    Home-Made Jelly
Same with buns or brown bread - - 4c
Sliced Chicken Sandwich - - - - 10c
Potato Salad - - - - - - - - 3c
Salmon Salad - - - - - - - 3c
Hard Boiled Egg - - - - - - - 3c
Apple Sauce - - - - - - - - 3c
Cream Slaw - - - - - - - - 3c
Stewed Prunes - - - - - - - 3c
Stewed Apricots - - - - - - - 3c
Cottage Cheese - - - - - - - 2c
Pickles or Olives - - - - - - - 1c

Fresh Buttered Bread per Slice - - 1c
Buttered Bun or Roll - - - - - 2c
Shredded Wheat Biscuit with Cream 10c

### DESERTS

Ice Cream various flavors - - - - 5c
Home Made Cake - - - - - - 5c
Home Made Pie - - - - - - - 3c
Home Made Doughnuts (each) - - 2c
Home Made Cookies - - - - - 1c

**FRESH FRUITS IN SEASON**

SHS luncheon menu, 1907

Shortridge cafeteria

pass to leave the building. Eating at school provided the most food for the least money, but it was more exciting to go out to the other places.

Although Margaret Noble was young for her class and therefore did not participate in a lot of school activities, she did sing in the Girls' Glee Club, which was a brand-new organization. She particularly remembers that she learned "The grasshopper's sitting on the railroad track singing pollywolly doodle all the day," and "There was a B I E I BEE lit on a B O Y E BOY. . . ." in the Glee Club because her children, grandchildren, and great-grandchildren have all been lulled to sleep with those songs. She also says in reference to her youth, "I wasn't allowed to have callers—boys, but I had friends who helped me."

· · · · ·

In 1906–07 Shortridge offered its first advanced placement college course. The September 26, 1906, *Echo* announced:

Saturday morning, October sixth, in Room 9 of the Shortridge High School, Mr. W. D. Howe and Mr. C. S. Thomas will meet all teachers and advanced students who wish to take the year's work in nineteenth century literature. Satisfactory completion of the course secures college credit.

From 1906 to 1908 virtually every auditorium program included music, along with talks on such subjects as "Football and Life" and many stereopticon lectures: "Rambles in the Old World" by Mr. Edgar T. Forsyth, of the History Department; "Shakespeare" by Mrs. George Hufford, formerly of the English Department; "Lexington Day" by the Rev. F.S.C. Wicks, pastor of the Unitarian Church. The orchestra continued to be directed by Edward Bailey Birge, while both the Glee Clubs and the Mandolin Club continued under the direction of Lynn McMullen. Music was still not formally a part of the curriculum, but it pervaded school life.

. . . . .

As did art. The class of 1906 dedicated their *Annual* to Roda Selleck, but all the *Annuals* contained expressions of appreciation to her, and the practice of donating art to Shortridge continued. The new building provided almost unlimited scope for enthusiastic artists. One of the first major projects is described in the 1909 *Annual* with pride:

> Prominent among the achievements of Shortridge students in the year 1908, stands the transformation of Room 3 [Charity Dye's room]. Where there were once bare, uninteresting walls, there is now an artistic decoration that has attracted national notice. This work was financially conducted by juniors, but pupils from various classes and departments of the school contributed their respective talents toward making this room beautiful.

The decorations began with the door, which was covered by a curtain of Greek design made by Lucy Shover. The room contained a bookcase made by four boys and topped by a cast of Dante's head. On the opposite wall was a shelf "in beautiful lines," also student-made. Below the shelf hung pictures of four of Miss Dye's favorite authors—Carlyle, Ruskin, Morris, and Tolstoi—a gift of the class of 1904. Around the room ran a frieze created by Alma Grumman, art editor of the 1907 *Annual*. The subjects were taken from Flaxman's *Homer*. On the front wall were the "Judgment of Paris," "Council of the Gods," "Four Gods Going to War," and "Archers Trying Skill." On the right were "The Chariot Race," "Hector's Farewell to Andromache," and "The Warrior." On the back wall was "Nausicaa Throwing the Ball," while next to her was "A Priest Making Sacrifice." On Miss Dye's desk was a copper desk set designed and made by yet another student.

The *Annual* report concluded: "It is the hope of all teachers and students that every room in Shortridge will soon be transformed as happily as Room 3 has been."

Decorations of Room 3

Ella Graham Marthens

The 1908 *Annual* was dedicated:

To

Ella Graham Marthens
whose Loyalty, Sincerity and Charm have
endeared her to us all, and whose Gracious Personality
and Inspiring Friendship we shall ever cherish as one of
the Brightest Influences of our high
school life

In the summer of 1910 Miss Marthens had her room decorated by her students. The funds for the project came from the Indiana Pageant, a new segment of which was given each year by Charity Dye's English V classes, and which was always a successful money raiser. Peter Scherer, head of the German Department, had his room decorated by the German Club.

At the end of the 1907–08 school year, Charles Swain Thomas resigned as head of the English Department. He had been a much admired teacher, the first to have an *Annual* dedicated to him (1903). He had taught the senior English classes, acted as censor for the Debating Club and for the *Echo*, and been the sponsor for the senior class. He left Shortridge for a similar position at West Newton, Massachusetts. He became a recognized authority on the teaching of English and an associate professor at Harvard.

William N. Otto

Thomas left a big hole, but that hole was filled by a man who soon took over almost all of Thomas's responsibilities and added a few of his own. William N. Otto became the debate coach, sponsor of the senior class and the senior class play, managing editor for all the *Echos*, censor of Wednesday's *Echo*, and the author of the first journalism textbook for American high schools. After a few years he was made head of the English Department, a position he continued in for many years.

No major changes in school activities took place in 1909. The debate questions were: "Resolved, that the U.S. should establish a system of subsidies and bounties for the protection and encouragement of the American Merchant Marine," and "Resolved, that the presidential term

Rousseau McClellan                    Angeline P. Carey

shall be extended to seven years and limited to one term." The *Annual*
was dedicated:

To
Rousseau McClellan
who has opened unto us the door of the true
fairyland of Nature; and while guiding us along
these unaccustomed paths, has given each one
the priceless treasure of a wholesome influence.

Miss Marthens and Miss McClellan lived together in a house at
Twenty-third and Pennsylvania streets. Practically nobody who went to
Shortridge in the forty years that they were both there fails to mention
their names in recalling their school years. Not only did they have *Annuals* dedicated to them, but for years on pleasant evenings groups of Shortridge boys would come around to serenade them.

The 1910 *Annual* was dedicated to Angeline P. Carey of the English
Department:

who by the truthfulness of her Conceptions,
the simplicity of her reasoning, and the
Habitual cheerfulness of her personality
has increased our devotion to worthy
achievements and inspired nobler
visions of life's poetry. . . .

It also mentioned among the 1910 graduates Joel Hadley, "a little red-headed fellow, the courteous, tireless business manager of the *Annual*—His constant optimism and readiness for work predict a successful career."

The big news in the spring of 1910, however, was the resignation of George Benton as principal of Shortridge. Thomas Carr Howe, president of Butler, speaking in an auditorium program just after the resignation had been announced said, "Things don't happen by chance around Shortridge. There is a clear-headed man in the office downstairs and I for one am sorry he is leaving." The students leaped to their feet and clapped their agreement.

Mr. Benton had encouraged and participated in many school activities. He had led the orchestra, promoted the *Echo*, researched other high schools in the interest of a new building, and he had been an outstanding chemistry teacher before he was made principal. When he left, he made a gift to the Science Department of one hundred books that he had used in teaching.

George Benton has been described as a widely read man with a charming personality. In addition to his duties at Shortridge, he had been active in the affairs of the public schools of the state. In 1908–09 he served as president of the Indiana State Teachers Association and, in that capacity, was the principal speaker for the Twenty-fifth Anniversary Meeting of the Indiana Academy of Science.

A close relationship existed between the Indiana Academy of Science, founded in 1885, and Shortridge High School. Mr. Benton was a founding member. So was former Indianapolis High School teacher David Starr Jordan, then president of Indiana University, along with physicist Joseph P. Naylor, who taught at the high school from 1883 to 1885, and psychologist Lillien J. Martin, who was on the faculty from 1880 to 1889. (Miss Martin was the only woman charter member of the academy.) A number of George Benton's papers on chemistry, originally presented to the Academy, were later published. In his twenty-fifth anniversary speech to the Academy, Mr. Benton expressed his desire for "fitting the highest development of scientific thought into the general scheme of education for all the people."

When Mr. Benton left Shortridge, he became the Indiana editor of the New York American Book Company, and shortly thereafter the editor-in-chief, a position he held for more than twenty-five years.

·   ·   ·   ·   ·

The first *Echo* of the 1910–11 school year ran a large picture of the new principal with a welcoming article:

George Buck

As the successor of George W. Benton, George Buck comes to Shortridge with the reputation of being one of the most progressive educators in the middle west. He was born in Cincinnati, but educated in West Alexandria, O. While still in his teens he taught in a country school for two years and then entered Wittenberg University, from which he received both a bachelor's and a master's degree. In due time he was graduated from this institution and received his Master's degree a year later. Mr. Buck then taught at Lexington, O. until 1891, when he was elected Superintendent of the Monroe Township schools. After building up a strong rural system, Mr. Buck went to Dayton, O., where he became teacher of mathematics in Steele High School. In 1901 he became assistant principal and in 1906 principal. From Dayton Mr. Buck went to Duluth, Minn., as Principal of Duluth Central High School, where he served until engaged by the Board of School Commissioners as principal of Shortridge High School. . . .

Mr. Buck does not come to Shortridge as a stranger. Besides having visited the school, he is well acquainted with Mr. Benton. For several weeks past he has been at his desk preparing and has met many of the teachers. . . . Mr. Buck will make his home in Irvington, where he has already taken up residence. The general policies of the school will remain unchanged under the new administration; Shortridge will continue to advance along all lines that have made it the school it has been in the past; and the new principal will receive the loyal support of faculty and students alike.

During George Buck's first year as principal, Shortridge had an enrollment of fifteen hundred students. There were more than twice as many girls as boys, but the boys managed to hold their own. The first *Echo* of the year reported that Bergen Herod, a 1910 graduate, had scored first place in the Yale entrance exam out of all the applicants nationwide. Four out of the five *Echo* editors were boys (the girl was Monday's editor, Edith Skinner), and boys' athletics received considerably more attention than the girls'. Some of the older boys were abandoning knickers in favor of long pants. Tuesday's editor, Nicholas Eastman, was described as "one of the numerous recruits of the long trousered brigade—he now looks more like Senator Beveridge than ever." Thomas A. Hendricks, Thursday's editor, was senior class president and winner of the boys' tennis championship. He took that victory proudly into the city tennis tournament, but lost in the first round to the reigning champion, Fred Appel '04. The girls had a tennis tournament, too, which was won by Dorothy Vestal. The *Echo* continued to be well supported by the student body (750 subscriptions) and by the local merchants. Some of the ads read:

MEET ME AT CRAIGS
***
TO BE WELL FED EAT TAGGART'S BREAD
***
KAHN-TAILORED CLOTHES
A rich man's apparel at a modest man's price
SUITS

To order
$20–$48

Ready for service
$15–$25
***

and Strauss Says: THEY ALL LOOK LIKE SENIORS IN THOSE
SHORTRIDGE MODELS

and THAT NOBLE HEAD DESERVES A BETTER
LID

The *Echo* noted that it had recently received a copy of a new daily newspaper published by the high school connected with the University of Chicago. The *Echo* editor welcomed the new publication, but feared that it did not have either enough advertising support or a wide enough readership to be able to survive. The somewhat patronizing comment proved to be correct.

Although the *Echo* was unfailingly upbeat in its accounts of school life, the fact of the matter was that Mr. Buck had a rough first year. The *Echos* and the *Annuals* dutifully reported great success for intramural athletics, but a lot of Shortridge boys still wanted to play "real" football against Manual. A lot of Manual boys felt just the same way. In direct defiance of the school board ruling against extramural high school sports, a team from each school, calling themselves "Insurgents," staged a game on their day of traditional rivalry, Thanksgiving. Both teams were supported by cheering sections. Mr. Buck suspended fourteen boys who participated in the game because they "had violated the school board rule and had exhibited a spirit of opposition to the rules of the school."

Suddenly Mr. Buck almost had a riot on his hands. According to the *News* of December 3, 1910:

> A number of Shortridge students are openly resenting the action taken by Mr. Buck. Yesterday afternoon many of them gathered in the main corridor of the building and cheered for George W. Benton, former principal of the school, as a reflection on Mr. Buck. Peter Scherer, a teacher, ordered one of the janitors to put the first boy out who cheered again, and this was followed by cheers for the "insurgents". . . .
>
> The janitor attempted to put John Irwin out of the building, but before he could do so Mrs. Angeline P. Carey, a teacher, addressed the boys and quieted them. Mr. Buck appeared, and was hissed. . . .
>
> A number of girl students also gathered in the hall and gave signs of approval of the attitude of the boys. . . .

Meanwhile parents of the boys called on various members of the school board, all of whom said they would not interfere with Mr. Buck's decision. The parents also called on Mr. Buck, who told them that the suspensions would stand until January 2.

Not a word of all this appeared in the *Echo*.

The *News* ran an editorial supporting Mr. Buck as "a man quite willing to assume responsibility and fully prepared to do his duty" and complaining that "the young boys and girls have been so coddled and flattered that they have come to look on the school as belonging to them." The editorial went on to decry the evils of high school fraternities and sororities and the general effort to "ape college students."

Reflecting this point of view, the school board issued a mandate: "Since both state law and school board rule forbid high school fraternities and sororities, those belonging to such organizations after February 1 will not be permitted to graduate." This was totally unenforceable, and there is no record that anyone ever attempted to enforce it.

Two relatively young teachers were becoming increasingly prominent in school activities, Frank B. Wade of the Chemistry Department and Edgar T. Forsyth of the History Department. Mr. Wade checked the report cards of all student officers and all participants in athletics, debating, dramatics, and other activities, and furnished teachers with eligibility lists. He addressed an auditorium on the subject of gems, which was his hobby, and his chemistry classes received considerable press coverage. One day they spent the period putting out various types of fires, and on another they all made baking powder, which they then took home for family use.

Mr. Forsyth conducted the spring vacation trips and was censor for Friday's *Echo*. He also wrote the words for the school song to the tune of *Annie Laisle* (the same tune as the Cornell University song). Several previous attempts to establish a school song had dwindled into nothingness, but once Shortridge began to sing "In the land of milk and honey . . ." it never stopped. Each incoming class learned the song as part of their introduction to Shortridge life.

Another popular addition to the faculty was Louis H. Dirks, who replaced Peter Scherer as a German teacher when Mr. Scherer became head of German language teaching for all the Indianapolis public schools.

The year 1911–12 was a tranquil one. The girls, led by Edna Schnull, swept the top ten spots on the honor roll, but they were still unable to pass the Women's Suffrage Amendment in the Shortridge Senate. The vote was 24 to 16 in favor of passage, three short of the necessary two-thirds majority.

College scholarships were becoming more available. The Harvard Society of Indianapolis offered a Shortridge scholarship of $200 per annum. A Columbia University scholarship was also available, as was one to Wesleyan University in Connecticut.

In 1912 the *Echo* ran a series of articles by alumni encouraging Shortridge students to plan to attend various colleges. Garvin Brown, class of 1904, urged the merits of Princeton. Ted Griffith, class of 1906, promoted Williams. Of particular interest is Griffith's statement that Shortridge students had certificate privileges with Williams, providing that they had completed the full high school course including four years of Latin. (A certificate privilege meant that the recipient did not have to take entrance examinations.) Vassar also admitted Shortridge students on certificate. Edmund Ertel, 1903, declaimed, "Go to Cornell! It will make

Louis H. Dirks

of you a man, self-reliant, vigorous and conquering." Similar pleas were made for Yale, Wesleyan, Wellesley, and the University of Chicago. More than 60 percent of the seniors had college plans, according to the *Echo*, the largest number heading for Butler and Indiana University, with a sizable contingent choosing Purdue.

In the summer of 1911, James Whitcomb Riley gave three lots at Pennsylvania and St. Clair streets to the Indianapolis Public Schools for a public library. In appreciation of this, the State Board of Education set aside October 6 as Riley Day in the schools. To celebrate the day Fritz Krull, a Shortridge alumnus, put "Raggedy Man" and a number of other poems to music. Miss Dye and some twenty students went out in the rain that night to sing those songs, as a serenade to the poet at his house on Lockerbie Street. Riley was in poor health, but he invited them all in. The *Echo* of October 9, 1911, reported:

> In a bower of flowers sent to him by the various schools of the city, he shook hands with every guest and greeted them all and smiled and said the words over as they sang "There's Ever a Song Somewhere, My Dear," and "The Raggedy Man."

The class of 1912 dedicated their *Annual* to Riley.

This was the first year that Miss McClellan's zoology students had to collect and mount at least fifty varieties of insects. The *Echo* reported that several students found over one hundred. In the spring, some of the same students recorded more than one hundred and sixty different birds seen on their bird walks. The insect collections and the bird walks were part of the zoology course from that time onward.

The work of room decoration continued with the adornment of Angeline Carey's room. The theme for the decoration was a quotation from Heraclitus, "Wipe not out the place of the torch!" The Art Department developed a design, which was executed by Alma Grumman, as the one in Charity Dye's room had been. The background was divided into panels, and between the panels and across the curtain at the back, the significant torch was painted. The quotation from Heraclitus filled the panel on the side wall opposite the windows. Alma Grumman's mural contained allegorical figures representing the progress of the arts. The 1912 *Annual* reported, ". . . various eminent art critics of Indianapolis and visiting committees of gentlemen have pronounced the decoration of this room superior to that in any other school room of which they had knowledge."

This was Charity Dye's last year at Shortridge. She resigned at the end of May, 1912, too late for the *Annual* editors to honor her, but a whole *Echo* was devoted to heartfelt tributes from colleagues and students.

Miss Dye had been interested in pageants as a source of instruction ever since she visited the Oxford pageant in England in 1907. She had written a number of Indiana pageants while she was teaching, and, after her retirement from Shortridge, one of her major projects was to write a more ambitious and detailed historical pageant about her native state. This was presented at New Harmony, Indiana, in 1915 and led to her appointment to the Indiana Historical Commission in time for her to mastermind the Indiana Centennial Celebration in 1916. In or out of the classroom, she was always an educator.

# The Years
# 1912 to
# 1918

I N THE FALL OF 1912 Woodrow Wilson was elected president of the United States, and Indianapolis opened its third high school. Irvington had been annexed in 1904, but no high school had been provided on the eastside. A history of Arsenal Technical High School by members of the faculty begins:

> Early in the winter of 1912, the overcrowded conditions in Short-ridge and Manual Training High Schools demanded relief. The Board of School Commissioners did not own property adjacent to either school sufficient to build an adequate addition. Besides an addition to one would not have relieved the congestion in the other. It was out of the question to buy a site and launch a whole new high school. . . . The only feasible plan seemed to be to find a location where a sufficient number of beginning pupils of both schools might be accommodated. . . .
>
> But our city has, from the first, been committed to the policy of allowing eighth grade graduates free choice of high schools. This makes it possible for our high schools to specialize in different lines, drawing from all parts of the city those pupils adapted to the work. But to cause an appreciable number of eighth year graduates to choose to attend a temporary school for beginners was a puzzle. It was evident that two conditions must be met to make the plan succeed. First, the management and faculty of the school must be such as to convince parents . . . that the work done would be on a par with that of the other schools. . . . Second, the location must be appealing enough in point of convenience and general attractiveness to make pupils willing to forego being with the crowd at Manual or Shortridge. . . . The first of these conditions could be met by making the new school an overflow of one of the others, under the same management. The decision was made to organize as an overflow of Manual Training High School.

It remained to find the right location. There was one site ideal from many standpoints. . . . This was the Arsenal Grounds. . . . The one very material drawback was the fact that the title to its possession was involved in litigation . . . and no lease even could be obtained except such as might be terminated within five days. To offset this, however, it was the city of Indianapolis which was claiming the right to hold the grounds in trust for practical school purposes.

One hundred and eighty-three 8A graduates were persuaded to choose the new school. They entered high school on a beautiful campus—the site of the Civil War arsenal on the city's near east side. There were buildings available and also some shop equipment. These buildings needed a great deal of remodeling and repair, most of which could not be done until the title had been secured. This took four long years, but the history relates that the students "seemed to accept the situation in the spirit of pioneers, counting every hardship only an incident to be expected in starting a thing worthwhile."

Those who began at Tech continued on to graduation. Like their predecessors at Shortridge and Manual, they developed a strong school spirit, and Tech would become Indianapolis's largest high school.

Edgar T. Forsyth

Meanwhile, at Shortridge the year 1913–14 saw the birth of a new musical organization, the band. It was composed of twenty-eight pioneers under the direction of Mr. Birge, who also led the orchestra. The band was organized in December, 1913, and made its first public appearance before the student body on Wednesday, March 5, 1914. According to the next day's *Echo*, "the band took the school by storm." Its next appearance was at the indoor track meet, on April 16, followed by another program at the outdoor track meet two weeks later. Finally, the new musical group accompanied the team to the state track meet. Track was still the only sport in which Shortridge was allowed to compete with other schools, so track meets provided the best showcase for the talents of the band.

Another new organization was the Press Association, which was formed in the fall of 1912 to bring the staffs of the *Daily Echo* into closer contact with each other and to introduce them to the profession of journalism. That first year they were addressed by Indianapolis journalists: Anna Nicholas of the *Star*, Hilton U. Brown of the *News*, and Horace H. Herr of the *Indiana Daily Times*.

Rapport between teachers and students continued high. The class of 1914 dedicated its *Annual*:

To<br>
Edgar T. Forsyth<br>
Whose<br>
Untiring Years of Service<br>
As Teacher, Guide,<br>
And Leader<br>
Make Him Worthy to be Honored<br>
Whose<br>
Talent as a Song Writer<br>
Has Heralded Far and Wide<br>
The "School of Many Virtues"<br>
Whose Companionship<br>
And Cordial Smile<br>
Distinguish<br>
His Winning Personality<br>
And Endear Him<br>
To Shortridge Hearts

Mr. Forsyth replied:

To the Shortridge class of 1914

Not of gold nor of silver consists<br>
the teacher's greatest gain<br>
Those things are material and<br>
pass away

> Rather in association with the
>    age that is forward-looking
> And in knowing Youth at its
>    best comes the richest reward;
> These things are eternal and
>    fade not away
> During these years spent
>    with you,
> Bountiful has been my reward,
> May the benefits of our asso-
>    ciation have been mutual.
>
> > Your sincere friend,
> > Edgar T. Forsyth

That *Annual* also opened with a straightforward defense of bragging by senior class president, Robert M. Brewer: "The critic will have to excuse the graduate if he seems too egotistical, as his egotism only shows that he has the spirit which makes things go, and that is the kind of spirit to have."

One of these expressions of spirit by the class of 1914 was about its senior play:

> Deviating from the typical high school play, the class of 1914 presented George Broadhurst's famous success, "The Man of the Hour." . . . the play is one of such fine construction, high dramatic power, well-balanced parts, and vividly realistic character roles, that it proved peculiarly adapted to the excellent theatrical talent possessed by the class. . . .
>
> Tryouts were held late in March, one hundred and thirty-three expectant Thespians appearing before Mr. Harry Porter, who was chosen as coach, and Mr. W. N. Otto, censor of the senior organization. . . . Five days . . . passed before the final cast of seventeen characters was satisfactorily filled. . . .
>
> All of the parts were portrayed with an intelligence, grace and "polish" which is seldom found in amateur theatricals.

Among the seventeen polished actors was Clarence Efroymson (long-time professor of economics at Butler) who played the office boy. He is also listed as an outstanding member of the Senate.

The *Annual* reports that the 1913–14 Shortridge Senate ably discussed such measures as the Increased Navy Bill, Income Tax, Railway Regulation, Repeal of the Chinese Exclusion Act, and Home Rule for the Philippine Islands.

The year 1914–15 saw the formation of the Therapon Clubs. The boys' club was directed by Mr. Buck and the girls' by Mrs. Carey and Miss Mary Anne McCoy, registrar. The purpose of these organizations was expressed in the definition of their name: Therapon—"The doing of service, fostering and cherishing, friendship, loyalty, and service." Their initial project was for the upperclassmen to help the freshmen.

That was also the year that Shortridge first participated in the state basketball tournament. Shortridge had four intramural boys basketball teams, and interest was high. Many of the players proved to be ineligible under the tournament rules, but coach E. Carl Watson assembled a varsity team that went to Franklin for the sectional, the first interscholastic competition in seven years. The team won its first game against Broad Ripple High School, but lost to Southport in the next round.

Shortridge students and faculty continued to express appreciation to those who furthered education. The 1916 *Annual* contained a tribute to Nebraska Cropsey by Laura Donnan which said in part:

> The greatest asset of a city is a good public school system. The superiority of the Indianapolis public school system was attested several years ago when, at a national convention of the city superintendents of the United States, a vote was taken to decide which city, in the opinion of the convention, had the best schools—Indianapolis received the greatest number of votes.
>
> The Indianapolis public schools . . . are to a greater degree the work of Miss Nebraska Cropsey than that of any other one person. Miss Cropsey was an educational constructionist of the highest type. . . . She was an enthusiast, but one whose enthusiasm was controlled by common sense. Too wise to hasten, too firmly grounded in fundamentals to be unduly influenced by revolutionary movements, she remained, during the whole fifty-two years of public service, steadfast to the conviction that the corner stone of education is the mastery of the *printed page*.

That same *Annual* recorded the decision of the class of 1916 to honor the former Shortridge custodian, Mr. James Biddy, with a memorial tablet. The plaque was designed by artist Gordon Mess, class of 1918, and featured a picture of James Biddy with an inscription on each side.

|  |  |
|---|---|
| | HE |
| SEEST | DIGNIFIED |
| THOU A MAN | LABOR |
| DILIGENT | FOR HE KNEW NO |
| IN HIS | MASTER BUT |
| BUSINESS | DUTY |
| HE | HAD NO COMRADE |
| SHALL STAND | BUT TRUTH |
| BEFORE | DESIRED NO |
| KINGS | APPROVAL |
| | BUT |
| PROVERBS | SELF RESPECT |

James Biddy

The school board policy of "allowing eighth grade graduates free choice of high schools" so it would be "possible for our high schools to specialize in different lines, drawing from all parts of the city those pupils adapted to the work," meant, for Shortridge, that those students who were most academically inclined and who were probably college bound were steered toward Shortridge.

All three high schools were comprehensive schools; a student could go on to college from any of them, but Shortridge offered little in the way of vocational training. Both Manual and Tech offered a great deal. Shortridge's specialty was liberal arts. It was possible, for instance, to take, along with four years of English literature and composition, four years of Latin, four years of German, four years of French, and two years of Greek.

One student who actually took all these courses was Allegra Stewart, class of 1917, who went on to become a distinguished scholar and a professor of English literature at Butler. One reason she could work in so many languages was that she entered Shortridge with five credits from grade school: English, civics, Latin, German, and algebra. A large number of her classmates did likewise. The way the system worked was that academically talented children were sorted out in grade school and given instruction in certain subjects for high school credit. They were then encouraged to enroll at Shortridge, and when they were admitted there, they were automatically part of an advanced group.

Allegra Stewart kept a "girl graduate book," which paints a picture of an almost cozy environment in a school of sixteen hundred students and sixty-eight teachers. She records that she and various of her friends were entertained by a number of teachers. Miss Marthens took them to English's to see Minnie Maddern Fiske in *Erstwhile Susan*. Mr. Jennings took them to see Raymond Hitchcock in a musical entitled, *Betty*. Miss McClellan of the Zoology Department, Miss Grace Philputt of the French Department, and Miss Ruth O'Hair and Miss Harriet Sawyer of the English Department all entertained students in their homes. In every instance Allegra reported they had "a perfectly wonderful time."

Her favorite of them all was the French teacher, Grace Philputt. A Shortridge graduate and a noted basketball player in the class of 1904, Miss Philputt had majored in French at Indiana University and then spent a year in France before beginning her teaching. She was herself acutely conscious of the plight of France during the years of the First World War, and she conveyed this concern to her students. They were, therefore, active in raising money for French war relief even before the United States entered the war. Allegra used the money that she received as a graduation present to adopt a French war orphan of her own. At the end of 1917, Grace Philputt married the head of the Romance Language Department at Indiana University and left Shortridge for Bloomington. She was succeeded by Gertrude Weathers.

Byron K. Elliott, president of the class of 1917, later Marion County Superior Court judge, and still later chairman of the board and chief executive officer of John Hancock Insurance Company, wrote in 1984 about his high school life and times:

> The auto's invasion of America extended into even the classical segments of education. . . . When Miss Claybaugh's first-year Latin class was interrupted by four men carrying in a big flat object covered with a canvas, curiosity rose to a fever pitch. It was placed on the floor beside the teacher's desk and the canvas tied on tight. There it was to remain a mystery for three days, and on the fourth, there would be no assignment, for the object would be unveiled in the presence of the class, who would have permission to touch it, whatever it was. This much was disclosed however: the object had many parts and the names for forty-one of them had Latin roots.
>
> Word circulated, and classes in other subjects were regretfully told "no visitors." The Principal received a number of phone calls from parents asking if they could attend. Only the Principal, a school board member, and a half dozen other teachers, and one hundred per cent of the class were present when the appointed day arrived and two sturdy school janitors approached the object and pulled off the canvas.
>
> There it was, in all its mechanical nudity, a complete Ford chassis! On top was a placard bearing the name of each of 117 parts and materi-

als and the statement that 90 names were words with Latin roots and that anyone wanting to pass the course had better show up in 30 days with a list of 45, including their Latin origin. Parents were allowed to help—Miss Claybaugh saw a chance to point out to parents how basic Latin was to our language.

The entire ploy was a probable success with the girls, who didn't need much help, and a positive success with the boys, who needed a great deal. The boys had no special affinity for Latin, but they certainly did for a Ford chassis.

Enthusiasm, excitement and resourcefulness distinguished the faculty of Shortridge High School. Most of the teachers were strong personalities, as was Laura Donnan. She taught American Constitutional History. . . . On the first day of her class she directed that all notebooks be placed on the left side of the students' desks with name and seat number clearly marked. Then she would produce a market basket, walk up and down the aisle collecting the books and telling the students that the knowledge they acquired in her class was to reside in their minds, not their notebooks. She also informed the students that no one would pass who had not recited from memory, piece by piece, the entire United States Constitution, and none ever did.

During the war, Miss Donnan wrote every former student of hers who was in the military service a newsy letter. They were duplicates, of course, and said to have reached nearly a thousand soldiers and sailors. They were warm, supportive, and contained just enough advice so you recognized the author as Laura Donnan. I know about them. I still have mine.

Another student of those days who always had "a perfectly wonderful time" was Art Shea, who has lived many years in Greenwich, Connecticut, but has retained warm memories of Shortridge. He entered Shortridge in the fall of 1914 at the age of fourteen, along with his brother Bob, aged eleven, who became Shortridge's first Rhodes scholar. Art has recorded his recollections of Indianapolis during his high school years. His first memory is of entering Shortridge on a bright, sunny day, feeling both nervous and excited. Almost at once he encountered his favorite teacher in his favorite class. This was Louis H. Dirks teaching German I. In that class were a couple of older girls who worked on Wednesday's *Echo*. After a few weeks, Art told them he thought the *Echo* was fine, but he would like to see his name in it. Much to his surprise (he was a freshman), this was reported to the editor of Wednesday's *Echo* who asked him to submit a story. He wrote a parody of one of George Ade's *Fables in Slang*, adapting it to the Shortridge scene. Not only was Art's parody printed, but he was asked to write another and another. He never stopped writing for the *Echo*, and in his senior year he became an *Echo* editor himself. He liked the rivalry among the staffs of the various days of the week and still has no doubt that his *Echo*, Wednesday's, under the censorship of Mr. Dirks, was the best of all.

The Indianapolis that Art recalls was still a relatively small city with much of the flavor of a small town. His father was in the grocery business, and every morning before school Art drove his father down to the commission market to buy the produce for that day. The grocery truck was one of the first in Indianapolis, and it lumbered down the streets, driven by a proud teenager and powered by a two cylinder engine. The Murat and English theaters were the principal centers for entertainment. Rosie English was a friend and sometimes invited him to sit in the English family box. The Circle Theatre, a motion picture palace, opened in 1916, but movies were not yet an important recreation.

Art describes his teachers as "remarkably proficient." In addition to Mr. Dirks, he particularly remembers Miss Marthens, Mr. Otto, Miss Donnan, and his drawing teacher, Marie Todd. He rather enjoyed being scared of Miss Donnan. He also thought highly of "kindly, wizened Harry Porter," who coached and directed all the school plays. He did not take chemistry, but he spent a lot of time in the chemistry department, both because he liked Mr. Wade and because his friend Irv Page (later Dr. Irvine H. Page) was the assistant in the chemistry lab.

By this time Frank Wade had become a nationally recognized authority on gems. During the war he helped the Nordyke-Marmon Company in the purchase of industrial diamonds to tool Liberty airplane engines and supervised their mounting. During the school day, his students often had the startling experience of seeing Mr. Wade reach into his pocket and casually bring forth a handful of diamonds.

Dr. Irvine H. Page, director of the Lilly Laboratory for Clinical Research, then director, Research Division of the Cleveland Clinic, author of many books, and the recipient of countless awards, recalled Mr. Wade in 1984:

> Mr. Wade was a top notch teacher because he could make such pedestrian things as analyzing vinegar interesting. As his assistant, I followed Baird Hastings, who subsequently became the distinguished Professor of Biochemistry at the Harvard Medical School. By some oddity I was unaware that I had succeeded Hastings at Shortridge until one evening in a Toronto restaurant we started comparing notes only to find we both came from the Wade entourage. This entourage was also bound together by all of us purchasing our engagement rings through Mr. Wade. He had a habit of carrying a fortune in diamonds to be reset in a piece of folded paper in his coat pocket. Tiffany was one of his best customers. Almost everyone who was taught by Mr. Wade bought a ring from him. The bride received a book on diamonds by Mr. Wade.

A Wadian cult has subsequently grown up held together by respect and affection for Frank Wade.

I also served as assistant to Elizabeth Rawls in the botany department. She and Frank Wade and Rousseau McClellan were all first rate science teachers by any standard. Miss Rawls seemed the most forbidding, but later in life when I knew her socially she was an altogether different person—I still had trouble calling her "Bess." She lived long enough to see at least two of us get elected to the National Academy of Sciences in Washington.

Another of Art Shea's recollections is about the social clubs which, while still forbidden, were still going strong. He said that the faculty expressed disapproval of the clubs, but probably with their fingers crossed, as there was absolutely nothing they could do about them. Art belonged to the Hill Club. His brother, Bob, was a Corpse Club member, and Ott Frenzel belonged to Alpha Omega. The principal girls' club, in Art's recollection, was Beta Phi Sigma, which was rivaled by Tudor Hall's Sigma Beta Sigma. All the clubs did was to give parties, usually tea dances. They met once a month for general sociability and to plan these events. Pledges in boys' clubs were required to leap to their feet in the presence of club members and to address them as "sir," but that was about all that was demanded of them. Art remembers wearing his pledge pin with enormous pride and strolling past Tudor Hall and St. Agnes Academy in the belief that the girls would look out the windows and be dazzled by his shining emblem of success.

Harriet Brown (later Mrs. G. Vance Smith), also of the class of 1918, said that she did not join a social club, because she and her classmates had been told that anybody who belonged to such an organization in high school would not be eligible for a college sorority or fraternity. Several of her friends disregarded this warning, however, and when they got to college found that it had no substance. She is yet another who always had "a perfectly wonderful time" at Shortridge, and her favorite teacher was also Mr. Dirks. Prominent in her memory book, right in among all the dance programs, is a note to Miss Claybaugh, dated 11/13/17: "Miss Rupp and Mrs. Hankey are absent on account of illness. May I have Harriet Brown to take a class for me the 4th period? L. H. Dirks." Miss Claybaugh answered, "Yes."

Also in Harriet Brown's memory book is a clipping concerning Shortridge's new tennis star, under the heading: NOT 17, BUT A CHAMPION!

Driving the ball with force and accuracy that bewildered his opponent, Johnny Hennessey yesterday afternoon won the city tennis championship at the final match of the patriotic tennis tournament, which has been in progress for two weeks. . . .

Hennessey will be the most popular city champion in years, for he has established a new era in local tennis circles. Season after season Indianapolis followers of the sport have seen veterans in the final round. In this year's play, the youngster eliminated two old timers—Fred Appel and Charley Trask. Hennessey's development at the net has been fast. . . . If he continues to show his present form, he should be a hard lad to beat. . . .

Within a few years Johnny Hennessey was playing tennis for the United States on the Davis Cup team. While in Shortridge he also captained the 1918 basketball team, the first full season a Shortridge team had played since the 1907 ban on extramural competition.

. . . . .

In April of 1917 the United States declared war on the Central Powers. Shortridge students immediately began to raise money for the war effort. That year's senior play was Earl Derr Biggers's *Inside the Lines*. As usual, the production was reported in the *Echo* to be a brilliant success. The seniors then undertook to present it again as a benefit performance for the Red Cross. According to the account in the *News* of June 9, 1917:

After the performance of "Inside the Lines" was fairly under way at the Murat last night, the audience had no reason to feel nervous. Before the first act had been completed those who had feared there would be embarrassing hitches were ready to relax and sit back for an evening of entertainment, and they were not disappointed. . . .

The performance moved smoothly from the first.

Leading roles were played by Kathryn Turney, Max Recker, Pauline Marshall, and Robert Axtell.

This was just the beginning. By the following spring the *News* gave this report:

A complete report of the war work of Shortridge High School for the last year shows that $22,555.49 has been contributed through the school alone. . . . The total does not include Liberty bonds or outside contributions to war activities. Cash contributions were: Sale of Thrift stamps by school, $20,020.61; sale of tickets for Shortridge moving picture benefit, $1,196.23; Liberty Friday collections, $566.15; gift of junior (1919) class, $65; Italian relief campaign, $102.50; Italian ambulance fund, $55; Christmas gift campaign for French war orphans, $50; sale of art department Christmas cards, $50; American Red Cross memberships, $450.

Twenty-one pupils enlisted in the army or navy from September, 1917 to May, 1918. . . . Six French war orphans are supported by individual pupils, and 135 are contributing to the support of French war orphans (through the French Club). 715 knitted articles were completed by 321 pupils.

For the first time in the school's history knitting was permitted during Shortridge auditorium programs, and a number of the boys knitted along with the girls. In addition, one hundred Shortridge girls worked regularly in the Shortridge Red Cross shop and made over sixteen thousand surgical dressings. The Art Department made four hundred ninety posters, and the business students mimeographed some five thousand cards and twelve hundred circulars and wrote five hundred letters. In addition to all this, Shortridge, as a school, gave $1,000 in gold to the Indianapolis War Chest. They did it dramatically:

In one of the most inspiring exercises ever participated in by Short-ridgers, and one which will go down in the history of Indianapolis, the student body of Shortridge High School presented $1,000 to the Indianapolis War Chest. The school marched in a body to the Monument for the presentation ceremony. . . . This donation has made SHS "go over the top" 100%, with a record which has not been equalled by any other school. . . .

The procession was headed by the American Flag, followed by the flags of the Allies of America—England, France, Italy and Belgium. The SHS banner then came, followed by the Shortridge Service Flag. The parade proper was headed by the senior session rooms in order, as follows: 19, 9, 7, 5, 4, 3, 11. The next division consisted of the Shortridge banner, followed by Mr. Osbon, Mr. Buck, Miss O'Hair and the guard with the gold. The junior session rooms then followed and after them the underclassmen session rooms, closing the parade with the Shortridge banner. Each session room was headed by an American Flag. . . .

The Shortridge service flag contained 421 stars. At Christmas time Mr. Buck sent the following greeting:

To the Shortridge Boys in the Service:

We salute you. A short while ago you were under our care and we gave you such service as we had to give. But now conditions are quite reversed. We are now dependent upon you; we are now in your care; you have now become our defenders and you are making the supreme sacrifice, such sacrifice as only the brave and courageous of all time have made.

We, whom you have left behind, shall follow you in support; we shall follow you in thought; you will not be out of our minds day nor night; our spirits will cross the seas to wherever you may be, to give you courage, to give you patience, to cheer you and help you to victory. We shall pray that you may return to us strong and virtuous men, whose achievements shall be our glory, whose character shall be our emulation, and whose courage shall be our inspiration.

Sincerely yours,<br>George Buck

The 1918 *Annual* contains, along with Mr. Buck's greeting, some letters to Shortridge from men overseas and a thank-you note from the mother of one of the French war orphans. Sergeant Benjamin D. Hitz, Lilly Base Hospital No. 32, wrote:

> I . . . believe it more firmly than ever now that America will never really feel the war for a long, long time. Thousands of individuals . . . have felt the pangs of parting and separation, of course, but the Nation as a whole has not felt it and will not feel it until the big casualty lists start coming in. Looking back from here, I am impressed with the fact that America has been playing at war. The novelty of our wheatless days and meatless days has not yet worn off. . . . America's most wheatless day would be a luxury any time in France. France has war bread every day . . . there is no white bread in France—there is no cornbread, nor graham, nor whole-wheat nor rye; no soda-crackers or biscuits, and from now on no pastry of any kind. There is this difference between America and France in almost everything.

As a result of the war, German was dropped from the public schools of Indianapolis at the end of the 1917–18 school year. This did not, however, interfere with the popularity of Mr. Louis H. Dirks, who became first an English teacher and then a vice-principal. Loyalty to teachers ran high. The 1918 *Annual* was edited by Herbert R. Hill, who had already begun to work for the *News* during his senior year, and who was afterwards a regular *News* columnist and then for many years its managing editor. In retrospect, he spoke well of all his teachers and of the general discipline of the school under Mr. Buck, but he said firmly that the person who really made everything go was Mr. Otto. That opinion has been echoed by a number of later students, among them John Collett, class of 1920: "The teacher I remember best was William N. Otto. . . . He insisted that I enter into debating and he taught me the art of public speaking which I have found invaluable. I went on to do debating at Wabash College and found his training had been of the best."

·  ·  ·  ·  ·

During the 1917–18 school year George Hufford died. Tribute was paid to him in that year's *Annual* by Laura Donnan:

> George W. Hufford was a man teaching. With him teaching was not a stepping-stone but a goal. He was fitted for his chosen work both by his attainments and his character. Beginning his education before the days of specialties, the foundation of his scholarship was broad. By the best use of spare minutes he made this broad foundation the basis of many scholarly attainments. The Greek, Latin, French, German and English languages and literature were at his command; to him higher mathematics was by no means a stranger; the facts of science were his acquaintances and history was his friend. Democratic by nature and imbued with the love of learning, he was ever on the alert to discover and help any person seeking an opportunity to train his faculties and increase his knowledge. With Mr. Hufford there was no aristocracy of intellect. He recognized no barriers to education except the lack of a desire to learn and the failure to make the necessary application. . . .

In the same year that the ex-principal died, a future principal joined the faculty. Joel W. Hadley, class of 1910, had become an ardent naturalist and bird lover at Shortridge, under the influence of Rousseau McClellan, as well as a competent chemist, under the influence of Frank Wade. Joel had been unable to go to college following his graduation. Instead, he took a job as an assistant chemist for the Indianapolis Water Company. He worked there for a couple of years and saved his money. Then, under the prodding of Mr. Wade, he enrolled in Wesleyan University in Connecticut, Mr. Wade's alma mater. During the summers he continued to work for the Water Company. In the summer of 1916 he was called into the office of the president, Clarence Kirk, to receive a telephone call. The call was from General Gignilliat of Culver Military Academy offering him a job in the Culver woodcraft camp. Hadley said, "Thank you very much, but I couldn't possibly do it. I am working for the Indianapolis Water Company."

Mr. Kirk interjected emphatically, "I think you were much too quick about that."

"Well, I couldn't just walk out on my job here," said the startled young man.

"I've been watching you," replied Mr. Kirk, "and I think anybody who can get a bunch of Water Company ditch diggers excited about *birds* ought to seriously consider teaching. This is a real opportunity for you. I'm willing to promise that if you want to work here next summer you'll have a job. Call General Gignilliat back."

Hadley did. Except for the summer of 1918, when he was in service, he taught at Culver every summer until 1925. He became a member of the Shortridge faculty in the fall of 1917 and devoted the rest of his life to education.

Josephine M. Cox

# CHAPTER 8

# Normalcy

THE FALL OF 1918 was an eventful time. School had been in session barely four weeks when Indianapolis, along with the rest of the country, was struck by the worst flu epidemic this nation has ever had. Many people died. All the schools were closed for a full month, October 5 to November 5, and everyone who went into any public place or used public transportation was required to wear a flu mask.

Jim Gloin, class of 1919 and later president of L. S. Ayres, the well-known Indianapolis department store, remembers this as the time that he and his friends spent in Jim Sargent's basement becoming excellent pool players. Just three days after they had ripped off their masks and returned to school, word flashed through the building that an armistice had been signed and the war was over. The Shortridge students formed themselves into a parade behind the Cadet Corps and marched down to Manual, in the 500 block of South Meridian, to get their peers out of school. Then they all headed for the Circle and general celebration. It was exciting and joyous, even though it turned out that the peace rumors were false and the war was not yet over. When the armistice actually was signed on November 11, it came as something of an anticlimax.

With the end of the war, an era of expansion began for Shortridge and for Indianapolis. The 1919 *Annual* took service as its theme. It was dedicated:

To

JOSEPHINE M. COX OF THE DEPART-
MENT OF HISTORY, A WISE AND UN-
DERSTANDING INSTRUCTOR, A CHEERY
FRIEND AND ONE WHO HAS CONSIS-
TENTLY STOOD FOR ALL THAT IS BEST
IN LIFE. . . .

Mrs. Cox responded:

> Service has thrilled our hearts, service loyal and true;
> Service has been our watch-word the whole war through.
> But now the war is done, and service is forgot,
> Or mentioned lightly as a thing to give or not. . . .
>
> . . . .
>
> Service to country is due in time of peace as in war
> But lacking the flaming incentive, the duty is harder far.
> O, be not parasites, my Class
> And do not give half hearted service;
> "Live up to the hilt" for your country's weal
> Until you sink to the hero's rest.

The art editor of the *Annual*, Richard C. Lennox, said:

> This year has opened a new era in the world—the era of Progress, the ideal of Democracy, which every high school student must feel in order to reach the goal of true citizenship. The Art Staff of the *Annual* has endeavored to combine the new idea of Progress in art with the idea of Service. The cover design stands for Service and Chivalry. On the shield is the American eagle, while in the distance may be seen the Tower of Shortridge. . . .

The students continued to sponsor projects for the relief of war victims and for the poor at home. One such project was a "Chickadilly" participated in by both students and faculty. The Chickadilly was a costumed musical entertainment staged to raise money to reestablish poultry in war-torn France. A clothing drive was held for needy Rumanian children. In May, 1920, a benefit picture show, *Luck of the Irish*, was presented at the Ohio Theatre to raise money for the Armenian Relief Fund—Joel W. Hadley, sponsor. The Art Department established a class in toy making, to produce toys for those children who would otherwise not have them. Mr. Wade accepted the chairmanship of the Indianapolis Commission on Smoke Prevention and Fuel Conservation.

Jim Gloin's favorite teacher was Angeline Carey, who "taught me more English than I ever learned in college." He says he can still hear the sound of her voice saying, "James, you are not doing as well as you are capable of doing." Mrs. Carey was determined to maintain standards of excellence. She also enjoyed expressing herself in verse. She combined these interests in a letter to Santa Claus for the faculty page of the 1919 *Christmas Echo*.

Dear Santa, I'm a teacher here
In Shortridge school, and need, this year,
From out your well-assorted pack
Two gifts which pupils think I lack.
So if you do not heed my call,
How can I go to school at all?
I need a conscience, Santa dear,
Of modern type, of which I hear,
A '20s model, not the kind
That suited Puritanic mind,
But pliant, supple, yielding, mild,
That sees no fault in any child.
The conscience I have used till now
Is all worn out—I'll tell you how,
I've stretched and stretched it, with good will,
To make it cover all that's ill,
And so blot out, because it's sad,
Distinction plain 'twixt good and bad.
But 'tis old-fashioned conscience yet,
Too hard for it the task that's set.
A conscience rubber-lined I need
To stretch and fit a naughty deed,
And form it into something fair
Without regard to wheat or tare,
That looks not with partiality
But covers all with charity.
My other need I now put down.
It's something that will banish frown,
For smiling face, the modern say
The child, of course, must see alway.
So bring me, Santa, a sweet smile,
With which all errors to beguile.
I want a smile that won't come off
To flash upon the careless soph.
A smile to meet the bluffer's stall,
Or e'en the star in basketball,
Who holds me up for passing mark
As though school life was all a lark. . . .
Perhaps, kind friend you'd better put
Into my Christmas stocking-foot
A contract that will make secure
My teacher's job, for I'm most sure
That if you tell for what I call
They will not want me here at all.

Idealistic efforts from both students and teachers continued as strong as ever, but in the country as a whole, and certainly in the state of Indiana, the desire of the majority was for "normalcy."

"Normalcy" in Indiana turned out to include a strong movement for racial segregation in both schools and housing. The 1869 education law, which first admitted black children to public education, gave local authorities the option of maintaining segregated schools or of allowing members of both races to attend the same school. The 1877 law amended this to read that whenever a child attending a black school showed that he was prepared to be placed in a higher grade than that afforded by the black school, he was to be admitted to a white school. The Indianapolis school board exercised its option to maintain segregated grade schools, with only a few exceptions where neighborhoods were integrated. The black schools were staffed primarily with black teachers, but no black teacher was allowed to teach in a school that contained any white students. The student bodies of the high schools had been integrated from the time that Abram Shortridge escorted Mary Ann Rann into Indianapolis High School in 1872.

By the early 1920s Indianapolis's Negro population had grown considerably. There were about eight hundred Negro students enrolled in high school, many of them at Shortridge, where they constituted 10 to 15 percent of the student population. The proximity of the city's traditional Negro neighborhood, just northwest of downtown Indianapolis, gave considerable impetus to the movement for transplanting Shortridge farther north. There were other reasons, of course. The population of the city was expanding northwards, and most of the area around the high school was no longer residential. The majority of students came to school on the streetcar.

Still, building a new Shortridge and building a new all-black high school were interrelated projects. The city, in the early 1920s, had, in addition to the Ku Klux Klan, a White Supremacy League, a White Citizens Protective League, a Capitol Avenue Protective Association, and a Mapleton Civic Association, all of which were dedicated to preventing Negroes from moving out of their overcrowded neighborhoods and into better housing in neighborhoods which had been traditionally white. The school board, which had been elected with the backing of the newly formed Citizens School Committee, a civic group devoted to the improvement of public education, demurred at the language of some of the petitions it received, but it stiffened the requirements for school segregation as requested.

A principal argument for establishing separate schools for Negroes was based on their poor housing conditions. A resolution presented to the Indianapolis Board of School Commissioners in 1922 on behalf of the Federation of Civic Clubs pointed out that, while Negroes constituted only about one tenth of the total population of Indianapolis, about one fourth of the deaths in the city were among Negroes. "For years," it asserted, "the Marion County Tuberculosis Society has emphasized the care of incurable consumption among the colored people as the greatest social need in this city." Because crowded housing conditions made it impossible for tubercular patients to be cared for adequately at home, a large number of cases of incipient tuberculosis were believed to exist among black school children. Therefore, for the protection of white children the school board was asked to establish separate schools for all Negro children and to staff them with Negro teachers. This included the establishment of an all-black high school. The Chamber of Commerce submitted a similar petition, but included the proviso that the new building should be a modern and well-equipped school.

The movement for a separate high school met with strong opposition from the Negro community. A petition from the Better Indianapolis Civic League, representing Negro civic and ministerial groups, declared that the public school system was the most powerful factor in American society for the "engendering and transmission of sound democratic ideals." It emphasized that "no one section of the population" could be "isolated and segregated without taking from it the advantages of the common culture." Since money for the public schools came from all the people, it was "unjust, un-American, and against the spirit of democratic ideals that one section of the citizenship should subvert the funds of the common treasury to discriminate against another section solely on the basis of ancestry."

The board responded on December 12, 1922, with a declaration that the enrollment of over eight hundred Negroes in the city high schools showed a "laudable desire on their part and on the part of their parents" for an education, but that a "new, modern, well-equipped high school" of their own would provide them with the "maximum educational opportunity" and the fullest opportunity for the development of initiative, self-reliance, and the other qualities needed for good citizenship.

The school board resisted a petition to use the old Shortridge buildings for the new Negro high school "in the interest of economy," and went ahead with the construction of a school which was substantially equal to new schools being built for white students. The hope was that the new school and the employment of Negro teachers would make segregation less offensive. There was indeed an increase in enrollment of black high school students when Crispus Attucks opened in the fall of 1927 at the corner of 11th and Northwest streets. The black community came to take pride in its high school, but not without a sense of discrimination.

Segregation was made absolute. No black student could attend any high school other than Crispus Attucks regardless of geographical location, and no provision was made for transportation. Graham Martin, class of 1937, later a teacher and football coach at Attucks, walked every day from 25th and Keystone, a distance of five and a half miles, in order to get a high school education. He says, "It was the Depression. There wasn't any money for carfare. It was the only way I could go to school."

The Indiana High School Athletic Association barred the black schools (Crispus Attucks and Gary Roosevelt) from play in the state basketball tournament or any IHSAA league. They had to arrange their own games with whatever schools they could find. In the case of Crispus Attucks these were mostly with black schools in Kentucky. This rule was in effect from 1927 until 1942. In the same year, 1927, the trustees of Butler University decided to limit the number of Negro students entering the university by allowing a maximum of ten such students to enroll each year.

At Shortridge in the early 1920s, at least among the white students, there was virtually no awareness that all this controversy was taking place. Jim Gloin says, "We didn't think anything about black and white in those days. I remember my zoology class under Miss McClellan. I liked the class and the field trips, but I wasn't good at lab work, and I nearly died when I was supposed to dissect a frog. I had a black lab partner who was a whiz. He took pity on me and dissected my frog as well as his own, but he did it too well. When Miss McClellan came around to inspect our work, she took one look and said, 'James, are you sure you did all this?' so I had to confess."

Frances Westcott, class of 1923, says much the same thing: "The black students were just there. They participated in everything. There was no racial tension. I remember that several served as president of the Senate. I suppose they did particularly like the Senate. It was Miss Donnan's club, and nobody who was closely associated with Laura Donnan could possibly be a bigot."

Dora Omo Atkins, class of 1921 (now Mrs. Cleo Blackburn), remembers it differently:

> We got a good education. I'm grateful for it, but there *was* prejudice at Shortridge. Miss Love, the English teacher, was one who always made us uncomfortable, but the gym teacher, Mrs. Steichmann,

was the worst. We were totally segregated in gym, and it was really unpleasant. My father was quite angry about it, but he couldn't get it changed.

.   .   .   .   .

When the school year opened in the fall of 1919, the student enrollment was 1,524: 492 boys and 1,032 girls, girls still outnumbering the boys more than two to one. Walter B. Hendrickson, class of 1920 and longtime history professor at MacMurray College, has written about his Indianapolis education in *The Indianapolis Years 1905–1941*. He believes he was the only boy in his class at School 43 to go to Shortridge or to any high school.

> At the time, children had to graduate from the eighth grade or be fourteen years old before they could go to work, and jobs for boys were not hard to find. So it was still the exception for boys to go to high school.

Walter himself had to work during his entire high school career of three and a half years and so was unable to take part in any extracurricular activities, but he remembers many of his teachers well. For one thing he lived next door to Miss Marthens and Miss McClellan. He took Latin from Miss Marthens and mentions with pride that she had studied at Columbia and that she also taught Greek. He also comments on several of his other teachers:

> In English I sat in the classes of Miss Flora Love, Mrs. Angeline Carey, and Miss Zella O'Hair, all older ladies who upheld the highest standards of reading and writing and who sought to inculcate in their students their personal joy in literature. . . .
>
> Miss Rousseau McClellan was the zoology teacher, and she also taught geology and physiology to selected students. It was considered an honor to be allowed to enroll in these latter classes, and it was a kind of seal of approval of a student's scholarship. Miss McClellan was another teacher who had studied at Columbia University. She was a fine teacher and science demonstrator who used the most recent techniques. Her specialties, geology and physiology, were not usually courses that were given in high school. . . .
>
> Although I never had classes with Miss Donnan . . . I was in her session room and found that she had a warm heart under her crusty manner. She was a strong advocate for the rights of blacks. She was very helpful and understanding when I had to arrange to leave school early in the day to go to my job. . . .
>
> Finally, there was Principal George Buck, whom I met only once,

Zella O'Hair

in the spring of my senior year. The registrars were completing the academic records of students preliminary to certification for graduation, and it was found that I had only thirty-one and a half credits of the thirty-two that were necessary. I was called to Mr. Buck's office, and the matter was discussed. I suppose he felt that Shortridge High School was in part to blame because my attention had not been called to the matter sooner. At any rate, when Mr. Buck saw that I had worked all the time I was in school and that if something was not done immediately, I would have to delay graduation until I could take another course and earn the required one-half credit, he discovered, much to his peace of mind and mine, that I had a credit in German from grade school. In the usual course of events, I would have had to take another semester of German to make use of the credit. But Mr. Buck said that he would make an exception and would count the grade school credit so I would have just the thirty-two credits I needed.

. . . . . .

For those who did not have to earn a living while going to high school, there were almost endless opportunities at Shortridge to pursue special interests. The Senate, the Press Club, the *Echo*, and the Debating Club were still going strong. The Wireless Club was new in the fall of 1919. As soon as wartime restrictions were lifted, the radio buffs applied for permission to have a sending station. When that was granted, they organized enthusiastically and put out a call for membership, including the statement, "Girls will be allowed to join." The Physiography Club, sponsored by Miss Mabel Washburn, took hikes every other week and collected rocks. On the off-weeks they met indoors for discussion. Mr. Walter G. Gingery's Math Club had forty members who met weekly to solve mathematical puzzles, create magic squares, and generally enjoy themselves. The Junior Drama League, coached by Miss Flora Love, had a large membership and put on various short plays throughout the year. Members of the Shakespearean Club met weekly to deepen their understanding of Shakespeare by reading and acting out some of his plays.

. . . . .

Along with all these activities, great expansion took place in the fields of music, art, and especially sports.

The Indiana High School Athletic Association was founded in 1903 in Richmond for the purpose of encouraging interscholastic sports and establishing rules and eligibility requirements. Its first president was Shortridge principal, George Benton. He served only one year in that capacity, but continued on the Board of Control until after the disastrous fight with Manual in 1907, when the Indianapolis high schools were withdrawn from competition in major sports. They came back in gradually. The first state basketball tournament was held in 1911, but Shortridge did not compete until 1915. During this period intramural athletics were strong. A larger proportion of the student body was playing basketball than was ever to play again, but the students still wanted the excitement of playing against other schools.

Participation in varsity sports and compliance with IHSAA rules required rearrangement of the intramural schedules. Mr. Buck approached the situation cautiously. Shortridge did not commit itself to a full basketball season until 1918, when it played Franklin, Danville, Richmond, Rushville, Brownsburg, and Evansville. The team won three and lost three, but, as was carefully pointed out in the *Annual*, it outscored its opponents 315 to 237. In the sectionals it defeated New Bethel in the first round and lost to Morgantown in the second. Shortridge did not win a sectional until 1925, but it never again failed to compete.

In the fall of 1920, football came back to Shortridge, and the school acquired its first athletic director, Russell S. Julius, generally spoken of as "Tubby." He coached both football and baseball. The school board had acquired some land at 34th and Meridian streets as a possible site for a new Shortridge, and Mr. Julius and his players used this as a practice field. Football came back quietly. Mr. Buck did not want the excitement of football and basketball to dominate school life. He need not have worried. The school did not have a winning football season until 1925, and only one winning basketball season, 1921. That year also produced a winning baseball team, but otherwise the *Annuals* from 1920 through 1924 simply present the athletic records as bravely as possible and congratulate the boys for effort and good sportsmanship.

The 1922 basketball season was the low point at 1–16. In the fall of 1922 Enoch Burton joined the faculty as a math teacher, and the next year he became the head basketball coach. His players were known as the "Battling Burtonians," and they improved every year. In 1923 they came up to 6–13, in 1924 to 7–7, and in 1925 they posted a 25–2 record and won the city championship, defeating arch rival, Manual, by a score of 35–29. The *Echo* reported the victory:

> With wild whoops of unbounded joy the verdant children, sophs, juniors, the solemn and dignified seniors and even the famous faculty trooped happily down Pennsylvania Street to tell the whole world that Shortridge had won the city basketball championship. Blue and white banners waved, streamers tossed wildly as twenty-six hundred hearty voices proclaimed the victory.

Orations were given on Monument Circle by Mr. Buck, Mr. Dirks, Mr. Burton, Mr. Julius, and several others.

Shortridge went on to win its first sectional victory by again defeating Manual, 22–20 in an even more dramatic confrontation. The crowd again "went wild with joy," but there were no untoward incidents.

Shortridge defeated Greenfield in the first round of the 1925 Anderson regional, but then lost to the Muncie Bearcats, thus bringing an end to a magnificent season. In 1926 Shortridge had only a slightly less impressive record, 18–8, and another sectional victory. In 1927 and '28 it was less successful—10–11 and 4–13—but interest remained high.

The girls' basketball team, on the other hand, had a steady habit of winning. In 1921 they won thirteen out of fourteen games. In 1922 they were again defeated only once—by Manual. All during the 1920s they never failed to have a winning season, and in 1929 they were unbeaten. But they never inspired orations and cheering crowds on the Circle.

Kate Lilly Steichmann
with her assistant Calley Rice

The best of the girl athletes were rewarded with numerals and sweaters which they earned in a rather complicated way. All Shortridge girls were rated on an athletic index devised by Kate Steichmann, head of the girls' athletic department. They competed for points in a gym efficiency contest and a posture contest in the regular gym classes. They also competed in sports—volley ball, hockey, and tennis (all intramural), as well as basketball, which was extramural. Players received points for participating in any of the sports, with extra points for winning. Whenever a girl had accumulated five hundred points, she was awarded an athletic numeral. If she could get up to a thousand, she received a sweater. These awards were presented in gym class, not in the auditorium, where the boys received their letters.

The outstanding girl athlete of the 1920s was Muriel Adams (Stahl), class of 1928, who played on the successful basketball teams during her time at Shortridge and was also Shortridge tennis champion. She went on to win the Indianapolis city tennis championship eight times. She says:

As athletes, we weren't just second class citizens. We were about fourth class, but we didn't think anything about it. We were brought up that way, and anyway we had a good time.

Success in football followed closely behind that of basketball. Alonzo Goldsberry, a football star from Wabash College, joined the faculty as a history teacher and football coach in the fall of 1923. He ran a camp for his players in August of the following year to get them into shape before the season began. They responded by giving Shortridge its first winning season (6–2) since football had returned to school in 1920.

In 1925, under Goldsberry's coaching, the team had a 9–0 record and won the city championship. In fact, there were only two points scored against them the whole season. The 1928 *Annual* points out proudly that "no team ever crossed the SHS goal line." In the fall of 1928, the Shortridge team won a second city championship with a 9–2 record, but unfortunately they got a little overconfident. They challenged another school with an outstanding record, Gary Froebel, to play a "Mythical State Championship" game. Gary Froebel accepted the challenge and clobbered the Shortridge heroes 70–0. In the fall of 1929 Shortridge earned its third city championship in a row, but this time the team rested on its laurels.

Tennis was considered a minor sport, but it was important for both boys and girls. The 1921 boys' tennis tournament, won by Julius Sagalowsky, had one hundred players. The golf tournaments were much smaller, but interest increased during the decade. Tennis was coached by John Kuebler. In 1924 and 1925 his teams were state champions in both singles and doubles, and the outstanding Shortridge player, Kenneth Christena, won the national interscholastic singles championship at Ann Arbor, Michigan, in the summer of 1925.

Shortridge's best girl tennis player was written up in the *Indianapolis News* in the spring of 1928:

> Added laurels to Shortridge's long list of tennis triumphs were announced when Muriel Adams, a senior, by her brilliant play in the Michigan State and Western Clay Court tournaments, was rated ninth in the women's singles by the Western Lawn Tennis Association. She and Dorothy Stephenson were placed fifth in the Women's doubles. . . . In a field of this size, comprising some of the largest cities of the United States, this ranking is noteworthy, particularly as the group in which Muriel competed was composed mainly of women between the ages of twenty and thirty. Muriel has never played in a girls' tournament, but since the age of thirteen has competed in women's doubles and singles events. She is undoubtedly the youngest Hoosier to have attained such an honor.

Two other minor sports produced state championships in the 1920s: gymnastics in 1927 and swimming in 1928. The swimming team, led by star Frank Kennedy, participated in the national meet in Chicago. They finished fourth in the country, but Frank won several first-place trophies.

.    .    .    .    .

Interest in art at Shortridge continued to flourish during the postwar period. One of the new organizations in the early 1920s was the Art Appreciation Club. Its stated purpose was "To know and feel the principles of art, to study the resources of art in the community, and to enjoy friendship on the common basis of high ideals." During the first year of its existence the club made an intensive study of the architecture of the Indianapolis Central Library. Interest in architecture was high because everyone knew that there was going to be a new Shortridge, and this time it was going to be designed and built as a complete high school, not just an addition to old and unsatisfactory quarters.

Janet P. Bowles was the founder of the Art Appreciation Club and continued as its sponsor for many years. Mrs. Bowles was an expert silversmith. She taught a course in art metalwork and was instrumental in enabling a number of student craftsmen to create remarkably attractive silverware. Several *Annuals* carried pictures of handcrafted pieces of silver produced by the Art Department. This work received extraordinary recognition. The May 24, 1920, *Echo* reported:

ART METAL DEPARTMENT
ASKED TO EXHIBIT WORK

New York Firm Asks For Five
Pieces of Original Handi-
work From S.H.S.

Shortridge talent is to be represented in five pieces of art metal work which are to be sent to R. L. Gorham of the New York firm, the exhibit to take place at the Fifth Avenue Art Gallery in June. An honor is paid to our institution because only six schools in the country have been asked to exhibit and only five pieces from each school will be accepted. Those schools selected are: Pratt Institute, Columbia University, Peter Cooper Union, Rhode Island School of Design, Chicago Art Institute and Shortridge High School.

Also in May of 1920 Shortridge put on an art exhibition as part of the celebration of Indianapolis's centennial year. The *Echo* reported that the exhibits featured "free-hand drawing, toy-making, commercial art, figure work, jewelry and pottery. For figure work, both children and adults posed as models, and were drawn in pencil, pen and ink, charcoal and water color." There were also posters and zinc and copper plates, such as were used for printing Christmas cards and the cover of the *Christmas Echo*. The commercial art classes regularly received samples of merchandise from local stores—L.S. Ayres, Wm. H. Block, and L. Strauss—from which they created advertising copy for use in the *Echo*.

· · · · ·

The Music Department now had two faculty members: B. P. Osbon, head of the department, who directed the orchestra and the Boys' Glee Club, and Claude E. Palmer, who was in charge of the band and the Girls' Glee Club. The band was closely tied in with another new Shortridge organization, the R.O.T.C. The Shortridge Cadet Corps did not become a unit in the R.O.T.C. until the fall of 1920, but the band, as an important part of Shortridge life, began in January, 1919, with the arrival of Lieutenant Palmer, newly returned from his work as a band leader overseas.

B. P. Osbon

Through the early years the Shortridge musical organizations had tended to appear and disappear (the band formed in 1912 had only lasted a few years). In the 1920s, however, the musical groups were really stabilized for the first time, according to the *History of Music at Shortridge*, written in her senior year by Ann Linstaedt, class of 1945. Mr. Palmer, who became head of the Department of Music at Ball State Teachers' College in Muncie, wrote Ann about his "six and a half happy years" at Shortridge:

> My memory of work at Shortridge is very pleasant, both because of the agreeable faculty with which I was associated and the fine attitude of the boys and girls who participated in music work. Of course, in those days we were in the two buildings down on Pennsylvania at North Street. My office was in one corner of Caleb Mills Hall, which was located in the center of the newer building. We had all band and orchestra rehearsals on the stage of that hall. That was often the cause of consternation in some of the neighboring classrooms, especially when the band was warming up, because there must have been at least a dozen doors opening out in all directions from this old Caleb Mills Hall. But in many ways it was a fine room in which to rehearse, and I put in many busy and delightful hours there with the Shortridge musicians. We had class instruction in instruments, and sometimes a teacher had difficulty in finding an unoccupied place in which to teach his class. Some of our groups met in the boiler room in the basement. These boilers were not used, and one teacher chalked exercises for our drummers on the black ends of the boilers.
>
> We also had some singing groups that did lovely work. I often think of the time that the girls' glee club gave the operetta, "The Wild Rose." The students were fine to work with and cooperated wonderfully.
>
> As I recall, Miss Rousseau McClellan used to help the senior boys with their class stunt each spring. I was frequently called upon to help them with some of their songs, and I recall the gusto with which one or two groups sang "Old Man Noah". . . .

In another note, Mr. Palmer remarked, "Robert Shultz was one of the best cornetists to play for me during those years—and a good musician."

The band was not exactly part of the R.O.T.C., for it was always under the Music Department. However, band members wore R.O.T.C. uniforms, and the R.O.T.C. boys marched to its music. In 1920–21 it had a membership of forty-two players and performed in the auditorium for pep meetings and at the football and basketball games. It also participated in the massed concerts given by Indianapolis's three high school bands.

The orchestra in 1919 was a forty-three piece group under the direction of Mr. Osbon. It grew by a few members each year. Shortridge began to grant credit for outside musical study, and the quality of the music improved. The musicians played frequently for auditorium programs, offering such selections as Franz Schubert's "Military Marches," Ethelbert Nevin's "Venetian Suite," Franz von Suppé's "Light Cavalry Overture," and Jacques Offenbach's overture to *Orpheus in the Underworld*.

They also began to play for graduation exercises and established a tradition that lasted as long as the school. Over the years Shortridge commencements were held in a number of different places including Tomlinson Hall, Cadle Tabernacle, and the Hilton U. Brown Theatre on the Butler Campus—but always the graduates made their entrance in time to the Triumphal March from Giuseppe Verdi's *Aïda* and left to the strains of Sir Edward Elgar's "Pomp and Circumstance."

Two outstanding musicians of this period were Christine Houseman (White) and Arnold Davis. Davis, class of 1922, was the son of a violin teacher and was an excellent violinist. He was concertmaster of the orchestra during his entire three and a half years at Shortridge. He describes B. P. Osbon as a short, slightly pudgy man with fat, pink cheeks, who was universally referred to by his students as "Bo Peep." As he remembers it, none of them ever knew what B. P. actually stood for. Davis also describes Mr. Osbon as a fine musician and an excellent pianist. In addition to the programs presented by the full orchestra of fifty-one members, Mr. Osbon, Arnold Davis, and a cellist comprised the Shortridge Trio, which gave numerous concerts both in and out of school. Davis also let Mr. Palmer talk him into playing with the band, although he was not familiar with any band instruments. He started out clashing cymbals but worked his way up to playing a drum. He was willing to do this because it could be substituted for R.O.T.C., which, in turn, could be counted as a physical education credit.

Christine Houseman was an extremely talented pianist. She was chosen to accompany the orchestra and the school soloists during her last two years at Shortridge, and she also played in one of the downtown theater orchestras. When she was not playing the piano she sang. The fall after her graduation she was asked by Mr. Osbon to come back to Shortridge as the faculty pianist, a position she held for twenty years, until she left in 1942 to study music therapy.

The music teachers performed in each other's groups. In 1922 Mr. Osbon sang in the Boys' Glee Club, which Mr. Palmer directed, and Mr. Palmer played in the orchestra, which Mr. Osbon directed. It was Mr. Osbon's last year at Shortridge. The next year Mr. Palmer was head of the Music Department and conductor of the orchestra, while a new teacher, Lyndon R. Street, became the leader of the band. On January 18, 1923, the Shortridge High School Music Department under the direction of Mr. Palmer gave a concert for the Shortridge Parent-Teachers Association. The groups participating were the Orchestra, Brass Quartet, Shortridge Trio, Boys' and Girls' Glee Clubs, the String Quartet, and two vocalists. The next year a Girls' Band was added to the list of musical groups.

When Claude Palmer left Shortridge at the end of the 1924–25 school year, his place was taken by a man who was to oversee the school's music for many years to come, Will F. Wise. Mr. Wise showed his abilities as a conductor right away when, in his first year, a group from the Girls' Glee Club won the state contest for glee clubs. He was joined the following year, 1926–27, by another member of the music faculty who was to stay at Shortridge many years, Mrs. Laura C. Moag, who directed many of the singing groups. For some reason the boys were required to take a course in music history, while the girls took one in chorus. A great many of both sexes participated in one or more of the musical organizations. By the middle of the decade they also had a new outlet for singing and dancing—the Junior Vaudeville.

CHAPTER
9

# The Last Years at Old Shortridge

S HORTRIDGE IN THE 1920s was certainly not a neighborhood high school. What remained of a residential neighborhood was being cleared in order to make room for the World War Memorial. Indianapolis architect, David V. Burns, class of 1929, says that this involved more moving of houses to new locations than has ever been undertaken in Indianapolis at any other time. Students could look out of the classroom windows almost any day and see houses being moved up and down the street.

Most students came to school on the streetcar, and they tended to identify themselves with their streetcar route. Isabel Layman (Troyer), class of 1925, lived in Irvington next door to Mr. Buck. She talks about the "Irvington gang." Once in a while they got a ride from Mr. Buck, but most of the time they took the Washington streetcar. When they went on Miss McClellan's bird walks in the spring, they followed the ride into town with a ride on the College Avenue car out to 56th Street, before walking to Bacon Swamp. They spent a lot of time together.

Frances Westcott, class of 1923, lived at 42nd and Winthrop. This was a relatively new part of town, served only by the Broad Ripple streetcar which ran infrequently. All the students who lived northeast had to be on the same streetcar in the morning. They developed a lot of group feeling, too. Miss Ruth Allerdice, the botany teacher, was a neighbor. She drove an electric car, and sometimes students got to ride with her.

David Burns took the Peoples Motor Coach Company car. He reports that by the time he boarded in the morning at 42nd and Central the car was always so crowded that he had to stand on the outside step and hang on. He made his friends in other ways.

Insofar as Shortridge had a neighborhood it was downtown Indian-

apolis, which was a lively place in the 1920s. The Metropolitan School
of Music was across the street, and many Shortridge students went over
there for instrumental instruction. The band drilled regularly on North
Street and paraded at every opportunity. There were plays at English's,
concerts at the Murat and at Caleb Mills Hall, vaudeville at Keith's,
and, by far the most important to high school students, there were the
movies. These were still silent, so the theaters all provided musical
entertainment in addition to the films.

Jessie Strickland (Burns), class of 1929, particularly remembers going to the Ohio to hear Charlie Davis's orchestra, which featured singer
Dick Powell. Charlie Davis was a cousin of Arnold Davis, concertmaster of the Shortridge orchestra. Davis played "Song of India" at
the Ohio, as well as for the Shortridge graduation. Later Charlie Davis
moved to the new Indiana Theatre. Dorothy Lambert (Otto), class of
1926, has stronger recollections of going to the Circle Theatre. She says
that whenever anything special happened, such as a big win, a huge
crowd of Shortridgers would descend on the Circle and generally get
in free. She also went frequently to plays at English's on Saturday
afternoons.

Mr. Buck was a theater buff, who believed that theater was important for teachers as well as for students. The manager of English's
was a good friend of his and frequently gave him a block of tickets.
Elizabeth Matthews (Helm), class of 1918, who became a Latin teacher,
remembers that Mr. Buck would check the teachers' schedules to see
which of them had a late lunch period and only one after-lunch class.
He would then come around to inquire whether they could make arrangements for their last period class, so that they could attend the
matinee. She says the teachers all helped each other out, so that a group
could take advantage of these opportunities. Sometimes Mr. Buck went
with them, sometimes Mrs. Buck.

In this atmosphere of enthusiasm for the performing arts the Shortridge Junior Vaudeville was born. The senior play had long been a
major event in Shortridge life. Now the juniors wanted a project of
their own. The junior class censors were Nell Merrick Thomas and Joel
W. Hadley, both of whom provided a lot of encouragement for the new
endeavor. The first class to stage a junior event was the class of 1923,
which put on the Junior Carnival on March 25, 1922, the day before
spring vacation. They had looked through old *Annuals* and learned
about the Puritan Supper, the Street Fair, the Book Fair, the Chinese
Fair, and the Arabian Fair, all senior projects. Their carnival was rather
like those with one important difference. They had booths and special
attractions all over the school, as had the earlier classes, but they also

had a show in Caleb Mills Hall. The Boys' Glee Club performed; Frances Westcott gave a humorous monologue; and a group gave a skit of faculty impersonations. The *Echo* reported that Ben Koby as Mr. Osbon and Paul Bartlett as Mr. Eugene Mueller brought down the house.

The following year the class of 1924 followed a similar format, but with a longer auditorium show. The program lists a Faculty Stunt, followed by a Debate, a Fashion Show, a Rube Band, a String Quartet, a Comic Recitation, and finally a Dance by Seven Girls. The class of 1925 staged a Junior Circus. The audience in Caleb Mills Hall was treated first to a Hippodrome Show, then a Jazz Band, a Minstrel Show, a scene from *The Charm School* (the upcoming senior play), an Indian Dance, a Magician, and a Debate.

The next year, 1925, the juniors staged a Nottingham Fair. On the main stage were first a play, *The Real Thing*, put on by members of the Junior Drama League, then a performance by the orchestra, then a "Wild West Melodrama" performed by faculty members Joel W. Hadley, Simon P. Roach, Alonzo E. Goldsberry, Edward H. Carpenter, and Enoch D. Burton, and finally "Selections from *Bab.*" *Bab* was the senior play.

All the classes from 1923 through 1926 claim credit for launching the vaudeville, but there is no question that the first real Shortridge Junior Vaudeville was put on by the class of 1927. The 1926 *Annual* reports:

### A "VIGOROUS, VIVACIOUS" JUNIOR AFFAIR

ON SATURDAY evening, February 27, the Junior class produced its annual money-making project. This year, the class of 1927 presented a new and novel scheme, offering a "vivacious, vigorous Vaudeville" in eight acts. From the opening strains of the overture by Harold Warren's dance orchestra, until the last dance of the faculty stunt which closed the program, the audience of nineteen hundred had its fondest expectations realized. The acts in which almost one hundred juniors participated, were individually organized each with a student chairman and faculty advisor. These acts played in competition, the audience, by its votes, awarding to the "At Charleston" act directed by Don Whittinger, the fifteen Sectional tickets which were the prize for the best stunt.

All of the acts were of high calibre and offered many original and humorous features. "The Wishing Well" including artistic dances—ancient and modern—and a clever ensemble song, opened the program. In "So's Your Old Echo" many of the *Echo's* third page columns came to life before a huge reproduction of the first page of the paper. "The Follies of 1927" was a dance revue. The next on the program was "The

Indiana Home for Mental Unfortunates" containing many "hits" at Shortridgers. This was followed by the prize winning act which included the Charleston and several song and dance numbers. "Woof" was a very cleverly arranged radio act. "The Noble Lover" which won second place, followed. It was a burlesque of slow and fast moving pictures. The eighth act was a true snappy Fashion Show.

Norris Houghton, the General Chairman, was assisted by John Waltz, Stage Manager, who designed the artistic stage setting. To the junior censors, Mrs. Thomas and Mr. Hadley, as well as to the eight faculty members who aided materially in coaching the acts, the junior class expresses its appreciation.

Norris Houghton added to the distinction of being Shortridge's first vaudeville chairman, by becoming a playwright, an author, a student of Russian drama, a professor of drama at Vassar College, and the director and producer of several off-Broadway plays.

In 1927 the junior class presented the second annual vaudeville to a packed house of one thousand nine hundred persons; four hundred others were turned away. First prize went to "Shortridge Blues," directed by Malcolm Snoddy. The next year, the last in the old Caleb Mills Hall, was the first vaudeville to include intermission acts. Charles Fell's "Four Nitwits" "kept the audience in an uproar between acts with their various antics." That year the juniors gave two performances, the afternoon and evening of March 25.

The Junior Vaudeville had become another major Shortridge tradition.

.   .   .   .   .

As a result of a dramatic basketball confrontation between Shortridge and Manual, the quick action of an unidentified Shortridge girl, and the fertile brain of math teacher and former coach E. Carl Watson, Shortridge acquired its mascot. The story was repeated often in the Shortridge Blue Book and elsewhere.

It was the year 1925—February was the month—and Shortridge and Manual, bitter rivals, were about to clash on the hardwood. The Blue Devils were considered the "dark horse" candidates, so it was a most critical event—Shortridge must uphold its prestige. The crowds were roaring and Manual was in the lead at the half. Suddenly all eyes were turned on a minute figure, darting across the floor. He was a bright red mass of canine fur, a mascot for Manual. Finding the players rather unsociable, he pitched camp nowhere other than in the large circle in the middle of the gym.

This was too much for the Blue and White enthusiasts; they too must have a representative. There was much commotion, and from the stands emerged a cat, cradled in the arms of a Shortridge girl. It was placed alongside the Manual dog, and the anxious spectators gasped. The dog sniffed at the object beside him, found it a dull companion, and sauntered off the floor.

The Shortridge team was inspired and so was Mr. Watson. The players roared back to win the game, and Mr. Watson went home to write a favorite Shortridge poem:

> The Manual dog and the Shortridge cat
> Side by side in the circle sat.
> 'Twas seven o'clock and what do you know
> The stands were crowded, row on row,
> And the old dark horse in his near-by stall
> Neighed and informed us one and all
> There was going to be an awful spat.
> (Now I was there and saw it through,
> And what I here relate is true.)
>
> The Manual dog barked a mean bow! wow!
> And the Shortridge cat gave a snappy Meow.
> And then for about an hour or so
> The stands were frantic, friend and foe.
> And the old dark horse in his near-by place
> Could scarcely keep a sober face
> For he had all of the dope, somehow.
> (Now I was there and I'll say to you
> That this is absolutely true.)
>
> The Manual dog was at times ahead
> And then all the air was filled with Red.
> But the Shortridge cat knew a thing or two
> And soon the shade turned White and Blue.
> The Manual dog had a cast iron jaw
> But the Shortridge cat swung a wicked paw.
> And the fight went on as I have said.
> (And the old dark horse just watched the ball
> And laughed and laughed till he shook the stall.)
>
> When the gun went off—in the smoke and fog
> Not a trace could be found of the Manual dog.
> On the self-same spot where the two had sat
> There was nary a thing but the Shortridge cat.
> Now the truth is this about that pup—
> The Shortridge kitten just ate him up
> And set the South-side folks agog.
> (And the old dark horse—how that nag did laugh
> When the Cat came back in the second half.)

The now-famous cat was immediately adopted as the Shortridge mascot, and since he had already proved lucky, the school full of Latin scholars gave him the name of Felix. The Art Department and the print shop pooled their talents to produce his likeness. From that time on the perky little cat always represented Shortridge.

At the end of the 1928 season Mr. Burton gave up coaching basketball, so it was necessary for the "Battling Burtonians" to become something else. The *Echo* held a contest to choose a name. David Burns came out on top. He remembered some French soldiers who had come to this country during World War I to raise money for the war effort. When they were in Indianapolis, they stayed with the Burns family. They belonged to a special regiment called the Blue Devils, and young David found them dashing and heroic. He therefore made the winning proposal that all Shortridge athletic teams be given the name of the Shortridge Blue Devils (rather than Blue Jays, Blue Aces, or Bluebirds). As a reward, he received a season ticket to all the athletic events for the next year.

.  .  .  .  .

Scholarship at Shortridge was heightened by an important new institution in the early 1920s. Mr. Buck enjoyed all the school activities, but he said frequently, "Whatever we teach here we are teaching you to *think*." As one of a number of high school principals who were interested in seeing greater recognition of scholarship, he was instrumental in founding the National Honor Society. Shortridge was one of its first members, receiving the twenty-third national charter in 1921–22. Students were elected to the Honor Society by the faculty, and election was based on the four criteria of character, scholarship, leadership, and service. Mr. Forsyth, the head of the History Department, was the first faculty sponsor, and he saw to it that those elected had a good time along with the honor they received. The 1924 *Annual* recorded the Honor Society's calendar which listed a banquet at the Spink Arms Hotel, a party at the home of Elizabeth Hurd (McMurray), and several theater parties as "the main part of the numerous social functions."

The Honor Society also provided Mr. Buck with the opportunity to exact an appropriate penalty for membership in high school fraternities or sororities, which were still illegal and still going strong. If a student belonged to one of the forbidden social organizations, he or she could not be received into the Honor Society. A number of alumni recall vividly being called to Mr. Buck's office, one by one, and quivering as they made a formal statement that they had no such affiliation.

Mr. Buck was a strong authority figure, or, as one alumnus said, "a presence." Those who flouted the school rules or who did not make the grade scholastically were always in danger of being expelled by Mr. Buck. If that happened, it was not easy to get back in. The culprits were expected to enroll in one of the other high schools. There was a saying around school, "Never do Manual labor or make a Technical error."

One hapless student who was judged by Mr. Buck to have made a "Technical error" or laid himself open to "Manual labor" left Shortridge in 1923, and, as he departed, said to Mr. Buck, "I'm going to make you respect me some day." Twenty years later, after Mr. Buck had retired, the ex-student called him up and took him on a tour of his impressive business establishment.

One day a particularly daring person exploded a stink bomb during a speech in the auditorium. It was not possible to identify the villain, but Mr. Buck made sure he did not become a hero. First he ushered the speaker out; then he pulled a chair up to the front of the stage in the horrible-smelling hall and said, "I can take it, can you?" Everybody sat there and suffered until the end of the period. There were no more stink bombs.

Mr. Buck gave his faculty lots of encouragement. Latin teacher Elizabeth Matthews Helm says that it was always a pleasure to have him visit the classroom and that he always took part when he was there. She also said that he liked to be advised of any special projects and would look in on them if he could.

When Mr. Gingery, head of the Math Department, left Shortridge to become principal of Washington High School at its opening in the fall of 1927, he wrote for the *Echo*:

> I have been happiest at Shortridge. . . . Shortridge is an outstanding ideal high school in the individual relationship between teacher and pupils, between the teachers themselves, and between the teachers and Mr. Buck.

Along with new traditions and institutions came influential new teachers. Minnie Lloyd first came to Shortridge as a Latin teacher just

# National Honor Society of Secondary Schools Charter

## Shortridge Chapter, Shortridge High School
## Indianapolis, Indiana

### Know all Men by these Presents, that

**Whereas**, character, scholarship, leadership and service are cardinal qualities worthy of encouragement in all schools, therefore the National Honor Society of Secondary Schools gives, grants, and delegates through the authority of this **Charter** the right, privilege, and power to establish, conduct, and administer the Shortridge Chapter as a local Chapter of the National Honor Society of Secondary Schools

This Charter, Number 23  is given and granted this fourth  day of August  Nineteen Hundred Twenty-two by the National Council whose signatures are affixed below.

C.P. Briggs   S.W. Brooks   H.V. Kepner

M.R. McDaniel   Lewis W. Smith   Merle Prunty

Edward Rynearson   E.J. Eaton   Wm. E. King

A.W. Church   Secretary.

Minnie Lloyd

before the United States entered World War I, but when war was declared, she left to enter the Vassar training camp for nurses. She was
assigned to the Philadelphia General Hospital, "The famous old institution where Evangeline found Gabriel" and was there all during the flu
epidemic. When the war was over she became executive secretary of the
Red Cross in Warsaw, Indiana, for a year, before returning to Shortridge
to teach Latin, to found the Roman State, and to serve as its "dictator"
until she turned to history as her major teaching field.

In a school committed to scholarship, Miss Lloyd instantly became a
star. Everybody who remembers her remembers her enthusiasm for both
teaching and learning. To her background in Latin and history and her
nurse's training she added a master's degree in sociology from Indiana
University, followed by further graduate work at Indiana, Butler, and
the University of Chicago, principally in the field of social economics.

In the years that she taught Latin, Miss Lloyd took charge of the
annual Roman State banquet. The *Echo* of May 21, 1923, reported:

> Last Friday's banquet topped the climax of the year's entertainment
> given by the Roman State. With statues, couches, flowers, urns, and
> decorated pillars, the lunch-room was transformed into a typical Roman

banquet hall. The program was very well planned, and the dancing and music especially appropriate. The food was served by Greek slaves dressed in brown tunics.

Finger bowls were passed around before the first course, according to the Roman custom. The appetizer, consisting of pickled eggs on lettuce leaves and vinum, was first served.

There was piano music during the first and last course, dancing after the "prima mensa," and singing after the second course. Two trios played during the later courses. All this was followed by speeches from Miss Marthens, Mr. Buck, and Miss Lillian Berry, professor of Latin at Indiana University. Miss Berry said that "the excellent example set by the Shortridge Roman State was being followed by high schools all over the state." About two hundred and fifty attended the banquet.

After Miss Lloyd became a history teacher, the Roman State was taken over by Miss Anna Claybaugh of the Latin Department. Each year she put on a Saturnalia, as had Miss Lloyd. The 1927 *Annual* describes this gala event:

Hundreds of Roman citizens arrayed in bright carnival costumes formed a magnificent parade, that was led by trumpeters and drummers, through the halls to the Corso (auditorium).

On the platform draped in rich hangings, the king and queen, surrounded by attendants, were seated on a dais. [First they were carried

Officers of the Roman State

down the halls, seated precariously on a large board which was held aloft by their minions.]

The pagan part of the program consisted of skillful fencing, dancing, bareback riding and magic tricks. A thrilling chariot race around the auditorium made a fitting climax for this exciting celebration.

During an intermission refreshments were served and the king and queen presented worthy awards to the winners of the various events.

A beautiful Christian observance of Christmas completed the program. After the Christmas story was read, a representation of Corregio's "Holy Night" was shown while an unseen choir sang "Silent Night."

In the spring, the Romans celebrated more moderately with a Liberalia. This took place after school in the auditorium. First the presiding consul welcomed the *praetexti* (freshmen), then stood with the citizens and declared the *praetexti* citizens.

A few years after Minnie Lloyd joined the Latin Department, Mary Pratt returned to Shortridge to teach English. She had graduated from Shortridge in 1901 and had been an early *Echo* editor. Four years later she graduated from Vassar, where she was editor of the yearbook. She then went on to earn a master's degree in English from Indiana University. From 1911 to 1915 she taught in the seventh and eighth grades of the Indianapolis public schools. From 1915 through 1918 she taught at Tudor Hall, a private school for girls, and from 1919 to 1922 she was an English instructor at Indiana University. Then she joined the English Department at Shortridge, and school became more fun for everybody. She was made the sponsor for Tuesday's *Echo*, and she also became social chairman for the school. No alumnus who reminisces about Shortridge from 1924 to 1942 fails to mention Mary Pratt.

While the 1920s brought new activities to the school, the old ones continued to flourish. In 1926 the Senate had sixty-four active members. Some of the bills which were introduced and hotly debated provided for: entrance of the United States into the World Court, establishment of a separate air force, government ownership of the coal mines, and establishment of a federal Department of Education. In 1926 Collier Young, president of the senior class, won the State Oratorical Contest with a speech entitled "America's Gift to Constitutional Government." He was also one of the debate team, which also included Bill Otto and Gordon Thompson, that won the Tri-State debating cup for Shortridge in 1926. (The Tri-State debate teams were from Walnut Hills of Cincinnati, Louisville Male, and Shortridge.) Their subject was: Resolved, that an amendment to the Constitution giving Congress power to regulate the labor of persons under sixteen years of age should be adopted. (Collier

Young became a playwright and script writer, best known for the TV series "Ironsides." Gordon Thompson became headmaster of Orchard School, an Indianapolis country day school, and served in that capacity for forty-five years.) Shortridge was acquiring debating cups on a regular basis. In 1924 they had won permanent possession of a Tri-State silver debating cup as a three-year victor.

Much of this success was due to Mr. Otto's system of team preparation, which was more often used by colleges than by high schools. He sent his debaters out to libraries to research their question from both the affirmative and the negative sides, so that they would always be prepared for quick rebuttal. The debaters enjoyed tremendous student support. The auditorium was always jam-packed for debates.

A Girls' Debating League was organized in 1922. Like the Boys' Debating Club, it was coached by Mr. Otto, who was still head of the English Department, managing editor of the *Echo*, and senior class sponsor along with his debating responsibilities. The Girls' Debating League tackled such subjects as: a six-year term for the president, farm relief, uniform marriage and divorce laws, and Philippine freedom. Shortridge students still did not have enough opportunity to debate, so Clarence C. Shoemaker of the English Department created a Junior Debating League, which was only for freshmen. They debated the pros and cons of installment buying and automobile liability insurance. John Kitchen was president.

·    ·    ·    ·    ·

The last years at North and Pennsylvania brought an end to two remarkable careers. Roda Selleck died in 1925. Her funeral was held in Caleb Mills Hall, which was not large enough to accommodate all the mourners. She is described by all who remember her in her later years as old and frail and "wispy," but still totally interested in students and in art. Isabel Layman (Troyer), who was editor of Tuesday's *Echo* under Miss Pratt, who had the lead in the 1925 senior play, *Bab*, and who considered Miss Lloyd, Miss McClellan, and Miss Marthens all to be marvelous teachers, still says that the best thing that happened to her at Shortridge was taking pottery from Miss Selleck:

> Miss Selleck related art, in this case pottery, to culture and to the whole world. As we made our various bowls and things, we learned from her and from each other. There was a Jewish boy in the class, and from him we all learned about the high holy days and bar mitzvah. From an Indian boy we learned Indian traditions. He even danced for the pottery class. Miss Selleck was so devoted to her craft that she frequently spent the night in the school basement tending to her kiln so

Roda Selleck in her potter's apron

that the pottery would be fired properly. This seemed perfectly reasonable to us.

After saying all this, Isabel Troyer asked her husband, John, class of 1922, "Who was your favorite teacher?"

"Mr. Otto," he answered firmly. "He awakened me to reading and I am endlessly grateful to him."

The second loss was reported in the February 28, 1927, *Echo*:

> William Perry Crockett, a member of the Shortridge Physics Department, was killed . . . by a cave-in of a ditch which he was digging with his sons Harold and Austin, both Shortridge students, in the rear of their home at 419 West Forty-ninth Street. . . .

Mr. Crockett, then forty-six years old, was a native of Logansport and a graduate of Wabash. He had taught at Crawfordsville High School before coming to Shortridge. He had been at Shortridge for eight years, and he was considered one of the best physicists in the state, as well as an outstanding teacher. He left a widow, seven sons, and a daughter.

In response to this tragedy the faculty held a benefit, the proceeds of which went to establish a faculty memorial scholarship fund. From that time on, for many years, whenever a teacher or ex-teacher died, contributions were made to the faculty memorial fund. Interest from the fund was used to provide first one and then two scholarships to graduating seniors in memory of the last three Shortridge teachers who had died. The first recipient of the Memorial Scholarship was Bob Shultz, class of 1927, who had been Mr. Crockett's assistant in the physics lab. He received $100 which covered his first year's tuition at Butler. Mr. Shultz still regards Mr. Crockett as the ideal teacher and says he could have taught practically anybody practically anything. As he remembers, William Crockett was actually licensed to teach ten different subjects. After his death, Mrs. Crockett became a matron at Shortridge and successfully educated her eight children.

Vice-principal Louis Dirks left Shortridge in 1926 to become the dean of men at DePauw. His place was filled by Mr. Gingery, head of the Math Department, who left at the end of a year to become the first principal of Washington High School on the city's west side. Emmett Rice of the History Department then became vice-principal, a position he held until 1943.

At the end of the 1927–28 school year, the last in old Shortridge, three of the teachers who had come to Shortridge in 1882, whom Mr. Buck had dubbed the "Shortridge Immortals," retired from their classrooms. They were Angeline P. Carey, Laura Donnan, and Amelia Platter. There is evidence that Miss Platter taught too long. During her last years in the classroom, she frequently yielded to the impulse to throw erasers at students who had not done their work properly and sometimes rapped knuckles with a ruler, and at least once she threw an inkwell at one of her girl students. This brought a strong protest from the girl's father, but Miss Platter was such a Shortridge institution and so close to retirement that she escaped with a reprimand.

Mrs. Carey was a vital teacher right up to her last class, and she continued to write poetry and to maintain high standards. She wrote a poem of dedication to be enclosed in the cornerstone of the new building.

Miss Donnan's only concession to the passage of time prior to her retirement had been to give up her sponsorship of Monday's *Echo* in November, 1926. She sat for her portrait that year at the request of a group of alumni, headed by Mary Pratt. The *Echo* ran a picture of the portrait and underneath it a poem:

> THE SHORTRIDGE SPIRIT turned the ECHO's pages
> And read: "She censored Monday's ECHO years and ages"
> Amazed, he said, "From this it doth appear

She censored ALL editions for a year!"
The SPIRIT cried, "This record makes me weep;
Pray when did LAURA DONNAN get her sleep?"

Her GUARDIAN ANGEL smiled. (There is a rumor
That guardian angels have a sense of humor.)
And quoth, "Wait till you hear the total of it all;
She coached the high school girls in basket-ball;
Her SHORTRIDGE SENATE (still it's to the fore)
She's censored weekly thirty years and more!
And what an endless file of lads and lasses
Have yearly passed through her SIX HISTORY CLASSES.

Not mentioned in the poem was Miss Donnan's devotion to keeping order in the halls and on the stairs. The rules said: "up on the right side, down on the left side, stairs to be taken one step at a time and no running in the halls." She positioned herself in the hallway between classes, a small but indomitable figure. Don Knight, the track coach, and a new member of the History Department, was almost late to class one day. He rushed to the stairs and bounded up two at a time.

"Young man, come back," said the voice of authority, "You are to go up the stairs one at a time."

"Why, I'm on the faculty," he protested.

"All the more reason for you to obey the school rules."

Mr. Knight came back to the foot of the stairs and went up one step at a time.

There are any number of similar stories, but none that tell of anyone defying Miss Donnan. One student wrote a speech full of praise of her, which nonetheless indicated her formidable personality:

> One, whose many followers may be found throughout the world, whose hand has guided many a man and woman to honor and fame, and whose useful life has been spent in defending, and in teaching others to defend, that law, which has ever been the highest ideal of the human mind, that of Liberty, Justice and Equality! . . . she modestly attempts to conceal the admirable generosity of her spirit by blunt, frank speech, which has sent many a blundering loafer scurrying to his seat.

Miss Donnan was not the only one to devote herself to strict order in the halls. Mr. Mueller and Mr. Scherer regularly stationed themselves at either end of the Bridge of Sighs. Some students went all the way down to the boiler room in order to cross from building to building rather than come under their scrutiny.

Another colorful Shortridge faculty member was Frank Wade, head of the Chemistry Department, who came to the school in 1903. He

*William W. Davis*

Frank B. Wade

nearly always had surprising objects in his pocket. Bill Otto, class of 1926, remembers the day that Mr. Wade came into the chemistry class taught by Dorothy Arndt, class of 1920. He had just returned from a national chemistry conference. He spoke to Miss Arndt for a moment, and she called for the attention of the class.

First he asked the class, "Who can name the rare gases?" The answer came back quickly: neon, argon, helium, krypton, and xenon. "That's right," said Mr. Wade, "and there has just been a major technological breakthrough. We are now able to extract neon from the atmosphere." He put his hand into his vest pocket and pulled out a sealed vial. "I have here," he said, "one fourth of the pure neon available in the world."

"So what?" piped up a brash voice from the back of the room.

"We really don't know," replied Mr. Wade calmly. "It's too new, but we do know that if we apply high voltage to it it produces a bright pinkish glow."

Most often the famous pocket produced semiprecious stones. Frank Wade was an internationally recognized gemmologist. Besides contributing many articles to such publications as the *Jeweler's Circular Weekly*, the *Mineralogist*, and the *London Gemmologist*, he was the author of

*Diamonds: A Study of the Factors that Govern Their Value* (1916) and *A Text-Book of Precious Stones* (1918), both published by G. P. Putnam's Sons, which were standard works for many years. He also explored for and collected Indiana precious stones. Whenever he lectured on his hobby, he wore a tie pin containing a 1.33 carat Hoosier diamond which was picked up in Morgan County by a man panning for gold. The stone weighed a little over three carats, before Frank Wade undertook to cut and polish it. Wade, himself, found a ruby in the rough in Brown County and a blue sapphire from the bed of Gold Creek, in Morgan County. He said none of the stones really belonged in Indiana. They must have been carried down from Canada by glaciers, but they had, nonetheless, ended up here.

One of Frank Wade's outstanding discoveries was how to prevent the loss of color in turquoise. He undertook the research in response to a plea from a Nevada turquoise miner who was about to go broke. Wade had an idea. He had noticed a paragraph in a chemical journal mentioning that a researcher had spilled some copper ammonia compound in a jar of silica jell, that it had turned the jell blue, and that the researcher had been unable to wash the blue out. He ground a piece of turquoise which the miner had sent him and soaked it in silica jell. Then he dipped the stone in copper ammonia, let it dry and polished it. (The stone remained a bright blue from that time on, and Mrs. Wade wore it in a brooch.)

Wade gave the trade secret to the Nevada miner, and then several years later reported his findings to the Indiana Academy of Science. No one there quite knew why the process worked. On his way home from that meeting it suddenly hit him that there might be ammonia in the stone. As soon as he got back to the Shortridge laboratory, he collared the first chemistry student he saw. "Take this turquoise," he said—of course he had a couple in his pocket—"and go break it up in mortar. You go in that room and I'll go in this. I'll break up another piece. I'm going to test for ammonia and you do the same." Fifteen minutes later they rushed to tell each other that they had each found ammonia. After that some sixteen advanced chemistry students worked systematically on turquoise, and at the end of the year their findings were reported to gemmologists all over the world.

.   .   .   .   .

By the fall of 1927, as it anticipated moving to its new location on 34th Street, Shortridge was no longer one of three Indianapolis public high schools; it was one of six. During the time that plans were being made for a new Shortridge, a new all-black high school, and probably a high school for the west side, Indianapolis had somewhat reluctantly acquired a high school on the far north side.

In June of 1922, the city annexed the town of Broad Ripple, which was to the northeast, but the land on which Broad Ripple High School stood was carefully omitted. This caused so much anger and protest that after a year a special ordinance was passed affixing Broad Ripple High School to the school city of Indianapolis, making it the city's fourth high school. Karl Von Ammerman, vice-principal of Manual, was named principal. The enrollment was only ninety-four students, and the school board had hoped to be able to amalgamate them with Shortridge in the projected northside building. But the community of Broad Ripple was growing fast, and the building project was proceeding slowly. By the time Shortridge actually moved to 34th Street, Broad Ripple had 425 students. It was much smaller than the other high schools, but it was here to stay.

Crispus Attucks and Washington High Schools both opened in the fall of 1927.

Shortridge moved to its new home in the fall of 1928.

# CHAPTER
# 10
# 34th Street

ALTHOUGH THE TRACT OF LAND on the east side of Meridian Street north of 34th Street was purchased by the Board of School Commissioners in 1921, debate over the site for the new Shortridge continued until April 30, 1926. Other considered locations were West 40th between Illinois and Meridian, 1155 East Maple Road (eleven acres then occupied by the Hawthorne Tennis Club), a section of land on Meridian between 50th and 52nd streets, and, the most strongly supported alternative, a sizable tract south of 46th Street between Central Avenue and Washington Boulevard. The arguments for the 46th Street site were that it was larger and that it would combine with Butler to form an educational belt in northside Indianapolis. The arguments against it were that it would cost twice as much as the 34th Street tract and that it was less accessible by public transportation. On April 13, 1926, the board actually voted to build the new school at 46th and Central and to sell the 34th Street property. At the next meeting, however, that decision was reversed, and the matter was finally settled in favor of 34th Street.

There were still important decisions to be made, however. The school commissioners were engaged in building two other high schools—Washington and Crispus Attucks—and several new grade schools, and so were under a lot of pressure to hold down costs. At one time the board voted to build a new Shortridge with a student capacity of eighteen hundred instead of twenty-five hundred, as originally projected, and to cut the funds from $1,200,000 to $900,000. At their next meeting they received a letter from the Shortridge faculty petitioning them to reconsider. This petition was supported by the PTA. The teachers and the parents carried the day, and the faculty was given a major voice in the plans for the new school.

A group including Mr. Buck, Mr. Forsyth, Mr. Otto, Mr. Gingery,

Mr. Wade, and Mr. Julius worked extensively before they met with the architects. Each Shortridge department head provided roughly sketched plans to be translated into blueprints by architects J. Edwin Kopf and John A. Deery, who, along with the faculty, were committed to accessibility and simplicity as well as classical education. Kopf's goal was to place each department logically and keep it self-contained. The final design was a 280 × 420-foot hollow rectangle enclosing a 100 × 180-foot open courtyard.

From the fall of 1927 until the fall of 1928, Shortridgers and the rest of Indianapolis watched this design materialize. On November 3, 1927, the new building's cornerstone, which contained the school archives—"a great variety of material which should prove to be of historical value in the years to come when the box is opened"—was laid with appropriate ceremony. All the students were there for the occasion, along with faculty members, alumni, school officials, city officials, and interested members of the public. They listened first to the Shortridge band, the chorus and the glee clubs, and then to the dedicatory poem by Angeline Carey of the English Department, a copy of which was included in the contents of the cornerstone along with copies of the first *Echo*, the Honor Society charter, and a complete list of all the students currently enrolled. The poem read in part:

> In our fair land the school-house stands
> Deep-rooted as our forest trees,
> As native as our hills
> It humbly stands beside the road,
> Or towers superbly to the sky.
> Whate'er its form or place, it means
> A land of educated Youth,
> America's ideal.
>
> So as we watch New Shortridge rise,
> We see a high ideal take form,
> And bow in reverence.
> Now as we stand around this stone,
> The past and future looking on,
> We dedicate ourselves anew
> To cherishing and making true
> This national ideal!

The spectators then heard from Mr. Buck:

> Three words shine as the meaning of Shortridge—light, power and service. Shortridge aims to enlighten students; aims to give the students power from their enlightenment, and from these two principles aims to have its students give service to mankind.

They also heard from architect John A. Deery:

> Possibly no school was ever designed with such an abundance of
> valuable information as was available when we started on the plans for
> Shortridge High school. When school is started in the new building you
> will find all departments and activities that have been so dear to you in
> the past. It will not be like starting all over again in a school that is
> entirely different. The only difference will be that everything will be
> modern and up-to-date and the arrangement will be better than it has
> been in the old building.
>
> I wish to congratulate the citizens of Indianapolis on the erection of
> this fine modern structure. . . .

Dr. Herbert T. Wagner, class of 1903, spoke for the alumni:

> The new school is to inspire a spirit of sacrifice and service and to
> educate for brave leadership. The new Shortridge stands for broad cul-
> ture, square dealing and traditions and accomplishments that are inspi-
> rations to all of us.

The program concluded with a short speech from James H. Otto,
class of 1928, representing the students. (Otto later became head of the
Science Department at Washington High School and author of a widely
used biology textbook.)

The building proved to be both functional and handsome. The architecture is Corinthian, with the front entrance consisting of a statuary
court with a center colonnade and arch, including six columns representing the "Temple of the Winds." Panels high above the doors are inscribed with the components of a classical education—painting,
sculpture, music, poetry, drama, education, culture, commerce, industry, philosophy, ethics.

Practically all the materials used in construction were from Indiana.
The stone was from the Bloomington/Bedford area, and the brick, made
in Flemish bond for the main walls with a pattern in five shades, was
burned in Indianapolis. The interior was finished in golden oak and the
walls were sand plaster.

The building is actually three buildings in one. Each of the three
could stand alone having its own entrances from the outside. Each, of
course, could be entered internally. One building was the new Caleb
Mills Hall, on the southeast, with entrance on 34th Street. It differed
from its predecessor in that it was larger and was designed for theatrical
productions as well as concerts. (In the old hall there was no way to
hang a curtain except from the ends of the horseshoe-shaped balcony,
which meant that persons sitting in the balcony could see down over it.)
Now there was a handsome proscenium arch bearing the quotation

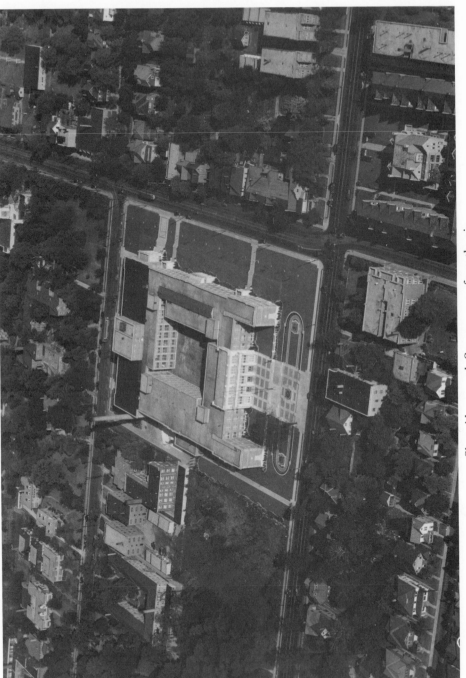

Shortridge at 34th Street as seen from the air

from Caleb Mills, which Shortridgers would read again and again: "A disciplined mind and cultivated heart are elements of power."

A second building, located on the northeast, with entrance on Pennsylvania Street, housed the athletic plant. It featured two gymnasiums separated by sliding doors to provide separate facilities for boys and girls. When these doors were thrown open for interschool basketball games, the seating capacity was twenty-four hundred. Both Caleb Mills Hall and the athletic facilities were especially located and designed so as not to interfere with classroom recitations.

The third, or academic, building, with its wider entrance on Meridian Street, was the most carefully planned of all. The library, which was considerably larger than most high school libraries and became the largest high school library in Indiana, was placed centrally on the west corridor of the second floor directly over the first floor foyer. Five windows fronted on Meridian Street for maximum natural light. An aesthetic atmosphere was achieved from the many books, the beamed ceiling, scribed walls, and electric sconces. It was built to accommodate two hundred students at a time and was named for that great lover of books and learning, Charity Dye.

The height of the library was increased beyond that of the classrooms to allow for the stacks. Because of this extra height it was necessary to go up a few steps from the third floor corridor to a series of five small rooms over the library, especially designed by Kopf for language study. The lower ceiling and small size gave the rooms an accoustical advantage as well as intimacy for communication.

Kopf located the Music Department higher than the other classrooms so that the sounds coming from it during rehearsals would not disturb other pupils. Since, according to Indiana law, the maximum height of school buildings was not to exceed three floors, the architect took the position that it only appeared from the inside that the music department was on a fourth floor. However, music students generally believed that they climbed three flights of stairs.

Among the many features that were special to Shortridge, reflecting its history and particular interests, was the large print shop on the first floor, well-equipped with a linotype machine and full press, which was used to train boys in printing as well as to produce the *Echo*. The large circular table from the old building was moved into the *Echo* office on the second floor and served as a copy desk and for folding the *Echos*.

Another special feature of the building was the beautiful art gallery on the third floor, named in memory of Roda Selleck.

. . . . .

Mr. Hadley and the new electric printing press

Shortridge High School moved into its new quarters at 34th and Meridian during the Thanksgiving vacation in the fall of 1928. It was a time of feverish activity. David Burns was the assistant in the physics lab; he also had a "tin lizzie," so he got the job of moving most of the equipment from the old lab to the new. Other students and teachers were driving back and forth with materials from the other labs, the classrooms, the Art Department, the Music Department, and, of course, the library. On Friday, November 30, and Saturday, December 1, there was a continuous parade of cars back and forth. They got the job done.

The *Indianapolis Times* reported:

> On the morning school was begun in the structure, George Buck, principal, allotted thirty minutes for the pupils to become acquainted with the plant and to "orient" themselves, as he said—after which the regular routine of the classes was begun and the school functioned without any perceptible confusion.

The article went on to say:

> Classical beauty and dignity of the main facade fronting Meridian street has become apparent since the high board fence was removed

about two months ago and the work of landscaping, not yet completed, was begun. . . .

*Echo* reporter, Joe Coffin, class of 1929, reported more fully in the issue of December 28, 1928:

Some dreams come true, for here we are in the new Shortridge. It reminds me of a new suit; it looks excellent, but does not feel comfortable yet. I wondered what the rest thought about it, so searchingly down one of the long corridors I went. First I saw John Forney and William Hoffman gazing into the elevator shaft.

John being asked to give his views concerning the new Shortridge said, "The building is well planned and already the students seem to have the school spirit. But, oh! If we could only use the elevators."

William Hoffman added, "I enjoy the out-of-town neighborhood atmosphere here. I consider the Auditorium the best feature of our school. The accoustic properties of Caleb Mills Hall are excellent."

Mr. Hadley came gaily down the hall and, by the expression on his face I expected him to yell, "Whoopee," or some other joyful exclamation. Instead, he said, "Isn't it fun! This school is just like a new toy to me. I like to explore around in the halls and stairways. After climbing a small stair yesterday I found that I was on the roof. To think we even have a roof garden now. I discovered the Press Room also yesterday."

Librarian Nell Sharp with Mr. Rice, Mr. Hadley, and Mr. Buck

Then on down the hall he went until he came to another stairway which he proceeded to explore.

Mr. Knight was just entering his classroom when I overtook him. He remarked, "It is a pleasure to coach a team in such a place as our new gym. Speaking of a gym, you will have a hard time finding a better one in Indiana." . . .

Miss Allen thought that it was remarkable the way the students had settled down to work, and found their lockers without much trouble. . . .

Mr. West, one of our best-liked janitors, was heard to remark: "This is sure the biggest building I ever tried to get around in." . . .

Miss Lloyd said that everyone got adjusted so quickly it seemed as if we had been here for months.

Miss McClellan was thrilled with her laboratory, about which she said, "It is the best equipped and most beautiful part of the school to me."

As I walked on down the hall I thought to myself, "If the teachers and students continue to enjoy this school as much as they seem to, we will soon have one of the best schools in the country."

And then I remembered, "Why it always has been the best school! It's Shortridge!"

The new building was generally a great success, but there was still much to be done. What had been envisioned as "the beautiful inner courtyard" was still just a mass of sand and gravel left over from the excavation—with no money in the budget to cover any landscaping. Under the sponsorship of Elizabeth Rawls, of the Botany Department, and with the encouragement of the *Echo* editors, the students started bringing shoe boxes full of top soil from their own yards to deposit in the barren courtyard. These offerings had to be brought through the teachers' cafeteria, which had the only entrance into the court.

In spite of good will and enthusiasm, covering eighteen thousand square feet of ground with the contents of shoe boxes proved to be impossible, so the Latin classes started taking up collections to buy a whole truckload of dirt at a time. (This also had to be wheeled in through the teachers' cafeteria.) By the following year the school board was so impressed with all this activity that they managed to find the funds to finish the job. This entailed sending a couple of horses and a plow through the well-traveled teachers' cafeteria to make the area ready for planting.

Indoor beautification received attention, too. With the move to the new building, Shortridge established a Fine Arts Society to which every pupil was asked to make a voluntary contribution of a nickel a week. The objective was to acquire works of art for each department and eventually for each classroom. Interested citizens also contributed some major art works to the school.

Patron of the arts Carl Lieber donated a portrait of Roda Selleck by the distinguished portrait artist Wayman Adams, which became the centerpiece of the Selleck Gallery. Lieber was a founder of the Art Association of Indianapolis and chairman of the John Herron Fine Arts Committee, as well as treasurer of H. Lieber and Company, a long-established Indianapolis art store.

Wayman Adams had been anxious to paint Miss Selleck for years, but she was reluctant and shy about it. Finally, her colleague, Mrs. Bowles, invited her for lunch and the afternoon, and when she arrived, there was Wayman Adams. She gave in and sat for her portrait. Carl Lieber bought it for $4,000 and had it in his home for five years before donating it to Shortridge. There it took its place along with other faculty portraits, including those of Abram Shortridge, George Hufford, and Laura Donnan. Another picture was given in memory of Miss Selleck by George Calvert, a local connoisseur. This one by Ronald Selfridge, entitled *Industry*, was a still life showing a variety of pottery vessels. George Calvert said he made this selection to commemorate Miss Selleck, because of her great love of pottery. The Portfolio Club of Indianapolis also donated pictures in memory of Roda Selleck.

By the fall of 1929 the *Echo* reported:

> Eleven sculptural and mural decorations that graced the halls of Old Shortridge are soon to find their proper places in a new home.
>
> Such pieces as the Zodiac Frieze, the panel of the Holy Grail and the picture of the Dutch Burgomasters have been unearthed. . . .
>
> The locations of many of these works of art have already been determined. Pictures of the Rheims and Amiens Cathedrals are going to Rooms 209 and 313, respectively. A bronze drinking fountain by Barnholme is to be used later in the court.
>
> A bust of Webster will be placed near study hall 241 and that of Lincoln goes nearby. Mr. Van Voorhees has suggested that the Biddy Memorial Plaque be located on the wall of the corridor close to Room 210. . . .

The graceful bronze statue, *The Sower of Ideas*, by the French sculptor, Picault, which had been the gift of the class of 1900, and which had stood at the head of the stairs in the old building, now took its place in the office of the Art Department.

The principal student money-raising effort was directed towards acquiring an organ for Caleb Mills Hall. The Charity Dye Library also

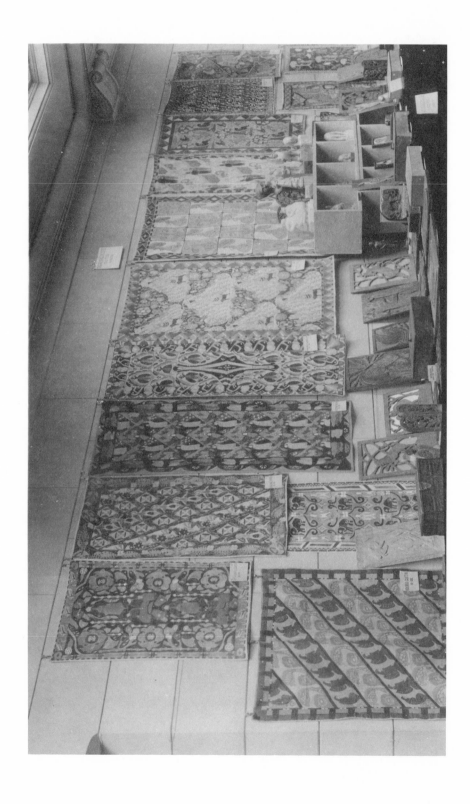

Student art work displayed in the Selleck Gallery

"Loved by Old and Young"

received attention. "Friends of the Library" held a Tea and Book Shower in the Selleck Gallery on February 13, 1929, which produced 325 new books and cash donations of $40.

In much the same spirit, Julius Sagalowsky, tennis champion of Indiana and member of the class of 1922, presented his entire collection of tennis awards to Shortridge. This included a Butler blanket, nine medals, and sixteen silver cups, four of which were won while he was at Shortridge. They went on display in the athletic office window.

The Shortridge athletes and debaters were quick to do their part to fill the new trophy cases. The football team won the city championship in 1929 for the third year in a row. The debate team won another Tri-State cup. The gymnastic team won a state championship; so did the swimmers. Girls basketball had a 9–1 season, and tennis and track were both strong.

# Shortridge in the 1930s

I N OCTOBER, 1929, the stock market crashed, but the ensuing depression caused no visible dampening of spirits at Shortridge.
Money was provided by the Parent-Teachers Association to help
needy students stay in school. New organizations sprang up and
flourished alongside the older established ones. The athletes experienced
considerable success. The musical groups expanded. Scholarship remained high, and many students also managed to have a good time.

Charles Feibleman, class of 1932, editor of Wednesday's *Echo*, and
Shortridge correspondent for the *Indianapolis News*, reviewed his high
school years for students in 1957:

> The Shortridge Class of '32 was acutely aware of a problem that I
> hope today's generation will never know—a depression. . . . Yet if it
> taught us nothing else, we learned to be considerate of each other, and
> to make plans on a basis that would not put too heavy a financial strain
> on the generous, but harassed man who came up with the weekly
> allowance.
>
> I remember when Shortridge played a special post-season football
> game with Cathedral in Butler Bowl on Thanksgiving morning, with all
> proceeds going for unemployment relief in Indianapolis. I remember
> the All-School Dances in the gym on Friday afternoon, that beloved
> Miss Mary Pratt sponsored—where admission was 10 cents, and you
> could buy your date a coca-cola after the dance and walk her home, and
> have a whale of a big time for a total outlay of 30 cents. . . . And the
> big debate in the Student Council was over the question of whether the
> organ for Caleb Mills Hall should be bought on the installment plan, or
> whether everyone should go on working for the Organ Fund for years,
> to make sure that once the purchase was made, there would be no
> threat of repossession.
>
> I remember the happy experiences in helping publicize Shortridge

life as correspondent for the *Indianapolis News*. Miss Grace Shoup
checked us in every day to make sure no newsworthy item was missed.
No one could become President of the Mythology Club, or Stamp
Club, or Fiction Club without rating at least an inch in the metropolitan
dailies. Best of all, tolerant City Editors like Wayne Guthrie and C.
Walter McCarty insisted on a clear, simple style of who, what, when,
where and how that had permanent carryover value. We even got paid
for those news items that were published.

War clouds were remote. We read about the "Manchurian Incident" in 1931, and studied the Stimson Report, little realizing that there
was the beginning of World War II. . . .

Maribel Snider Stark, speaking for the fiftieth reunion of the class of
1934, made a similar comment. Just before the reunion in 1984, the
*Indianapolis Star* had carried an article which remarked that "Shortridge
was built for rich kids." She said, "I just looked at that and laughed.
Hardly any of us had any money. But on thinking it over I decided that
we *were* rich—we had the finest school filled with the best teachers—and
indeed we did have everything."

"Everything" included a large handsome building which, by 1933,
though only five years old, was already extremely overcrowded—thirty-
one hundred students in a building planned for twenty-five hundred.
The state of the economy was partly responsible for the increased enrollment. Many students who could not afford to go to college and who
could not find jobs continued in high school as postgraduates. The administration coped with this situation by allowing some of the students a
shortened school day. Those who kept their grades up could have a
schedule of periods 1 through 5, which let them out at 12:20, or 1
through 6, which kept them in school until 1:10. They could then go
home for lunch and the rest of the day, or come back for special activities. Similarly, those whose classes fell at the end of the day could come
in later. These schedules were offered as a special privilege, which had to
be earned, and did not create the sense of a divided student body that
had resulted from the morning school and the afternoon school at the
turn of the century.

Clubs were almost too numerous to list: the Photography Club, the
Sketch Club, the Art Appreciation Club, the Poetry Club, the Mythology Club, the Stamp Club, the Shakespeare Club and, of course, the
Roman State, the Debating Club, and the Senate. The Roman State was
the largest, with 1,220 members. All the Latin students belonged, and
they continued to stage an annual Saturnalia and also a Liberalia. Always
there were plenty of Shortridge students who liked to argue, so the
Debating Club and the Senate were as popular and vigorous as ever.

The 1929 *Annual* reports:

> The Student Council is perhaps the newest organization of Short-ridge. It has been organized only since the past February. The council is made up of five Senior representatives, four Juniors, two under-classmen, and Mr. Hadley and Lt. Naylor acting as the faculty spon-sors. The aim of the student council is to be a connecting link between the faculty and the student body. The main project that this organi-zation has been undertaking this year and will continue in years to come is the raising of funds for an organ. . . . The council sponsored the first student party in the new Shortridge and the first moving picture. . . .

Another new organization was the Radio Club, sponsored by Her-man H. Siemers of the Physics Department. Students had not yet begun to write radio scripts—that came with World War II—but some of them learned to operate the public address system, which was controlled from Room 304 in the Physics Department. The switching system controlled loud speakers in the auditorium, study halls, cafeteria, and the principal's office, as well as a monitor in the physics shop.

In the fall of 1938, Bob Merrill, class of 1939, student assistant in the physics lab, was working with the radio tuned to the World Series when a messenger appeared to say that he was to report at once to the prin-cipal's office. Filled with apprehension he rushed downstairs. This is his story:

> Mr. Buck was awaiting me outside his office door; and with a stern look, he asked, "Bob, do you have that radio playing upstairs?"
>
> Feeling blood rising to my face, I meekly replied, "Yes sir."
>
> "You have it on the World Series, don't you?"
>
> With my heart now going like the proverbial trip-hammer, I again replied, "Yes sir."
>
> With the rumble of authority in his voice, Mr. Buck asked, "Did you know that the speaker in my office was on?"
>
> "No sir." I noticed a slight flash in his eyes, but I couldn't tell what it meant.
>
> "We have really got a problem here." Mr. Buck said, "Lets go inside for an explanation." As he opened the door I could see about fifteen teachers seated around the room, all staring at me with icy ex-pressions. As I braced myself for what appeared to be an imminent court martial, I heard above the ringing in my ears, "We are all here during our lunch hour, but we cannot hear the radio very well; could you go upstairs and turn it up a bit louder?"
>
> At that point, a ripple of laughter floated across the gathering of teachers, and I heard myself reply, "Yes sir, oh yes indeed, sir, I shall do it right away, sir," and I got back up the stairs even faster than I had come down.

All school activities continued to be reported in the *Echo* which had two supporting organizations: the long-established Press Club, composed of all the *Echo* staffs, the agents who gathered subscriptions, and the members of the Journalism Department; and the Editorial Board, to which only the *Echo*'s editors and associate editors belonged. This latter organization met every two weeks under the sponsorship first of Mr. Otto and then of Miss Nora Thomas, both of whom constantly promoted and encouraged journalistic talent. *Echo* editors came to school early and left late.

Another project designed to encourage writers was the Hufford Collection. A group known as "Friends of the Library" helped to fill the shelves of the Charity Dye Memorial Library, but an especial friend was Lois Hufford, once head of the Shortridge English Department and the widow of former principal, George Hufford. Mrs. Hufford undertook to form a "Shortridge High School Honor Roll in Literature." She began this project in 1933 when she was eighty-seven, and within a year she had gathered more than ninety books, all written by Shortridgers, either faculty or alumni. According to her plan the books would comprise a

Nora Thomas

library separate from the general one, to be kept as a sort of literary museum and not for general circulation.

Mrs. Hufford received an enthusiastic response from three distinguished members of the class of 1885. Perhaps best known was George Andrew Reisner, professor of Egyptology at Harvard and director of the Harvard-Boston Egyptian exposition. Mrs. Hufford made contact with him through the Harvard-camp, Pyramid post office, Cairo, where he had supervised excavations for a number of years. He wrote back, expressing great approval of the project, and said that he was instructing his publisher to send some of his books. One of his classmates, who was a colleague as well as a fellow writer, Wilbur Abbott, a professor of history at Harvard, also sent several books. So did Louise Closser Hale, actress and author.

Among Mrs. Hufford's literati was Mary Ritter Beard, class of 1893, wife of historian Charles A. Beard. She is probably best remembered now for the books she wrote in conjunction with her husband, but she was described in the *Indianapolis News* in 1934 as "one of the most distinguished woman writers of the country." She sent several books to Mrs. Hufford, including her most recent one, *America through Women's Eyes*. Claude Bowers, class of 1898, then U.S. ambassador to Spain, sent copies of his widely read histories and biographies and an enthusiastic letter in support of the project. So did his high school friend, Myla Jo Closser, sister of Louise Closser Hale.

Ernest Lynn Talbert, class of 1897, professor of psychology at the University of Cincinnati, sent copies of his writings on psychology, and Dr. Morris Fishbein, class of 1906, then editor of *Hygeia Magazine* and later president of the American Medical Association, contributed his books on medicine.

Some of the Shortridge faculty represented in the original collection were Carolyn Ashbrook and Janet Bowles, both of the Art Department; Dr. Alembert W. Brayton, former science teacher; Angeline Carey, Laura Donnan, Charity Dye, Rosa M. R. Mikels, and Grace Shoup, all but Miss Donnan from the English Department; and Emmett Rice, vice-principal.

Booth Tarkington was included in the list by his own choice, because he had studied with Mr. Hufford, although he was not an alumnus. His time at Indianapolis High School had involved so much truancy that his parents had sent him to Exeter. Indianapolis's other well-known novelist of that day had a similar relationship to the school. Meredith Nicholson started at Indianapolis High School, but quit, according to one account, because he had to take math; actually it was for financial reasons. He also wanted to be included as a Shortridge writer.

When the original list of the Hufford Collection was published in the *News*, July 21, 1934, Mrs. Hufford was just getting started. She only lived another year, but she added many more authors to her roster, and she succeeded in establishing the tradition. The *Echo* memorialized her on her ninetieth birthday:

> Many Shortridge teachers have recollections of Mrs. Hufford's personality, teaching methods, and early classes.
>
> Miss McClellan, of the zoology department, remembers the theme of "the dear old lady's life work" as being, "Gladly will I learn and gladly teach."
>
> "Mrs. Hufford was a great teacher and an inspiration to the students," Miss McClellan recalled. "She was one who believed in thorough work, and that boys and girls were able to appreciate the best in literature." . . .
>
> Miss Washburn tells of a recent visit with the "wonderful lady."
>
> "I mentioned to her that it was too bad her condition confined her to her bed. She replied, 'I am so thankful that I can read and think.' She has a very keen mind and showed a great interest in Shortridge." . . .

Mrs. Hufford died shortly after this, but the Hufford Collection was placed on special shelves in the Shortridge library as an inspiration and incentive to aspiring writers. There turned out to be a number of them, some in fields which Mrs. Hufford did not envision, and the collection grew. It is now in the Indiana Division of the Indiana State Library.

Madelyn Pugh (Davis), class of 1938, best known as the coauthor of the "I Love Lucy" television series, was a sophomore when Mrs. Hufford died. Television scripts never became part of the Hufford Collection, but Shortridge alumni all over the country were electrified on a Sunday evening in early 1963 when "Lucy," now trying to become a reporter, pretended to have gone to Shortridge in order to get an interview. She was terribly nervous but finally managed to spit out "Mr. Hadley" and "Shortridge Blue Devils," and that proved to be enough.

Madelyn Davis says of her own Shortridge experience:

> I took it for granted at the time. I just thought that was what high school was like, but as I look back it was a marvelous experience. I'll always remember how much fun we had on Mary Pratt's Social Committee and how stimulating the Fiction Club was under Ruth Armstrong.
>
> I was planning to be a newspaper person. I just got into radio and then television because that's where the job was. For somebody who wanted a career in journalism, the opportunity at Shortridge was almost unbelievable. *Echo* editors were given huge responsibility, although al-

ways under the eye of the faculty sponsors. We wrote, assigned the stories, planned the layout, everything, and we certainly felt impelled to do a good job. [Madelyn was editor of Friday's *Echo*.]

The journalism class under Grace Shoup was a great experience too. She was really tough with us—absolutely no sloppiness—but she also cheered us on. We all learned to turn in clean, crisp copy.

Another teacher that I think of often is Bess Rawls of the botany department. She was totally against "sloppiness" too. We had to make neat drawings, and for those drawings we had to learn to print the way she wanted us to, a small, neat backhand print. I still use it.

Miss Rawls was tough; so were Mr. Forsyth in history and Mrs. Weathers in French. In fact, that whole building was stuffed full of teachers who managed to be tough and encouraging at the same time. We were very fortunate.

Just two years behind Madelyn was future novelist Kurt Vonnegut. He participated in many of the same activities she did. He was a fellow member of the Fiction Club, an *Echo* editor, and chairman of the Social Committee in his senior year. He speaks with similar enthusiasm about his Shortridge experience:

> Shortridge was so exciting and nourishing to me intellectually that I should really write a book about it. The best teachers there were revered as though they were full professors at a great university: Frank Wade in Chemistry, Minnie Lloyd in Ancient History, Rousseau Mc-Clellan in Zoology, and on and on. We used to sign up for courses because of the greatness of the teachers rather than the usefulness of the courses taught. . . .
>
> When I went East to college, to Cornell, and came up against prep school kids, I found myself better prepared than they were. And the playfulness I have with ideas I learned at Shortridge and it serves me wonderfully to the present day.

Kurt did not, however, share the general admiration for the coaches. He describes them as "brutal Darwinists" who did not find him or his friends among the fittest, and he says, "Our bodies could rot as far as the Athletic Department was concerned. Still, that left us to work on the *Echo* in the afternoons. . . ."

He also said in a speech at Butler University in 1983, "I was raised a pacifist and a socialist in the public schools of Indianapolis with the full approval of the school committee, as far as I knew. . . .

"Every joke I've ever told, every attitude I've ever struck, came from school 43 and Shortridge. I never needed any new material from any place."

While future authors were writing diligently in school, other stu-

# FACULTY

We'll tell you one little thing
It is a known fact,
Miss Campbell should be a race driver
And speed around the track.

There was a man in our
school
Who was so wondrous wise
He sat upon a flagpole
And shooed away the
flies.

WHAT A MAN

17930 5·9674    9002 71.36½

And here we have the strong man,
Oh! he is very tough
He can lift a thousand pounds or more
Without a single
puff!

What would you think if you should see
Miss Pratt, that teacher sedate
Riding around on top of a horse
And cantering at a perilous gait?

Here is a charming teacher
One whom you need not fear,
For her ambition is to be
The champion woman skier.

M. Bundren

Drawings from 1933 *Annual*

# FANCIES

MR. NIPPER WANTED TO GO TO THE FOOT-
    BALL FIELD
HE DID NOT WANT TO BE LATE
HE LOOKED AROUND FOR A WAY TO GO
AND FINALLY DECIDED TO SKATE

WHENEVER YOU GO OUT TO
    FISH
BE CAREFUL WHAT YOU
    PULL IN
FOR GRACIOUS! IT MIGHT BE—
MR. SIEMERS JUST DOWN FOR
    A SWIM

ONE OF THE THINGS WE'D
    ALL LIKE TO SEE
WOULD BE MR. KNIGHT
    PLAYING BALL,
BUT I SUPPOSE HE'D START
    THINKING ABOUT HISTORY
AND FORGET TO BAT AT
    ALL !

IF A GIRL KNOWS NOTHING ABOUT CHEMISTRY
    MR. GEISLER WILL NOT RAZZ HER
FOR ISN'T IT HIS DESIRE TO BE
    THE DEAN OF GIRLS AT VASSAR?

OF COURSE YOU KNOW OF THAT POPU-
    LAR CRAZE
'TIS THE JIGSAW THAT WE MEAN—
AND OF ALL THE JIG-SAWERS OF OUR DAYS
WE THINK THAT MISS LONG IS THE QUEEN.

M. FREEMAN

Drawings from 1935 *Annual*

dents were more interested in speaking and debating. Clarence C. Shoe-maker became debate coach in 1932. Shortridge won the five-year Tri-State debate cup in 1935. The question was: "Resolved, that the United States should adopt the essential features of the British system of radio control and operation." In 1936 the question was "Resolved, that all electric utilities should be governmentally owned and operated." By 1940 debaters were wrestling with: "Resolved, that the powers of the Federal government should be increased," and by 1941 they addressed themselves to: "Resolved, that the national government shall own and operate the railroads."

These were all assigned national debate questions. The Shortridge Senate chose its own subjects which closely paralleled those being dis-cussed in the Senate of the United States. The *Echo* says discussion became "tumultuous" several times during 1936 and '37, as the senators argued about the packing of the Supreme Court, socialized medicine (which was roundly defeated), and the sit-down strikes by organized labor. In 1940 the high school senators bravely endeavored to untangle the European crisis, balance the budget, and solve the unemployment problem. The next year they debated bills against war, against con-scription, and against liquor and tobacco advertising.

Those students whose particular interest was in public speaking rather than debating also were under the wing of Mr. Shoemaker, and they had opportunities to participate in contests and to appear on public platforms in support of such worthy causes as the Community Fund and the Smoke Abatement League.

Although Roda Selleck was gone, the Shortridge Art Department was thriving. It had greatly improved facilities in the new building and strong leadership from department head, Theodore H. Van Voorhees. Indianapolis architect, H. Roll McLaughlin, class of 1941, says of him:

> He always kept you stimulated and he wouldn't put up with any nonsense. He had a fine department. I particularly remember Gordon Johnson, who taught mechanical drawing and draftsmanship. He pro-duced a remarkable number of architects for Indianapolis, Al Porteous, Howard White, Harry E. Hunter, John Carmack, Harry Cooler. . . . He always wanted an industrial arts building at Shortridge and it was a regular class project to design such a building. We all had a crack at it. I liked to draw cars better than I liked to draw buildings in those days, and I remember that he once let me get away with a drawing that had a car in the foreground and a building in the background. The best of our drawings were exhibited in the Selleck Art Gallery. The gallery was a great stimulus to all the art students. Mr. Johnson was also a talented, dedicated photographer. He lived on 43rd street across from the football field and had a dark room which he let students use. He

Gordon O. Johnson

corresponded with me, and I'm sure with many others, all the time I was in service. I haven't forgotten him.

.    .    .    .    .

Shortridge activities on 34th Street were supported by an increasingly active Parent-Teachers Association. The association got started in 1917 when Mr. Buck asked Mrs. Frank E. Brown, mother of Harriet Brown of the class of 1918 and a past president of the School 60 PTA, to organize a chapter for Shortridge. She and her friends got right on the job. The first meeting was held on June 6, 1917, in the Shortridge Study Hall. Mrs. Brown was elected president, a constitution was adopted, and the members of the association immediately went to work with patriotic fervor. They played an active role in raising money for the war effort and participated in the Shortridge march to deposit $1,000 in gold in the Indianapolis war chest.

Next they turned their attention to the dilapidated condition of the buildings in which their children were being educated. They sent a committee to the school board in 1921 to say that the old structures and equipment were "wholly inadequate" and that "a new and larger school is a recognized necessity." They continued to press for a new building that would be large enough, as well as properly designed, to accommodate all the Shortridge projects.

Once they had the building, the Shortridge PTA launched programs to raise money to help needy students and to support school activities, especially music. The PTA contributed a sizable portion of the funds for the pipe organ for Caleb Mills Hall (thereby relieving the Student Council of the decision about installment buying and the fear of repossession). The organ was installed in 1931. Joel Hadley, chairman of the committee, presented the organ to Mr. Buck at an elaborate dedication service and announced that it had been named the "George Buck Organ" in his honor.

When Robert J. Shultz joined the Music Department in the early 1930s, and became director of the band, one of his greatest desires was to get his band members out of their R.O.T.C. uniforms and into something handsomer. Mr. Buck agreed with him about this, and they made a joint request for help from the PTA. It was successful. On Armistice Day, 1933, a Shortridge military band of one hundred and fifteen pieces played for the dedication of the World War Memorial. They were resplendent in new blue and white corduroy coats and leatherette hats of the same colors, which had been provided by the PTA. (The boys furnished their own white trousers.) The band now played constantly—for football and basketball games, pep sessions, auditorium programs, in the public parks, and in parades. They were the first Indianapolis high school band to march in formations and to create blocks and pinwheels on the field. They also blocked out an impressive Shortridge *S*. What

Robert J. Shultz

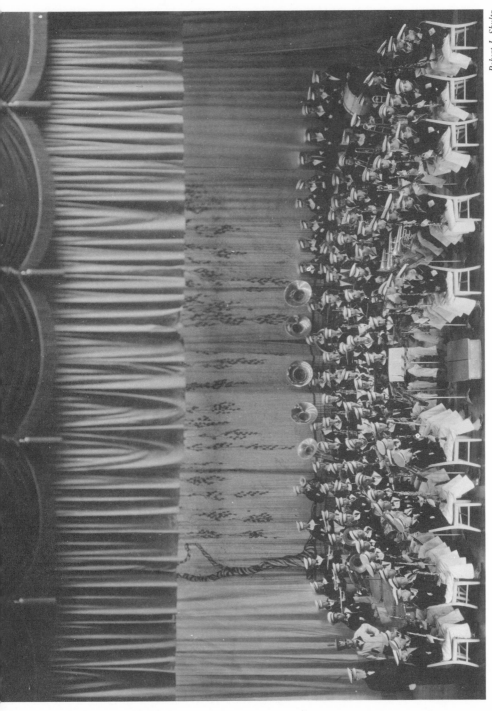

*Robert J. Shultz*

SHS Marching Band in new uniforms, 1933

Mr. Shultz remembers particularly is the new formation that went wrong. The band marched out to say HELLO. However, something happened, and the players who were to form the letter *O* did not make it onto the field. He found this a hard thing to explain.

Since the Junior Vaudeville was now firmly established as the junior project and the Senior Play as the senior project, the PTA felt free to take over the sponsorship of a traditional money-raising fair, similar to those staged by the seniors at the turn of the century and the juniors in the early 1920s. An article in the *Indianapolis News*, November 28, 1934, reports:

> Each year the Shortridge association gives one grand and glorious "show" of some kind to raise money for the organization.
>
> Last year the "Round-Up" was held, and this month the headlines of the Shortridge Echo proclaimed "The Old-Time Sociable," given under auspices of the P.T.A. Elderly and young combined to have a big night. In addition to dancing, with plenty of waltzes thrown in for the parents, there were a fish-pond, shooting gallery and many other attractions. From a small start the organization has reached vast proportions, for at the fall dinner meeting more than 2,500 fathers, mothers and teachers were present.

In 1933, besides furnishing the band uniforms, the PTA contributed over thirteen hundred dollars to help keep needy students in school. These fairs became another strong Shortridge institution. In 1938 they took the name of Family Frolic, and they raised larger amounts of money each year all through the depression and for many years thereafter.

. . . . .

The depression years at Shortridge were boom years for sports. By the early 1930s the staff was well in place. Russell Julius, head of the Athletic Department, had been at Shortridge since 1920. Lt. George A. Naylor, golf coach, came in 1921, and Don Knight, track coach, in 1926. Kenneth Peterman, varsity basketball coach, arrived in 1929, as did Howard Wood, the tennis coach. Claude Keesling, reserve basketball coach, joined the staff in 1930, and finally in 1931 Robert L. Nipper became the head football coach.

The 1931 basketball season was almost unbearably exciting. The Shortridge team won the Sectional and the Regional tournaments and found themselves among the sweet sixteen. The 1931 *Annual*:

> Shortridge entered with the select sixteen for the first time in the history of I.H.S.A.A. basketball and played the state champion Washington Hatchets in the second game of the morning. Playing a flawless

brand of basketball, Coach Peterman's boys outplayed and outfought the Friddlemen to build up what seemed sure to be a winning margin only to have Dave Dejernet, incomparable negro pivot man for Washington, score twice in the final thirty seconds of play to send the fighting Blue Devil crew down to a bitter but glorious defeat.

Coach Kenneth Peterman has in his first year as basketball mentor at Shortridge, enjoyed sensational success. . . .

"Pete," as he is affectionately known to his boys, will not only be remembered as the great net coach who took Shortridge to the State, but also as the man whose outstanding character and leadership will forever leave their imprint upon the boys under his supervision.

Still, only two years later Shortridge was even more puffed up with basketball pride. Jack Appel, sports editor for the 1933 *Annual*, reports:

The Shortridge High School basketball team of this year compiled probably the greatest record of any other basketball team in the history of the school. They won a total of twenty-five games, losing only four. In the state tournament they reached the semi-finals and bowed only in over-time.

The highest-scoring player was big Jim Seward, all-state center and winner of the Gimbel medal for sportsmanship during the state finals. He towers five and a half inches over the six-foot mark. Seward could shoot equally well with his right or left hand; he was a master of the pivot shot, and he was probably the cleverest center in the state. After a year of varsity competition, his defensive work improved greatly and in 1933 he was truly a star. Flanking Seward were two sharp-shooting forwards, Harry Yelch and Jack Berns. Harry Yelch, after two years' experience on the reserve team, developed into a sterling player this year. He was a sure shot from out on the floor and a hard-driving player. His under-the-basket shots were exceptionally good. Harry is six feet tall. Jack Berns, the other forward, is another six-footer with a year of competition under his belt. Jack was an alert ball-hawk and also a dead-eye for long shots. He was great following-in under the basket. Dick Robinson, who was probably the fastest, shiftiest man on the team, played floor guard. He improved greatly from last year, when he won his letter, and was the spark-plug of the team. Although he was only five feet ten, Robinson held some of the best men in the state, as well as driving under for many baskets. "Big George" Perry, six-foot two inch back guard, was the fifth member of the team. Perry played center on the reserve team of last year and so was a good man for taking the ball off the back-board. He was a good long shot and could also play pivot position.

It is no discredit to the other five men on the squad, namely, Dick Dempsey, Jack Kitzmiller, Joe Mooney, Jack Appel, and Bill Pensinger, that they did not see much action, as the first five worked together perfectly. . . .

One of the greatest assets of the team was their coach. "Pete," as Mr. Peterman is known, is one of the smartest, most sympathetic coaches in the country, and a large measure of the team's success is due to him. All through the season he worked with the team, always with them in victory and in defeat. Shortridge is proud of Mr. Peterman, a fine coach and, above all, always a gentleman. . . .

Jim Seward, reminiscing in 1984, echoed those sentiments:

Ken Peterman was a wonderful coach. We happened to have a bunch of good athletes in our class, but he certainly got the most out of us. He was one of only two Indiana coaches who ever had two Gimbel award winners. We learned the fundamentals of basketball from him and we certainly learned team play. Many of us played for our college teams, which says a lot for our high school coach. I played at Purdue, Jack Appel at Princeton, George Perry at Butler, and Jack Berns at Wabash. Jack Berns and I were both captains of our teams.

We were a close-knit group at Shortridge, probably somewhat cliquish. We didn't just play basketball together. We studied together and double dated together and partied together. We have all remained

Kenneth (Pete) Peterman

1933 basketball team (Gimbel Award winner Jim Seward in center)

good friends, and those of us who live somewhere near Indianapolis generally manage to get together several times a year.

Jim Seward remembers more about Shortridge than just playing basketball. He was a midyear student and a little young for his class. He decided right away to take four and a half years at Shortridge, because of his interest in athletics. His brother, Bob, who was also a good athlete, had entered Tech in the middle of the year several years earlier and had elected to graduate in three and a half years, thereby minimizing his chances for athletic prowess. Jim, with nine semesters, not only had time to grow extremely tall and play excellent basketball, he had time to take a lot of courses, too. Since he planned on an engineering program at Purdue, he took all the math and science he could get, but he also says:

> I think I took every art course the school had to offer. The art department was very impressive. I also particularly remember my Shakespeare course, although I can't think of the teacher's name right now. She had us do a lot of memorizing. In fact we answered the roll every day with newly memorized quotations. That's not fashionable now, but we enjoyed it, and I have had a lifelong enjoyment of and appreciation for Shakespeare that I think I might well not have had without that course.
>
> The math and science courses were so good that when I got to Purdue I tested out of eight hours of math and chemistry, and by the end of my freshman year I had forty-four credits. This almost got me into trouble later. I think it was my junior year. Right before Thanksgiving with the first basketball game only two weeks away the trainer, a rather elderly man, was taping my ankles when he said, "Do you realize you are ineligible?"
>
> I didn't realize it at all and neither did the coach, but the trainer was right. According to the rules at that time, as a student in the School of Mechanical Engineering, I had to be taking a full engineering load of eighteen hours to be eligible for varsity play. I was only taking sixteen hours, because that was all I needed to fulfill my graduation requirements. The next day I rushed around the campus and found a psychology professor who was willing to let me enroll in his class even at that late date. He said I could make up the missed work as best I could, and he would give me whatever grade I made on the final exam. That brought my course load up to eighteen hours and solved the problem, but it was a near thing.

The spring of 1933 was the great year for basketball, but the fall of 1935 was the climactic year for football, and the football players were every bit as ready to give credit to their coach, as were the netmen. The 1936 *Annual* reported in full:

Four years ago, under the coaching of the late Lieutenant Naylor the Shortridge freshmen beat the Tech frosh 19–6.

This year, the same team with few exceptions climaxed an unde-feated season with a victory over the Big Green by the identical score of 19–6, annexing the City Championship and the undisputed possession of the School Board Trophy. "How did they do it?" we ask. The team says, "Spirit!"

The School Board Trophy had been up for grabs ever since football had been reintroduced to the Indianapolis public schools in 1920. It was to go to the first team that won the undisputed city championship five times. When the rivalry began the city teams were only three: Short-ridge, Manual, and Tech. By the time Shortridge finally won it in 1935, Washington, Broad Ripple, and Cathedral had been added to the list. (Cathedral would not have been eligible for the School Board Trophy because it was not a public school, but it was a city team and could become City Champion.)

Tech almost wrapped up the victory in the first five seasons. They won every year except 1921, when the season ended with a three-way tie. Then Alonzo Goldsberry took over as coach of the Shortridge team, and Shortridge won four times in a row, bringing them toe to toe with

Coach Nipper

1935 championship football team

Tech. By 1930 the competition between the two schools was intense. They both expected that that would be the year that one or the other of them would take home the coveted prize. Instead Washington won the city championship. The next year it went to Manual and then to Washington again. The year 1933 produced another three-way tie: Tech-Shortridge-Washington. In 1934 it was just Tech and Shortridge who had to share the title. The School Board Trophy was still up for grabs.

By the fall of 1935, the Shortridge footballers were totally committed to winning the trophy, and they did! Wesley Martin, team captain, gives a fervent description of their dedication:

> It is hard to put into words the exact feelings of those boys. What had once been just a game, had become an obsession. Summer found many of them together and others holding an enthusiastic correspondence. That outfit had been eating and sleeping football before the season began. They returned to practice in the fall with an eagerness that made the old heart pound. The boys knew what they wanted and they were out to get it.

The *Annual* sportswriter was equally fervent about the coach:

> But although Nipper was not unaware of the new element that had found its way into his ball club, he still kept his distance for his experi-

The school board trophy

ence had taught him that there are those who can't stand too much prosperity and will take advantage. On that team there was no such person. Every one was ready to make any sacrifice, not just for a cup, but for a man. We wanted his trust, his complete faith. We wanted him to know we would never quit.

And we told him so. I have never seen a happier man. It was one of those precious moments when words are superfluous.

Practice the next day was indescribable. Nipper did everything but put on a uniform and scrimmage. We worked, we sweated, and we laughed together; and so we went through the season.

This was not the only team that worked their hearts out for Bob Nipper. In the ten years before coach Nipper left Shortridge to serve in the Navy at the end of the 1942 season, Shortridge had tied for the city championship three times and won it outright four times. His players all regarded him as the world's best coach. They said so at the time, and they still say so now.

The tennis team felt much the same way about Howard Wood. Dan Morse, class of 1933, says:

I think Shortridge almost always had the best tennis team in the state, and I'm sure we had the best coach. We traveled around a good deal, playing schools such as Culver and the freshman team at Indiana State. We generally stayed in a dormitory or in private homes. A lot of people don't realize what an outstanding tennis player Howard Wood was. He turned pro because he needed the extra income, but if he had continued as an amateur he would probably have been among the top twenty players in the country. We all enjoyed playing for him.

Not as many Shortridgers went out for golf as for tennis in the 1930s, but Shortridge produced an Indiana state golf champion in Dick McCreary, class of 1935.

The girl athletes were also a close-knit group, who formed warm friendships, worked hard at the sports program, and admired their coaches. They continued to be rated on Mrs. Steichmann's complicated athletic index and to be rewarded with letters and sweaters if they could accumulate a sufficient number of points. The various sports were under the direction of Thelma Armfield and Kathryn Thompson. Jean Benham (Tussing), class of 1937, recalls, "I particularly enjoyed playing hockey at Riverside Park, partly because I thought a lot of Miss Armfield, who was our coach. She was a Scout leader, too, and a wonderful person. Those of us who liked to get out and play hockey were all good friends and we had a really good time."

In addition to hockey, the girls played basketball, volley ball, and baseball, as team sports. Many of them were also swimmers, tennis players, and golfers. Mary Anna Butz (Beasley), class of 1935, was the outstanding tennis player during her four years at Shortridge. She won the tennis championship three times. Helen Lee Smith, class of 1934, was a national swimming champion.

. . . . .

One reason that so many who went to Shortridge during the hard times of the 1930s do not remember being depressed was the activity of Mary Pratt. At the turn of the century she had been a student of Laura Donnan's. She said that she wanted to be the same kind of teacher and in many ways she was. Like Miss Donnan, she was a great admirer of Abraham Lincoln, and although she taught English, rather than history, she made all her sophomore students keep Lincoln notebooks. This was an introduction to research. Students looked up literary references to Lincoln, called the Indianapolis Chamber of Commerce for information about his Indiana years, consulted newspaper references, and wrote to Lincoln memorials in Illinois and Kentucky and to Louis Ludlow, Democratic congressman from their congressional district, elected and re-elected in otherwise Republican elections. Ludlow apparently had an aide, one of whose principal duties was to clip articles and pictures relating to Lincoln and to save them for Miss Pratt's sophomores. All those

Faculty group, 1933
(*Top row, l. to r.*): Paul Lockhart, Lois Martin Cislak, Herman Siemers,
Margaret Brayton, Robert Shultz
(*Front row, l. to r.*): Essie Long, Mildred Campbell, Ruth Allerdice,
Mary Pratt, Walter Geisler

who wrote to him received a packet of Lincoln-related items, and no two were alike.

Miss Pratt differed from Miss Donnan in that she did not inspire terror, as Miss Donnan frequently did, but she resembled her in being a catalyst for much of what went on in school. She created the Social Committee and imbued it with her own inventiveness and enthusiasm. The Friday afternoon after-school dances were promoted as special occasions, each with its own title and theme—a "Hatchet Hop" in honor of Washington's birthday; a "Blue Devil Hop," complete with floor show, at the end of the basketball season; "The Kickoff" in the fall of '35 after the great football triumph; and, of course, the Bluebelle and Uglyman dances.

The first Shortridge Bluebelle, Clemence Dow, was crowned in 1931. The first Shortridge Uglyman, John S. Matthews, took his place on the stage in 1932. John was also editor of Tuesday's *Echo* (Miss Pratt's). He says of her:

> She was the heart of the school. She was there for everybody, always available. People with family problems found in her a degree of understanding that no one else could furnish. Students who felt unfairly treated could count on her to fend for them against all comers.

John's own experience came with an editorial he wrote for the *Echo* in February, 1931, when Shortridge had just won both the Sectional and the Regional tournaments and the whole school was clamoring for tickets to the State. Entitled "Students! Do You Object?" it suggested that favoritism entered into the allocation of those precious pieces of cardboard:

> Only students holding season tickets are allowed a chance on them. . . . The student body should protest vigorously. . . . May it be suggested that everyone wishing a chance on a ticket should put his name on a slip of paper and deposit it in a box from which will be drawn (without favoritism) the quota number. Since the number allotted is only 6 per cent of the student body, the tickets should indeed be distributed fairly and judiciously.

John S. Matthews

Mr. Buck summoned him to the office to tell him what a dastardly thing he had done, but Miss Pratt came, too, and stood firmly behind her editor. She said that he had stuck to the facts, that many students did feel that the system was unfair. She was perfectly willing to agree that the matter not be pursued any further in the *Echo*, but she thought Mr. Buck would do well to hold a public drawing as suggested. That is the way the matter was resolved.

Alex Clark, president of the class of 1933 and later mayor of Indianapolis, says of Miss Pratt, "She really gave of herself. I remember her taking a whole bunch of us, on a Saturday afternoon, up to the top rows of the peanut gallery in English's for fifty-five cents apiece, to see Ethel Barrymore in *A School for Scandal*. It was an experience I'll never forget."

Another alumnus who expresses his admiration for Miss Pratt is Gene McCormick, class of 1942. He says:

> She was a real scholar, who also had a complete understanding of teenagers. She was able to make literature come alive and make it understood. It was fun to be in her class, but we all understood that she was serious about the learning process and that we had better be serious about it, too. Her Romantic Literature class was always so full that she had to set up extra tables and chairs beside her desk and, since everybody wanted to sit there, she held a drawing to see who got those chairs.

Gene's other most-admired teacher was Mrs. Grace Morrison of the Latin Department. He wrote of her at the time of her death in October of 1965:

> She was indeed extraordinary. Exacting, tough-minded, meticulous, she taught Latin with a style that made it truly a living language. Intolerant of nonsense and impervious to bluff and ingratiation, she drew from callow minds a love for Roman history in all its variety, splendor and humanity. . . . Her unvarying insistence upon perfection, well garnished with sharp wit and ebullient spirit, was an inspiration. . . . The inscription over the stage of Caleb Mills Hall describes her best, "A disciplined mind and cultivated heart are elements of power."

. . . . . .

On July 2, 1939, Rousseau McClellan died. She had taught at Shortridge for almost forty years and had started many students on the road to distinguished scientific careers, but more than that, as Mr. Buck said, "She had something that the pupils of Agassiz had—the seeing eye and the understanding heart. Her passionate love of nature and its creatures fired the imagination of thousands of young people and led many of them into lifelong appreciation and love of the wonders of nature. . . ." The whole community mourned "Miss Mac."

One of those led into "a lifelong appreciation and love of the wonders of nature" was Albert W. Brown, class of 1923, now retired and living on St. Thomas in the Virgin Islands. He became so excited about birds while he was taking zoology with Miss McClellan that he could barely find time to eat or sleep. He remembers how outraged his mother was because he called Miss McClellan at 5:45 one morning to tell her that he had just seen a pileated woodpecker, although, of course, he was going to see her that day in class. He is still unrepentant: "I was excited. I knew she would be excited too, and she was." Albert received an A+ for his bird record book and a long note from Miss McClellan praising him for outstanding work and saying, "No matter what else you do with your life, it will always be important to you that you did this, and you are always going to love birds." He says, "She was absolutely right. I still have my Shortridge bird book with me on St. Thomas, and I still spend many happy hours watching birds."

Val Nolan, class of 1937, is another one whose imagination was fired by Miss McClellan's class. He says:

> I was always interested in nature. My brother [Alan Nolan, class of 1941] and I collected insects and frogs and such, but it wasn't until I went on Miss McClellan's hikes that I discovered birds. I am sure I would have loved birds anyway, but her eagerness and enthusiasm certainly helped to spark mine. I remember how carefully she taught us to make field notes, and I can still hear her saying, "the more time you spend in the field the more you are going to see."

He has been spending time in the field ever since. Although his formal education was in law and he has long been a professor in the Indiana University Law School, he is now also a recognized authority on birds and an Indiana University professor of zoology. He achieved this status without ever taking another zoology course after Miss McClellan's. What he did instead was to become a keen observer, to make careful field notes, as he had been taught, and to write about his observations. He says:

> I didn't want to just list the birds I saw; I wanted to know more about their habits and behavior. I began to read professional ornithological journals. I also made a special field study of prairie warblers. When I was through with that study, I wrote an article about it which was accepted by one of the professional journals. After that I was accepted too, and I have continued to observe and to write ever since. As far as the teaching is concerned, first I was asked to come over to the zoology department to give a lecture, then a series of lectures. After that I was asked to teach a course and then another. Now I divide my time about half and half between the zoology department and the law school.

Although Shortridge had lost Miss McClellan, the school still had a natural science teacher who was totally dedicated to field work. This was Mildred Campbell, class of 1924, now retired and living in Irvington, who has been a vigorous outdoor person from her earliest years. In her high school days, when the weather was nice, she usually chose to walk the five miles from her home to the old Shortridge at Michigan and Pennsylvania streets. She says, "I never intended to be a science teacher, because only God can possibly know enough about nature to teach it." Nonetheless, she studied science, first at Butler University, then at the University of Michigan, and finally at the Institute of Oceanography at Woods Hole, Massachusetts. At Shortridge, she taught botany and biological science. She describes her work, both at Michigan and at Woods Hole, as having been "all outdoors." She also says:

> At Woods Hole, I spent most of my time in the water collecting specimens. I also got to work in the very first laboratory, where David Starr Jordan worked. I have always admired him more than anybody. I had all his books on fishes, and I tried as much as I could to teach the way he taught.
>
> I used to take my students over to Crown Hill to identify plants and to the fish hatchery to study fishes. We went on foot. Both places were within walking distance, and I never wanted to be responsible for students driving. Crown Hill had a wonderful variety of plant life, and the officials were completely cooperative.

.    .    .    .    .

The school year 1939–40 was the seventy-fifth anniversary of Shortridge. The school expressed pride in its history through the 1940 *Annual* and through special events throughout the year. The Parent-Teachers Association presented its annual Family Frolic as an anniversary occasion and drew a crowd of over three thousand, but it was the next year's graduation that marked the end of an era. The members of the class of 1941 were the last to enjoy the "years between the wars" and the last to have Mr. Buck as their principal. The students said in their *Annual*:

> The Shortridge we take with us in our memory, the school our hearts have come to know so intimately, cannot be the same again. George Buck leaves Shortridge with the Class of 1941. . . .
>
> The thousands of men and women and boys and girls whom he has graduated concur in granting George Buck his diploma in life, summa cum laude.

The teachers' tribute was even more heartfelt:

> Since September, 1910, Shortridge High School has had a special climate of its own. This has been the air, kindly yet bracing, genial yet stimulating, that establishes itself in the neighborhood of George Buck. For more than three decades Mr. Buck's gifts of integrity, intellect, wit, sympathy, and authority have vitalized Shortridge life. This inspiring atmosphere the pupils have accepted happily and as a matter of natural

Mr. Buck conferring with students

right; the teachers happily and with a keen sense of their own and the school's good fortune.

Countless details over the years build up our picture of Mr. Buck—in the auditorium before the Shortridge Service Flag bringing home to light-hearted students in his beautiful and lucid English the patriotic ideal—in conference with a Parent-Teachers' committee on some project for the school's welfare—ably representing Shortridge and the schools in some matter of civic importance or in national education councils—in his office dispensing even-handed justice. How many a teacher, and pupil too, recalls these scenes with a smile—the teacher sure of the principal's backing, the pupil sure of a fair decision, and both right! Each sensed Mr. Buck's fairmindedness, his perfect willingness to change his decisions for good reason, and his steady courage in action.

Perhaps more revealing than any formal incidents are Mr. Buck's casual daily contacts as he walks through the halls, now stopping for friendly conversation with a faculty member, now checking some youth who is exceeding the corridor speed limit, now helping untangle some puzzled freshman's locker combination, now in the teachers' dining room making the daily luncheon a social occasion. In these and other glimpses of him one sees the real man; one sees how his qualities seem always to call forth answering qualities in others—loyalty for loyalty, professional zeal for professional zeal, friendship for friendship, and for understanding, devotion. . . .

For the long and happy connection of a great principal with a great school all Shortridgers are grateful.

CHAPTER

12

World
War II

I N THE FALL OF 1941, Franklin D. Roosevelt was in the first year of
his third term as president of the United States, Henry Schricker
was in his first term as governor of Indiana, Reginald H. Sullivan
was mayor of Indianapolis, DeWitt Morgan was superintendent of
schools, and J. Dan Hull was beginning his job as principal of Shortridge
High School. Young men were being drafted for military service. Factories were expanding production to meet the needs of a rapidly growing
military establishment. At every level the country was preparing for
war, while still trying to avoid it.

The new principal of Shortridge came at a difficult time to take on a
difficult assignment—following thirty-one years of the leadership of
George Buck. Dr. Hull was a native of Missouri with unusual academic
credentials. According to the 1942 Shortridge *Annual*, he had been principal of a high school even before he graduated from college, and from
that time on his entire experience as an educator had been gained in the
principal's office.

Born in Mountain Grove, Missouri, he [Hull] attended grade
school and high school there. In 1920 he received his bachelor's degree
from the University of Missouri. During 1918–19 he returned to Mountain Grove as principal of the high school there.

Shortridge does not have the distinction of being the first Indiana
school to claim Mr. Hull. From 1920 to 1924 he served as principal of
the Sullivan, Indiana, High School. Continuing his study at the same
time, he received his master's degree from the University of Chicago in
1923. . . .

In 1924 Mr. Hull returned to Missouri in the position of principal
of the Senior High School in Springfield, where he remained until
last summer. During this time he was able to continue his education,

Principal J. Dan Hull

and in 1933 he received the degree of Doctor of Philosophy from Yale University. . . .

Dr. Hull took over the principalship just three months before the Japanese dropped their bombs on the American ships at Pearl Harbor. The first major event of that school year, however, came before the outbreak of hostilities, and it was a glorious one for Shortridge. The Shortridge band made what the *Echo* described as an "historic trip" to Newport News, Virginia, during Thanksgiving vacation in the fall of 1941 to participate in the launching ceremonies of the U.S.S. *Indiana.* Here is the *Echo*'s account of that great adventure.

The band left Indianapolis November 19 on Governor Schricker's Special 30-car train. Its 102 members occupied five cars. After marching downtown to the Union Station, the band boarded special trains bound for Cincinnati. From here they headed straight for Newport News via Charleston, West Virginia. Arriving at 8 o'clock they were quickly whisked away to the shipyards. At 9:53 A.M. the big moment had arrived! It is here that the band played four times over a coast-to-coast hookup. It also played at the construction dock before and after the launching of the battleship.

The account in the 1942 *Annual* gives further details:

Full of pent-up enthusiasm, they [the band] were taken in chartered buses to the three-hundred acre shipyards. Here in these yards, where ships of many countries may be seen in repair, the great mistress of the waves was waiting to be launched.

The buses wound in and out among the buildings until the boys could see the mammoth superstructure which surrounded the U.S.S. Indiana. Inside the superstructure stood the impressive battleship, proudly ready to challenge any enemy. Flags and banners of all sorts were waving festively from her decks. This was a real preview of a real battleship.

The band hurriedly and eagerly assembled in a special stand built on the port side of the ship. On all sides were gathered thousands of patriotic Americans, including spectators, workmen, governmental dignitaries and shipyard officials.

Indiana's own Governor Schricker made an excellent speech, which was followed by one from Secretary of the Navy, Frank Knox. During this time the spectators could hear the knock-knock of invisible workmen beneath the ship, removing the safety catches preliminary to the launching.

When Secretary Knox had finished his speech, Mrs. Margaret Robbins, daughter of Governor Schricker, was introduced. It was her privilege to christen the ship with the traditional bottle of champagne. The bottle, encased in a vari-colored mesh covering, was hung from the top of the ship by a red, white, and blue rope. Small flags hung gaily from the rope at intervals.

At exactly 10:53 A.M., Eastern Standard Time, the high tide reached its zenith. Every onlooker (especially the Shortridge bandmen) was tense with excitement when Mrs. Robbins broke the beribboned bottle of champagne on the bow of the ship. Simultaneously, the Shortridge band struck up "The Star Spangled Banner."

In the same breathless moment the very last supports were knocked from beneath the ship, and the new colossal dreadnaught of the United States Navy—the U.S.S. Indiana—slid down the ways to the strains of the national anthem. It careened gracefully into the wide James River and for the first time actually split the waves that will wash its sides forever. . . .

At noon the bandmen were guests of H. L. Ferguson, president of the Newport News Shipyards, at a turkey dinner in the Warwick Hotel. Afterward they visited the famous Mariners' Museum. . . . Then they boarded a ferry bound for Norfolk, Virginia, where all one hundred of them were assigned staterooms for the leisurely boat trip up Chesapeake Bay, into the Potomac River, and on to the nation's capital.

During the trip, according to the *Echo*, they feasted on a "delicious lamb dinner" and afterward played a concert in the salon of the ship. The account continues:

> Sightseeing buses met them in Washington the following morning where they toured for several hours. The Jefferson Memorial, the Capitol Building, and the Supreme Court Building were only a few of the national shrines seen in Washington. Inside the Library of Congress they not only saw the Declaration of Independence and the Constitution, but also the Gutenberg Bible, the first edition of the "Star-Spangled Banner," and the Magna Charta. One of the many unexpected events that occurred was the seeing of Mrs. Roosevelt in her car. After the boys waved to her, she leaned out the window and waved back. The band completed the day by playing in front of the White House and then taking a tour of the Smithsonian Institution.

Accompanying the band, besides Robert J. Shultz, director, and Mrs. Shultz, were Emmett Rice and Joel W. Hadley, vice-principals, and Robert C. Grubbs, John Rouch, and Al J. Kettler of the faculty. Money for the trip was raised by a committee of fathers of the band members.

The band made its great expedition and received national recognition both because it was an excellent musical organization and because it was blessed with energetic and influential "Dads." The idea for the trip came first from Governor Henry Schricker. He had formed the habit of attending Shortridge band concerts during the previous years, when his son, Hank, class of 1941, had played the baritone horn. Now his younger son, George, a freshman, was playing in the B band and hoping to move up. The Schrickers were a band family.

When the Shortridge musicians marched past the reviewing stand in Indianapolis at the traditional Armistice Day parade on November 11, 1941, playing with all their usual skill and enthusiasm, the governor remarked loudly enough to be heard by all those around him, "My, how I'd like to have that band with me when we dedicate the U.S.S. *Indiana* next week." Another alert "Dad" on the reviewing stand, Herbert R. Hill, managing editor of the *News* and father of one of the band's drummers, began instantly to raise money to make the project possible. By the end of the day he had a considerable sum in hand and had organized an enthusiastic committee, composed of Leland Fishback, Bryant Gillespie, and John English, all of whom had sons in the band and a shared deter-

SHS marching band of 1941

Robert J. Shultz

mination that the young musicians should indeed go to Newport News and Washington.

Feverish preparations began. On the assumption that the necessary funds would be available, arrangements had to be made for travel and accommodations for one hundred and two band members plus the accompanying faculty and, of course, all the musical instruments. On November 17, just six days after Governor Schricker made his encouraging remark, Dr. Hull was able to announce to the school and to the press that all had been accomplished and the band would go.

Mr. Shultz recalls that at the last meeting before the trip Fred Flickinger, who was the captain of the band, said to him, "Mr. Shultz, would you please excuse yourself." Fred then proceeded to tell his fellow students that absolutely nobody was to misbehave in any way on this trip and that if anyone did, the officers of the band would take care of him. The one freshman member of the group tested this out on the train trip by running up and down the aisle after the boys were in their bunks and swatting everybody with wet paper towels. He was picked up and carried to the baggage car where appropriate discipline was administered. After that there was no more trouble. Mr. Shultz says, "I really didn't have to do anything on the trip except enjoy it. The boys took care of everything."

Fred, however, does not remember having exercised so much leadership. What he remembers most is how many concerts they played:

> It seems to me we began playing the minute we got off the train. We played and played and played, but it was all right. Mr. Shultz always kept us up to snuff. He saw to it that we were ready to perform any time any place, and we thought we were pretty sharp because we had new uniforms. He was a marvelous band leader, and it was a great experience. I will never forget how big that ship looked as it slid into the water.

Only a little more than two weeks after the musicians returned, came the Japanese attack on Pearl Harbor. The Shortridge Senate quickly declared war on Japan and Germany and created a War Production Board, but the first year of the war had only a minor effect on school life. The class of 1942 describes it this way in its *Annual*:

> On that fateful day, December 7, we gathered together with serious faces and listened to grim radio reports . . . and the Echo had a special edition with the President's speech, and America was in the war, and we were seniors and knew that it will be our generation who will pay . . . and we were intensely patriotic . . . we bought defense stamps at the bookstore . . . some of us bought bonds . . . we gave pencils to the U.S.O. and we gave pennies to the Red Cross . . . we

read through the papers carefully . . . and we started seeing the names of Shortridge graduates who gave their lives to their country . . . and we were proud. We made up slogans about our part being to stay in school now so we could be the trained men and women of tomorrow's world . . . and we began driving less and walking more because tires were rationed and cars were no longer sold.

But even though the war was always there behind us, we could forget it sometimes. We were young and we were seniors and the whole world awaited us. . . . We had our senior play and it was fun to watch our friends on the stage. We saw the candy machines installed in the cafeteria, and we worked in the chemistry labs and walked casually through the halls even if we were late to class. . . . We looked back on the year and remembered the funny Hallowe'en "party," complete with witches and prophecies on the stage . . . and the beautiful Christmas auditorium of America's first year at war and our last year at Shortridge. We had a big senior week . . . we scrawled autographs in *Annuals*, we went to the Vesper services, and we worked in the Class Day fun . . . we laughed at the giftorian's gifts and reminisced with the historian. . . .

By the next year the war was closer to home. Enrollment had dropped from 3,200 to 2,687. Many boys and girls were employed or in service, and graduations were speeded up. Ten members of the faculty had joined the service. They were listed in the 1943 *Annual*: Lt. Russell V. Sigler, Lt. (jg) Howard T. Wood, Lt. A. Atwood Bliss, Lt. James C. Beane, Lt. P. W. Holaday, Gordon O. Johnson, Capt. Albert C. Neff, Capt. Cohn L. Morrison, T. Sgt. Robert L. Campbell, and Lt. Robert L. Nipper.

Still, before Mr. Nipper became Lieutenant Nipper he had coached another Shortridge team to the city football championship in the fall of 1942. After he left, the freshman coach, Tom D. Woods, class of 1927, took his place and procured yet one more championship in 1943 with an upset victory over Tech, which was won in spite of the loss of two star players to injuries. The students had a new idol. Cici Hendricks (Hollowell) wrote a poem to him based on Kipling's "Tommy":

"T. D."

We all went out to Technical to see a game of ball
We weren't very confident that we could win at all
The papers told of woe to come to Shortridge ridin' high
For John and Fred were out you know, so we heaved a mighty sigh.
But it's "T.D." this and "T.D." that, and "T.D." win today,
For we place our faith in you, "T.D.," when Shortridge starts to play.

It was late in the fourth quarter, 'fore Shortridge got the ball,
And Technical was out in front, and our tears began to fall.

1943 football champions

For it looked so very hopeless, just as hopeless as could be,
With groans and moans and doleful tones, but not from our "T.D."

For its "T.D." this and "T.D." that, and "T.D." you're the stuff.
We'll stick to you in victory and when the goin's tough.

And their never failin' faith in you, kept our team upon the field.
And gave them power and pep and push, so they wouldn't yield.
So in the fleeting seconds (forty-five, the truth to tell),
T. Haggard snagged a touchdown pass, and with it rang the bell.

So it's "T.D." this, and "T.D." that, and "T.D." here's our hand,
And we'll ever stand behind you, as the best coach in the land.

· · · · ·

In September, 1942, partly in response to wartime pressures, Dr.
Hull announced that English teacher Al J. Kettler would sponsor all
editions of the *Echo*. This was a big change from the long-established
pattern of having a different faculty sponsor for each day of the week.
No one person had read all the copy since Laura Donnan was given the
help of some of her colleagues in 1901. Shortridge was always reluctant
to change tradition, but the new system worked well. Each day's *Echo*—
Monday's through Friday's—still had its own staff of student editors and
reporters, but now there was less competition among them. On a day
when there was too much copy to print, it was possible to shift something to the next day. Some students missed the great sense of loyalty
they had had for their particular sponsor. Still, the overall operation was
smoother.

Under the new regime, while the *Echo* sports writers were describing football triumphs as enthusiastically as always, other *Echo* writers were reporting war news. Enoch D. Burton, head of the Math Department, was appointed War Services Counselor to help students with their decisions about war work or enlistments. The *Echo* kept a file of alumni in service. In September of 1942 it reported there were 1,061 with eight casualties. More and more often during the next three years the grim news of a Shortridge casualty appeared on the front page; other times it was an account of an exploit. Jim Farmer, class of 1937, a former *Echo* contributor himself and later a journalist by profession, was astonished to learn that he had been written up under the headline "Shortridge Warrior Interviews Ernie Pyle."

For some it was difficult to reconcile the constantly upbeat quality of student life at Shortridge as reported in the *Echo* with the grimness of the war news. Ann Metzger, Junior Vaudeville chairman in 1943, wrote a letter to the *Indianapolis Sunday Star* expressing what she believed to be the feelings of high school girls everywhere:

> I am 16 and I'm a girl, and you may think that a girl of 16 thinks about nothing but clothes, dates, and looks, and that what she has to say isn't of much importance anyway—but you're wrong. I have plenty to say and I'm asking you to listen. . . .
>
> We know we can never fight; we know we must go to school to help rebuild the world for tomorrow. We're young, yes, very young— but we've got eyes that read about what is going on, how people and soldiers are suffering . . .; we've got ears that hear about those fights to keep us free and what so many people are giving up to keep kids like us from going through what they are; and we've got hearts like everyone else—hearts that know these things and want to cry, "let me go, let me help you, let me share a little of all this too," but can they? No. . . .
>
> We know we've got to do something; we know we've got to go out there and help these people or we'll go crazy, but what can we do? We can't fight; we can only pour our heart out in something like this and hope that the person who reads it or hears it won't think we're off our nut. . . .

Students were advised to stay in school, while simultaneously being asked to take jobs. Factories stepped up war production at the same time that they were losing employees to military service. Not only did a lot of women go to work for the first time, so did a lot of high schoolers and their teachers. Members of the Shortridge faculty supported the war effort by teaching in the local colleges and university extensions and also in the armed forces programs. DeWitt Morgan, superintendent of schools, issued a plea to students to work part time. They were allowed to adopt a four-four schedule—four hours of school and four hours in the work force. All the high schools accelerated graduations. Students could graduate at the end of summer school or in January. The spirit of this is shown by the following creed:

CREED

of the

JANUARY GRADUATES, 1944

WE ARE THE FIRST SHORTRIDGE GROUP IN MANY YEARS TO GRADUATE IN JANUARY—TO ENTER A NEW LIFE AND A NEW YEAR AT THE SAME TIME. AS WE ENTER OUR NEW LIFE AT SO CRITICAL A PERIOD, WE PLEDGE OURSELVES

1. TO SERVE HONORABLY OUR COUNTRY WHOSE NEEDS SUPERSEDE ALL OTHERS IN WARTIME.
2. TO APPLY OUR BEST ABILITIES TO POST-WAR PURSUITS.
3. TO DO OUR UTMOST TO PRESERVE THE VICTORIOUS PEACE WE SHALL WIN AT SUCH COST.
4. TO STRIVE TO BRING CREDIT TO OUR ALMA MATER THROUGHOUT THE YEARS, AS OTHERS HAVE DONE BEFORE US.

Floy Wilcox

As in World War I, the whole school cooperated in raising money for the war effort. The Art Department made posters and promotional fliers. The band played regularly for bond drives. The Commandos were organized in March, 1942, by Mrs. Della Thompson, dean of girls, for the purpose of collecting articles wanted by the armed forces. Twenty-two squads of twelve girls each worked to secure the desired items: cards, magazines, records, and cookies. The social clubs, of which there were now approximately fifty, baked and sold cookies and used whatever profits they made from this and various other projects to buy war bonds. The Radio Workshop, a new organization under the sponsorship of Mary Glenn Hamilton of the English Department, presented twelve programs over WIRE and WISH radio stations. Some scripts were written by the students; others were prepared by the United States Treasury Department to promote the sale of War Savings Stamps and Bonds. The homerooms also encouraged the regular purchase of War Savings Stamps. By the end of 1943 Shortridge, Washington, and Cathedral had all earned the right to fly the Treasury Flag, showing that 90 percent of the student body were buying war stamps regularly in support of the war effort.

But this was only the beginning. Ann Metzger, along with a lot of other Shortridge girls (and boys), found much else could be done. The Shortridge class of 1944 purchased a $1,000 War Bond with the proceeds of its Junior Vaudeville in the spring of 1943 and sold $450 worth of War Savings Stamps to its patrons along with their tickets to the show. The following year, 1944, the school as a whole undertook to sponsor an all-Shortridge war bond drive in honor of an illustrious alumnus, Admiral Raymond Ames Spruance, class of 1902, commander of the 5th fleet, headquartered on the flagship *Indianapolis*.

The original goal of the drive was to sell about $60,000 worth of bonds, enough to purchase a pursuit plane, but it went over the top right away, because the students received a promise of $50,000 in matching bond purchases from a secret patriotic benefactor. This added mystery and excitement. The already enthusiastic Shortridgers redoubled their efforts, and by the end of the drive they had succeeded in selling $1,302,224 in War Bonds—enough to purchase, in addition to the pursuit plane, two B17 flying fortresses, which were appropriately christened *Blue Devils*. At the rally in Caleb Mills Hall which climaxed the bond drive, Ann Metzger, 1944 Shortridge Bluebelle, was crowned Victory Queen for selling the highest amount of bonds, and the identity of the mystery man was revealed. He was Senator Homer E. Capehart.

Shortridge believed itself to be the top high school in the nation in its war bond drive.

CHAPTER

13

# Ranked among the Best

I N THE FIRST FLUSH of postwar victory, much of the United States was filled with a sense of prosperity, confidence, and enthusiasm. Shortridge certainly reflected these attitudes. The students were proud of their school's war record. They had formed the habit of successfully raising money for patriotic causes. They had enjoyed the experience, and they were quite willing to continue their efforts.

In 1945, high schools throughout the country were asked to sell $3,000 worth of victory stamps and bonds, enough to furnish a hospital unit for the care of returning wounded veterans. Shortridge was the first high school in the state to reach that goal. Encouraged by their success, the students continued their campaign and finally managed to raise enough money to cover the cost of seven such hospital units.

The era of World War II finally ended for the school with a special auditorium program on February 20, 1946, at which Admiral Raymond Spruance spoke to the school about his war experiences in the Pacific theater and then gave out hundreds of autographs to his enthusiastic listeners.

During the war, Shortridge had received enormous amounts of publicity, some of it national. This attention continued in the postwar years, as shown in this article from the *Echo* of February 12, 1946:

### VAUDEVILLE WINNERS NAMED; TALENT SCOUTS ATTEND SHOW.

Hollywood Representative Enthusiastic About Local Performance;
Interested in Several Shortridge Students

Honor and praise for a "show well done" were heaped upon those
who produced and performed in the Junior Vaudeville by scouts from

Admiral Raymond Ames Spruance

the major movie studios who came from Chicago to attend the show. This year's presentation attracted nationwide attention, and brought representatives from several Hollywood studios to Shortridge.

According to the sponsors of the vaudeville, they came to backstage after the show was over Friday night, and their enthusiasm and praise was most gratifying. One of the reviewers said that he had never seen a show to equal it in any high school or college or in any of the vaudeville houses on the western coast.

Representatives from the Warner Bros. studios . . . asked Bill Stephenson to send his picture to the studio. Other students in whom they were interested included Jack Metcalf, Charlene Butz, Joan Robinson, Robbie Robinson, Hillman Loftiss, and Dottie Webb.

None of the performers was actually summoned to Hollywood to perform in a movie in 1946, but the previous year, John Rawlings, son of English teacher Blanche Rawlings, had been mentioned favorably in *Life Magazine* and had worked as a script writer in Hollywood during the summer of 1945 as a result of his successful Vaudeville Act.

As soon as school opened in the fall of that year, John's impressions of Hollywood were recorded for the *Echo* by Bill Stephenson (whose photograph was requested by Warner Brothers the following spring):

"Hollywood is completely different from any other place in America," said John Rawlings, recently returned from the West Coast. "The

people there are all individualists. It doesn't matter about your background. There are no religious or racial barriers. If you have something
to contribute to the entertainment world, if you can do something well,
there is a place for you."

John explained more fully that the people who live there will accept
any new idea. The city has sprung up over night, practically, and people's minds are open. He remarked that this was the reason for the
many strange religious cults that flourish there. . . .

"The city of L.A. [Los Angeles] . . . is enormous. I lived twenty
miles from the studio, yet it was considered I was fairly close," he
remarked. Twenty miles is about the distance from Irvington to the
south side and back! . . .

Turning to the subject of his work, John stated, "I love it as much
as I love Hollywood. I stayed mostly in my office and wrote. Six short
stories about high school kids, a story for Shirley Temple, as practice,
and a script from the book *Portrait of Jenny*. My boss was Mr. Selznick's
right hand woman, Miss Keon. Officially she is a 'scenarist.' Then too I
spent some time in the art department designing sets." . . .

John said that part of his work was to watch a picture being "shot."

"The one I saw was 'Duel in the sun'," he remarked. "In that way
I got to know Joseph Cotten, Jennifer Jones, Gregory Peck and Lionel
Barrymore." . . .

"Speaking of those stars," he told the interviewer, "they act like
other people. . . ."

He stated that moving pictures are an industry. The actor is just a
part of it. Money and time are no object, as there is plenty everywhere.
True, some actors do chase around like they are supposed to, but not
many do. It is the technician who is the big character. . . .

Having Hollywood scouts attend the Junior Vaudeville was heady
stuff, and so was the continued success of the Shortridge athletes. The
Shortridge football team won another city championship in the fall of
1947, under the coaching of George Gale. Tom "T.D." Woods had
resumed the role of freshman coach when Mr. Gale came out of the
Navy and took over the varsity. Bob Nipper had also been discharged
from the Navy, and he had taken a coaching position at DePauw, but at
the end of a year he came to Dr. Hull and said, "I feel I belong at
Shortridge. I want to come back even if I have to come as a janitor." He
did indeed return, but to a position which was newly created for him.
The *Echo* announced on July 3, 1947:

> Robert L. Nipper, former Shortridge football coach, will return to
> SHS this fall as director of intramural activities. . . . Mr. Nipper was
> the Shortridge football mentor for 11 years before his resignation to
> accept the DePauw position. He had developed a championship squad

at Shortridge and acquired city-wide fame as a football coach. His present position involves the administration of the intramural program and he will act only in an advisory capacity with the varsity football and basketball teams.

Coach Nipper attended Technical High School and Butler University where he was a star athlete. From 1926 to 1931 he assisted Coach Paul Hinkle at Butler with football and basketball and was the head baseball coach. . . .

Two years later Russell (Tubby) Julius retired after twenty-nine years of overseeing Shortridge's athletic programs. Bob Nipper took his place as athletic director.

Soon after the news of Mr. Nipper's return, came the announcement of a new principal for the school. The *Indianapolis News*, August 27, 1947, stated:

One spring evening in 1910 a young man filed by with his fellow classmates to receive his diploma from George Benton, then principal of Shortridge High School.

Today, 37 years older, that young man himself is principal of the school, appointed by the Board of School Commissioners Tuesday night. And Shortridge seems to be smiling all over.

For Joel W. Hadley the pull has been a long one, but for the

Joel W. Hadley

quietly confident, self-effacing man it represents years of happy experience. . . .

All his adult life he has instructed children and been close to nature and its quiet grandeur, and he shows it.

With a quiet, almost frowning sincerity he will tell you what his new position at Shortridge means to him:

"While it means great responsibilities, I would be foolish not to admit it also means a great opportunity to help in leading the children of this community. With the cooperation of parents and faculty, on which I count heavily for success, we can do a wonderful job at this school. It's a privilege to have the chance."

Shortridge was indeed "smiling all over." J. Dan Hull had been an able administrator. He was a scholar who was determined to maintain academic standards, and to this end he had instituted a program of twelve-week tests to be sure that all classes were measuring up to his exacting standard. Still, he had not been particularly popular, although the students had dedicated their *Annual* to him in 1947. He had labored under the double disadvantage of coming in from the outside and of following in the footsteps of George Buck. Even Mr. Buck, who also had come to the principalship from outside, had experienced a difficult first year, and the other imported administrator, Lawrence C. Hull (no relation to J. Dan), had stayed only one year (1902–03).

Now Shortridge had one of its own at the head again. The first *Echo* of the year carried a huge picture of Mr. Hadley at the top of the front page accompanied by a long, enthusiastic article. On the third page was a much smaller picture of Dr. Hull with an announcement of his resignation and his plans to take a position with the Department of Education in Washington, D.C.

There were other changes in the faculty: Al J. Kettler, *Echo* sponsor, had left in 1944 to become director of publications for the Indianapolis Public Schools. His place was taken by Jeanette Grubb, class of 1920, of the Math Department. Miss Grubb remembers that one day as she was teaching summer school in 1944, Dr. Hull started to walk by her classroom and then pulled up abruptly to speak with her. He had just remembered that this teacher of algebra also had a master's degree in journalism. His problem was solved. Miss Grubb gave up teaching math and became director of publications for Shortridge, a post she held until her retirement in 1970.

Grace Buchanan (Vitz), class of 1917, became head of the Latin Department in 1942, after Miss Marthens retired. Nowhere in Shortridge was the continuity of school life more apparent than among the Latin teachers. Mrs. Vitz, Elizabeth Matthews Helm, and Josephine Davidson

Jeanette Grubb

(Bliss) had decided to become language teachers because of their admiration for those who had taught them—Miss Ella Marthens and Mrs. Grace Morrison.

They, in turn, had their admirers. Diana Harvey Jackson, class of 1947, now an editor in the Marketing Division of Eli Lilly and Company, reports that her strongest Shortridge memories are of Mrs. Vitz's Latin class:

> Vocabularies were memorized, nouns declined, verbs, even the deponent ones, conjugated and the pronouns marshalled in their proper order, all the parts of speech standing rank on rank along the walls of Room 109. On we marched like Caesar's soldiers, through the second declension, the third, the fourth, and finally the fifth.
>
> The semesters went on: Marcus Tullius Cicero declaimed in the senate, "O tempora, o mores!" At last it was time for Vergil, "Arma virumque cano. . . ." We looked through the doors of Room 109, and Aeneas had come to shore from his wrecked ship. Venus had made him good to look upon, and Dido was entranced with the handsome stranger. Later, amid much ceremony, they rode off together, clad in purple and gold, riding their white horses. I can see them yet. "Ave atque vale" Grace Vitz and Room 109. "Forsan et haec olim meminisse iuvabit—and perhaps, in time to come, it will be good to remember these things."

Diana's classmate, Dick Farrar, now an engineer with the Aerospace program, concentrated heavily on Shortridge's math and science courses, and he now finds it "good to remember" those who taught them, particularly Herman H. Siemers of the Physics Department, whom he characterizes as "an excellent teacher and a jovial disciplinarian." "I enjoyed my classes, but I didn't realize how good all those teachers were until I got to the University of Rochester and found how far ahead I was." He also remembers his fellow students:

> We didn't used to talk about "peer pressure," but it was important then, too, and at Shortridge it was on the side of achievement. One thing happened to me there that is still a sharp recollection: I graduated, I think, fourth in the class. On the day the rankings came out, I was a little late getting to the cafeteria for lunch. Of course, I had a group that I usually ate with, and when I got to the table, they all stood up for me.

The new football coach, George Gale, commanded as much respect as his predecessors. Sophomore Dick Lugar wrote a thirty-two page football history entitled *Blue Devils of '47*, which was printed at the school, bound in the regular Shortridge blue cover, and sold for fifteen cents a copy. He wrote it, he said, in the "hope that this record of the '47 football team will reflect and keep for posterity a part of the glory that was theirs." He attributed much of this success to George Gale:

> Although Mr. Gale will modestly say that the record of the team is entirely their record and not in the smallest part his, by watching other coaches and comparing them with Mr. Gale, one knows what a wonderful coach we really have at Shortridge. . . .
>
> Mr. Gale believes in quick, clever plays which go for yardage rather than the bulling bruising plays which, added to, may or may not make a first down. . . . Mr. Gale believes in thoroughness and overlooks nothing in preparation for a game. . . . Mr. Gale can do anything he asks his players to do himself. He was a great passer at Purdue and kicks and runs almost equally well. He is an excellent example of physical education and so are the boys he trains.

Other students seem also to have considered it a time of glory. Ted Steeg (now a film producer), who was one of the stars of that 1947 team—"the team's leading ground gainer . . . the backfield's leader"—wrote in 1984:

> I got to thinking about my own recollections. When you're a teenager, you enter a new outside world for the first time, and I suppose that's what makes my memories of Shortridge so vivid. It was like a self-enclosed mini-city for me, with all my friends as the population and government; all the world taking place within those four walls. I lived

just across the street on Meridian, and when I walked to school in the morning it was like heading for the Emerald City. There would be the band out there tootling away, Mr. Shultz in command, and our own little Defense Corps, the ROTC, swinging their wooden rifles.

Inside the building, I remember the smell of the ink and printer's forms in the print shop . . . the clang and rustle of lockers being opened and shut . . . the fine residue of chalk dust on the blackboard trays in the home rooms . . . the stern visage of Mrs. Betty Helm as she pounded the importance of Latin into our heads . . . immense Russell Julius, larger than life, growling out from the Athletic Office. . . .

So much of adult life was already present there! yet scaled to our own teen-age dimensions: Our own daily newspaper; our own Broadway (the Vaudeville); our own societies and clubs and politics; our own gradations of achievement and ambition and reward; our own young sagas of romance and heartbreak and discovery. . . .

"Our own societies and clubs"—social clubs, which had long been unsuccessfully banned, were admitted to full legal status in 1936, provided that they agreed to abide by school regulations—no hazing, no initiations. The strong, established organizations like Euvola for girls and Corpse Club for boys had never been much affected by the prohibition against membership. As a result of the new status, other clubs proliferated and with them, parties—mostly dances.

There were still all-school dances in the gym on an occasional Friday afternoon, which were cheap and well attended. The Bluebelle-Uglyman dance continued to be important, and, beginning in 1946, it was held at night. Dances put on by the social clubs were not held in the gym, but at places like Woodstock or the Murat ballroom, with Louis Lowe's or Chuck Smith's orchestra or an imported big band like Jimmy Dorsey's. Graduation dances were held at the Indiana Roof, and they always had a big band.

While social activity had slowed a little during the war, with peace and prosperity the pace increased. More social clubs were listed in the *Annual* each year, sometimes with pictures of the club pins. Some students belonged to four or five, each with its meetings and its parties. Many of the clubs had members from other schools—Broad Ripple, Park, and Tudor Hall. There was concern among the school administrators that the clubs were becoming overly important and making school life too social. An *Echo* story on December 3, 1947, remarked, "twenty-five orchids were counted in school Monday—two of them WHITE ones!" Both Congressman-to-be Andy Jacobs, class of '49, and Senator-to-be Dick Lugar, class of '50, disapproved of the social clubs as undemocratic and divisive, but they went to the parties.

The *Annuals* for 1949 and 1950 characterize the social clubs as "providing wholesome sociability and recreation" and thereby "discouraging delinquency." Until that time delinquency on the part of Shortridge students does not seem to have been a matter of concern and was not mentioned in print.

In October, 1951, the Student Board held an open meeting to discuss the clubs. Mr. Hadley attended but did not take part in the discussion. When he was questioned about his silence after the meeting, he said, "I have great faith in the abilities of high school students to solve their own problems."

A few years later he told the mothers of the incoming freshmen how he felt about the whole question of the clubs: "We try to discourage them, but they will always be with us, and most of the time they are harmless." Then he went on to describe his earliest experience with high school social clubs:

> I grew up at 11th and Park. When my older sister was in Shortridge, she and her friends formed a secret society. This was about 1904. It was the P.B.C. Club, and they took an oath never to reveal what the initials stood for. My father strongly disapproved of secret societies and secret oaths. He tried to get her either to reveal the secret name or to withdraw from the club, but she stood firm. She would not betray her friends. It was the worst thing we ever went through in our family, although we all survived it.
>
> My sister is almost seventy now. She visited me recently, and we were reminiscing about old times. I said, "I'll always remember how upset Father was about your secret club. I never did find out what mysterious thing P.B.C. stood for."
>
> "Oh, didn't you?" she replied, "Park, Broadway and Central."

"Our own gradations of achievement and ambition and reward"— Shortridge had always provided a variety of rewards for achievement. A beginning writer could try out for the *Echo*, become a member of the staff, perhaps a regular columnist, or even an editor. There was the elected job of *Annual* editor, a big responsibility, and dozens of other important positions on the *Annual* staff. After 1952 there was membership in Quill and Scroll, the national journalism honorary society. For this students had to be in the upper third of the class, do outstanding work in journalism, and have their work approved by the National Quill and Scroll Executive Committee at Northwestern University.

For those more interested in literature than in journalism there was the Fiction Club. Again, it was necessary to qualify for membership in this organization by maintaining an A average through English IVx and by submitting original literary material to be judged. Every year the Fiction Club held a short story contest with a prize of $5.00 and a promise of publication in the *Christmas Echo*. In 1946 sixty students submitted short stories for this contest. Ruth Louise Armstrong was a longtime sponsor of the club.

For those who liked to stand on their feet and express themselves, the Senate provided an opportunity for speeches, debate, and identification with national issues. The Debating Club offered its members a chance to make the Varsity Debate Team and possibly to bring another debating championship to Shortridge. Public speakers, coached by Mr. Shoemaker, had opportunities to speak on behalf of worthy causes, or to represent Shortridge in the state public speaking competition and perhaps bring back a trophy to add to the department's collection.

Art students could hope to have their work displayed or to be part of the annual Shortridge art exhibit, which drew many visitors and lengthy reviews in the metropolitan newspapers. All sorts of opportunities were open to musicians—the band or the orchestra, the glee club or the choir—all organizations which gave concerts for the school and for the public. The Junior Vaudeville provided myriad opportunities for recognition and success. The job of Vaudeville chairman, like that of *Annual* editor, was an elected office and a big responsibility.

Beginning with its early years Shortridge had offered certain classes in which enrollment itself was regarded as an achievement. Classes in Greek were open to the best of the Latin students. Physiology and geology could be elected only with the permission of the teacher. Physics III and Chemistry III were for outstanding students in those fields, calculus for the cream of the crop in math. Advanced composition was an invitational course for the most accomplished English students.

Incentives beyond grades appeared in the regular classes. Which zoology student could collect and mount the most extensive insect collection? Whoever it was would see his/her work in the display case, to be admired by all who passed, as well as written about in the *Echo*. Former botany students still remember how long they worked on their leaf collections and the sense of achievement they felt to have their work singled out and put on display. The more ambitious of the physiography students worked equally hard to amass large rock collections.

In athletics gradations of achievement, ambition, and reward were especially plentiful—teams to be made, games to be won, races to be run, championships to be achieved, varsity letters and special awards for outstanding performance to be earned—all this with maximum publicity. The *Echo* had an abundance of sports columnists. Novelist Dan Wakefield and U.S. Senator Richard Lugar, both class of 1950, wrote sports columns for Thursday's *Echo*. Lugar's was "Shooting the Works" and

Wakefield's was "SPORTLITE." The future senator often began his
column with a short verse. He also held a contest and offered a prize for
the student who could predict most accurately the scores of forthcoming
games. His system worked well and drew a good response. Trouble
came, however, when he decided to change his format so that he could
analyze and correct the problems of the school. He changed the title of
his column to "Straight Shooting" and on January 13, 1949, published
what was planned as the first of a series:

> Every Shortridger is proud of his school and its great achievements,
> but almost every school has problems which it must solve in order to
> maintain its high standing. This is true at Shortridge and to help ac-
> quaint you with our problems and to offer possible solutions, each
> Thursday Straight Shooting will pull no punches and hit hard, but at
> all times will try to present the problem fairly. . . .

The first problem he chose to hit hard was that some of the basketball players were breaking training; they were smoking regularly and
being encouraged to do so by their friends in the social clubs. This was
the only appearance of "Straight Shooting." Jerry Steiner, the basketball
coach, was upset. So was Mr. Hadley. Senator Lugar still remembers it
vividly:

> I was called down to Mr. Hadley's office and asked how I could
> possibly have done such a thing. This was the edition of the *Echo* that
> carried official notices and went to all the other schools. He was
> shocked and hurt by my column. It was just terrible, because Mr.
> Hadley was such a father figure and we all admired him so much. He
> made me feel as though I had cut the arms and legs off Shortridge and
> just left it bleeding, but, as a matter of fact, we all survived.

Miss Grubb, *Echo* sponsor, was called down to the office too. She
received much the same message, but was less disturbed by it. She says,
"It only caused trouble because it hit home. You can't censor everything,
and I didn't see anything wrong with that column except that it was too
wordy."

Still, it did not have a sequel.

The *Echo*'s statement of purpose casts light on this controversy and
gives support to both sides:

> The *Echo* strives for straightforward, unbiased high school journal-
> ism; chronicles the interests and activities of the student body; sustains
> unity between student opinion and administrative policies; interprets
> the life of the school to the community; encourages scholarship and
> sportsmanship; fosters the Shortridge spirit.

Dan Wakefield reports that he never had any feeling of censorship, but still he had not been moved to undertake any crusades:

> We just weren't rebellious. The *Echo* was a wonderful experience for me and central to everything I've done since. It was exciting to write and be published. I wrote a regular sports column and through that I got a job as a stringer for the *Indianapolis Star* and then a summer job on the sports desk, where I got my first byline. Most of my close friends came out of the work on the *Echo*. Kurt Vonnegut is ten years older than I so, of course, I didn't know him at Shortridge, but I heard about him. He was held up to me as an encouragement, and I made it a point to read his stories in the *Saturday Evening Post*. I didn't actually meet him until 1963, when he was living on the Cape and I was in Boston, but after that we corresponded, and he was instrumental in helping me to get my first novel published. We got together originally because of Shortridge.

Dan has warm recollections of school life and of many of his teachers:

> There was a mystique about it that is rare in my experience of anything. I knew it was special and that I was privileged to be part of it. Journalism and writing were the focus for me, and, of course, I have kept in touch with Miss Grubb, but other aspects were also very powerful. I particularly remember Roy Aberson's history class and his playing the record of Carl Sandburg reading "The People, Yes." I renewed my friendship with him when I was in Indianapolis in 1967 working on an article for *Atlantic Monthly*. Dorothy Peterson was another out-

Dorothy Peterson

Roy Aberson

standing history teacher who became a good friend. Florence Guild, who was for a while head of the English Department, was a most unusual and interesting woman.

From a practical standpoint one of the best courses I took was public speaking from C. C. Shoemaker. He was a fabulous guy, and he taught me how to stand up and give a public lecture, a skill I have been using ever since. We learned both how to prepare speeches and how to speak extemporaneously. Dick Lugar and I had a friendly rivalry over public speaking as well as over our sports columns. I won the honor of delivering the graduation address, which he also tried out for. It was about the only thing he didn't win. We also competed in a state contest called "I Speak for Democracy." He won that and I came in second. When we correspond we still address each other as "Dear SPORT-LITE" and "Dear Shooting."

The *Echo* provides an endlessly happy picture of life at Shortridge in the 1940s. Only occasionally does even a hint of controversy creep in. It can not have been quite that wonderful for everybody, but considerable evidence supports the idea that it was a fine time for quite a few people. Shortridge athletes are prone to reunite on every possible pretext. The football team of the class of 1941, which had a winning season, but won no championships, has been holding a reunion once a year for more than forty years. Alan C. (Buzzy) Levinson, an athlete of the class of 1944, which did have a championship football team and a winning basketball team, holds a reunion of athletes every year. In 1984, 250 attended, and they came from all over the country.

The *Echo* commanded loyalty, too. The year 1948 was its fiftieth anniversary. Miss Grubb and her assistants—teachers, parents, alumni, and students—planned a gala celebration. They began by taking a booth at the State Fair for the purposes of publicizing the achievements of the *Echo* and recording names and addresses of alumni. Downtown stores decorated their windows in honor of the event, and some featured the occasion in their newspaper advertising. Local radio stations scheduled special programs.

There was a memorial dinner, and the committee in charge wanted to do it in style. They hired waitresses from Ayres to serve what they expected to be about two hundred guests. Formality had to be abandoned, however, in the face of six hundred reservations. *Echo* alumni came from all over the country for a reception in the Charity Dye Library, followed by dinner, cafeteria style, in what was known for that evening as the Shortridge banquet room. A program in Caleb Mills Hall followed. The Shortridge band played, and there was group singing. The main feature was a series of tableaux, depicting the history of the *Echo*, both by decades and by days of the week. Frances Westcott, class of 1923, acted as narrator for the successful program:

### "SO THE ECHO RECORDS IT"

Narrator. . . . . . . . . . . . . . . . . . . . . . . . . . . . . . . . . Frances Westcott
Prologue–1898
Laura Donnan. . . . . . . . . . . . . . . . . . . . . . . . . . . Dorothy Jeffries
Fletcher Wagner . . . . . . . . . . . . . . . . . . . . . . . . . Jim Seidensticker
Mr. Hufford . . . . . . . . . . . . . . . . . . . . . . . . . . . . . . Larry Noling
1898–1908
Monday's Echo Staff . . . . . . . . . Barbara Redding, Marilyn Gernstein
A Football Player. . . . . . . . . . . . . . . . . . . . . . . . . . . . . Ted Steeg
Cadet Hop Dancers . . . . . . . . . . . . . . . . . Nancy Lazure, Don Wright
Orator, James Gipe . . . . . . . . . . . . . . . . . . . . . . . . . . John Mahrdt
1908–1918
Tuesday's Echo
   Censor, Miss Love . . . . . . . . . . . . . . . . . . . . . . . Betty Lou Stewart
   Staff. . . . . . . . . . . . . . . . . . . . . . . . . . . Margo Keltner, Jim Merrell
An Annual Editor . . . . . . . . . . . . . . . . . . . . . . . . . . Monica Lennox
Honor Students . . . . . . . . . . . . . . . . . . . . . . John Wood, Rebecca Lane

Senior Play
    Bob Wild.................................... Roger Sheets
    Mozelle Stubbs............................. Linda Wohlfeld
                        1918–1928
Wednesday's Echo
    Censor, Mrs. Mikels .........................Mary Obear
    Staff............................. Mark Colby, Warren Rich
Charleston Dancers ................ Barbara Redding, Dick Stout
A Sad Football Player .......................... Ted Schurdell
Junior Carnival..................................... Patty Joy
                        1928–1938
Thursday's Echo
    Censor, Mr. Kuebler ...........................Dick Lugar
    Staff......................... Janie Fouts, Peggy MacNelly
A Gentleman from the School Board .................Dick Russell
A Football Player............................Johnny Grimmer
A Gentleman from the I.H.S.A.A. ................. Bill Burnette
A Basketball Player, "Sunny" Jim Seward ............. Dick Stout
                        1938–1948
Friday's Echo
    Sponsor, Miss Grubb ............................. Herself
    Staff......................... Mary Lockwood, Don Jeffries
Jitterbug Dancers ................ Cynny Pittenger, Bob Robinson
Color Guard ...................... Bob Renick, Bob Christena,
                            Dick Stoeppelwerth, Tom Todd
                        Epilogue
The Present....................................Themselves

In 1952 Mildred Foster, who had been teaching English at Shortridge since 1936, succeeded Florence Guild as head of the English Department. She was strongly committed to carrying on the tradition of
literary excellence, but she also encouraged expansion into the field of
writing for radio.

Although Shortridge had had a Radio Club since 1929, broadcasting
took on new importance in 1954. The Shortridge PTA helped to finance
the purchase by the Indianapolis Public Schools of an FM transmitter.
This came from WASK in Lafayette. It was installed at Shortridge, and
the school went on the air as WIAN for the first time on October 1,
1954. Two new English teachers, Mary Sutherland and Alwyn Carder,
were put in charge of programming. They were joined later that year by
another new English teacher, Nancy Hendricks, who also supervised
programming. Mrs. Sutherland remembers that she could sit in Room
344, which was her classroom, and look through a glass window into
Room 343 which housed the radio station. Those first years the station

programmed mostly for the late afternoon, and it made use of Short-
ridge's large collection of classical records, and of the skits which had
been written by some of the English classes. Eager members of the Radio
Club were trained to act as disk jockeys and to take part in the skits.
Maintenance of the equipment was provided by physics teacher Herman
Siemers, longtime sponsor of the Radio Club. The station received its
permanent license as WIAN, the radio station for the Indianapolis Public
Schools, in March, 1955. Since, at first, its power was only 120 watts,
its programs could only be heard within a radius of a few blocks around
Shortridge. Nonetheless, it was an important part of Shortridge life, and
would be for sixteen years.

The city school administration wished to use the station as an instructional tool for the school system as a whole, so in 1958 they increased the station's power to 890 watts and put Arthur Van Allen, the
present director of WIAN, in charge of programming for all the classrooms in the city. The station continued to be essentially student operated, and since it was still in its original home in Room 343, most of the
students who worked under Mr. Van Allen were Shortridgers. The
other Indianapolis high schools, however, also sent their interested students to participate in the program, which generated a lot of enthusiasm
for broadcasting. However, in 1970 it ceased to be student-operated. Mr.
Van Allen describes the way the station developed:

Student at control board of WIAN in Room 343

For several years we worked hard at instructional programming, but, as instructional TV increased in importance during the sixties, instructional radio was phased out in favor of public service broadcasting. WIAN continued to be the radio station for the Indianapolis Public Schools, but it moved out of Shortridge in the fall of 1970 and into its present quarters at 931 Fletcher Avenue. The power was increased again, this time to eleven thousand watts, and the station became part of Public Radio, as it is today.

In the fall of 1956 Shortridge was the first Indianapolis high school to participate in the American Field Service program, which undertook to promote international understanding by placing foreign students in American high schools. These students lived with carefully selected American families who had high school students of their own and who

Exchange student from Holland saying goodbye to Shortridge student, 1965

supported the objectives of the program. In return, American students went abroad to live and learn with families in other countries. Eugenia Hayden, English teacher and dean of girls, not only supported the program enthusiastically within Shortridge, but was also instrumental in getting it started in other Indianapolis high schools. Knud Mork from Copenhagen, Denmark, was Shortridge's first foreign student, and David Otto was the first Shortridge student to go abroad. He went to Norway. The program was continued at Shortridge until the school closed.

·    ·    ·    ·    ·

Although the skies were blue and the horizons looked bright, clouds were gathering. Gradually, Shortridge began to notice that its enormous self-confidence and constant appearance in the limelight had engendered hostility in the other Indianapolis high schools. This was not a new problem. As early as 1920 the *Echo* carried an editorial deploring the fact that the other high schools (Manual and Tech) seemed to be drawing away from Shortridge. After the war, however, their resentment became acute.

An Inter-High School Council consisting of representatives from the seven Indianapolis public high schools was organized on November 15, 1945. It had three students each from Shortridge and Tech and two each from Manual, Washington, Broad Ripple, Attucks, and Howe. Its purpose was to maintain and encourage more cordial relations among the high schools. Emphasis was put on the broad field of public relations. This new organization was written up optimistically in the 1946 *Annual*, but it seems not to have been effective.

Shortridge athletic teams began to be booed when they appeared on the football field or the basketball court. This did not happen to any other high school. By 1950 they were even taunted with a yell, "Shortridge, Shortridge, you think you're it. S H for Shortridge, I T for it."

Resentment from the other high schools was not Shortridge's only problem. Enrollment was declining, and the student body was changing. Like the rest of the country, Indianapolis experienced significant shifts of population in the postwar years. Large numbers of relatively affluent families moved to the suburbs. The exodus had begun in earnest in the 1920s but was checked by the depression of the '30s. With the end of the war and the return of prosperity, the move to the suburbs boomed. In 1954 the editors of *Fortune* magazine estimated that over the United States nine million people had moved to the suburbs in the previous seven years, and that the total number of suburbanites amounted to thirty million, almost one-sixth of the total population.

For Indianapolis this national trend is illustrated by the census figures for Washington Township outside the city limits:

1930—34,739
1940—42,978
1950—62,147
1960—97,861
1970—126,136

Change was also occurring within the city limits. Early in the 1940s, the Board of School Commissioners adopted the principle of neighborhood high schools. This meant that eighth-grade graduates were required to enroll in the high school to which their grade school was assigned. They could no longer choose their high school as they had in the past. Shortridge was no longer the specifically academic school, nor was it any longer *the* northside school. Broad Ripple had become its chief rival. The principle of free choice was preserved to the extent that any student with a particular reason for choosing a high school other than the one to which he/she was assigned could petition for permission to transfer, stating his/her reasons for the request. Dan Wakefield, for instance, who lived two blocks from Broad Ripple and started there in the fall of 1946, asked to transfer to Shortridge on the grounds that he wanted to be a writer, and that he needed to be able to write for the *Echo*. His request was granted and, as he says, he enrolled at Shortridge, reported to the *Echo* office immediately, and got the chance to cover the Stamp Club.

In 1949 the state legislature passed a law to eliminate racial segregation in public education at all levels. In compliance with this legislative mandate the Indianapolis school board began a process of desegregation.

Shortridge was desegregated, gradually at first. By 1953 the black students comprised 15 percent of the student body, almost exactly the same percentage as had attended Shortridge before Attucks opened in the fall of 1927.

.   .   .   .   .

In the mid-1950s a major new rival appeared on the educational scene. Washington Township opened a senior high school and two junior high schools. The *Echo* of January 24, 1956, carried an account of this by journalism student Tom Green:

> Completing the dream of 35,000 people is the problem confronting
> J. Everett Light, superintendent of schools in Washington Township.
> Mr. Light, who previously was superintendent of schools in Rushville,
> Indiana, came to Washington Township six months ago to undertake

the building of three new schools, and to assume guidance of the schools already established in Washington Township. . . .

In 1953, Fall Creek, Delaware Trails and the White River schools were completed. In 1954, the decision to build a new high school and two junior high schools was made. This decision was promoted by the parents, who worked together in meetings to form their plans.

As a comparison, in 1945 there were 30 schoolrooms in Washington Township. Presently there are 133 classrooms. With the completion of three new buildings, there will be a total of 277 classrooms. . . .

The new pupils will name their new school.

It was named North Central High School, and it was immediately filled with students who, prior to the movement to the suburb, would have gone either to Shortridge or to Broad Ripple. The percentage of black enrollment at Shortridge began a sharp climb. By 1957 it was up to twenty-eight percent. Shortridge patrons and prospective patrons began to hear the buzzing of an ominous new phrase—"the tipping point." Theories varied as to just what the tipping point was, but many people made firm statements that once black enrollment at a school reached thirty or forty percent, no more white students would enroll there. Rumors flew around the city that the school board expected Shortridge to be all black within two or three years and was planning to turn it into a vocational school. These rumors were almost always followed by the statement that "Shortridge isn't what it used to be, anyway. It doesn't have the teachers it used to have."

In the face of all this, Shortridge patrons, particularly the PTA board members, turned themselves into a huge public relations group. They had considerable outside help.

The first year for the National Merit Scholarship tests was 1955. That year there were sixteen winners in Marion County, seven of them from Shortridge. In 1957 thirteen winners came from Shortridge, seven from Broad Ripple, three from Cathedral, three from Howe, two from Tech, and one each from Manual, Sacred Heart, St. Agnes, and Tudor Hall.

The successful launching of Sputnik by the Russians in 1957 shook the American public out of any complacency it might have had about its educational system. One result of this jolt was a series of efforts to identify excellence in high school education.

In the fall of 1957 Mr. Hadley received his first notification that Shortridge had been rated as one of the best high schools in the country. This rating was made by a Chicago educator, Dr. Robert Marschner, who had conducted a lengthy study and had compiled a list of thirty-eight outstanding high schools. Six of these were in the New York area and three near Chicago, with the remainder scattered around the country. Three were private schools.

This piece of recognition was followed by articles in *Time*, the *Wall Street Journal*, and the *Ladies Home Journal*, all of which rated Shortridge as among the forty best high schools in the country.

Although it was true that Shortridge did not have the teachers it once had (nobody lasts forever), it had an able faculty, and its institutions were flourishing. The *Echo* was as strong as it had ever been. During this period two outstanding journalists and authors got their start on the *Echo*, under the guidance of Jeanette Grubb and Doris Elkins. Wallace Terry, class of 1955, editor of Tuesday's *Echo*, has since been a Nieman Fellow, a Rockefeller Fellow, and a Howard University professor. He spent two years as deputy chief of the Saigon bureau of *Time* magazine, and he is the author of a recently published and widely acclaimed book, *Bloods*, an account of the experiences of black soldiers in Vietnam.

Jonathan Kwitny, class of 1958, editor of Wednesday's *Echo*, has long been an investigative reporter for the *Wall Street Journal* and was nominated for the Pulitzer Prize in journalism in 1983. He is also the author of five books, the latest of which is *Endless Enemies—The Making of an Unfriendly World*, an analysis of United States foreign policy, published in 1984.

Shortridge High School's college admissions counseling also continued to be exceedingly strong during the competitive years of the 1950s. Graduating seniors achieved admission to a wide variety of colleges (Harvard, Yale, Princeton, and Stanford among them), and many of those graduates gained scholarships as well. For a number of years, the college counselors had been Dorothy Peterson, class of 1924, for those who were planning to attend Indiana colleges, and Annalee Webb Miller, class of 1927, for those going out of state. Mrs. Miller was also sponsor of the Senate from 1941 to 1955.

In the fall of 1954, Elizabeth Evans, class of 1923, returned to Shortridge as an English teacher. The following year she began assisting Mrs. Miller with schedule planning, and when Mrs. Miller left in June of 1958, Miss Evans took over her responsibilities.

Dorothy Lambert Otto, class of 1926, who had been a member of the History Department at Shortridge from 1930 to 1935 before giving up teaching in favor of rearing a family, rejoined the faculty in the fall of 1956. Because Miss Peterson's illness that year suddenly left Shortridge short of both a senior class sponsor and a college admissions counselor, Mrs. Otto had to take on major responsibilities without having served any apprenticeship. She says of this:

Dorothy Otto (center), as senior sponsor, counting votes with students

It certainly was a plunge, but absolutely everybody helped me, especially in relation to the senior class. The more experienced faculty members were careful to remind me of anything they thought I might overlook, and Mr. Hadley kept assuring me that *of course* I could do it.

I didn't have any specific training for college counseling, except that I had reared four children, all of whom went to college, but I learned on the job. Mr. Hadley sent both Elizabeth Evans and me to meetings of organizations such as the Association of College Admissions Counselors, and we both learned from those. Theoretically, I worked with the students planning to attend Indiana colleges, and she worked with those planning to go out of state, but there was a lot of overlap. We shared an office and basically we worked together.

Jean Wells Whitcraft, class of 1940, was another alumna who joined the Shortridge faculty in the late 1950s. The 1940 *Annual* said about her, among other things; "Butler, English teacher." She did go to Butler, and she did become an English teacher. After teaching at Tech for fourteen years, she returned to her alma mater in the fall of 1958, and she later became head of its English Department.

Even as Shortridge was bringing in old students as new teachers, some of its more established teachers were having their talents acclaimed. For example, in 1959 advanced composition teacher Louise Wills Steiger, class of 1916, and several of her Shortridge writers received both national and local publicity. The *Indianapolis Times* on April 30, 1959, reported:

### Shortridge Writers
### Finish One–Two

Two Shortridge High School pupils have taken first and second place in what is probably the nation's toughest contest for fledgling writers.

Seniors Kirk Sargent and Elaine Reuben were named winners of the annual creative writing contest conducted by Atlantic Monthly magazine.

A third Shortridge senior, Ken Harker, took fifth place in the contest. Competing were 419 of the nation's top high school writers.

All of the winning pupils were studying under Mrs. Louise Steiger when they wrote their prize-winning entries.

Three other Shortridge pupils, Sandra Cheney, Jean Kammen and Evelyn Birge, won honorable mention in the competition.

Discussing Kirk's first-place entry, an essay on "Space, Time and the Sculptured City," the judges said:

"This paper has scope and depth, and represents a keen interest in

Jean Wells Whitcraft

the trends of architecture. It is very well planned and executed and is illustrated with meticulous drawings of some of the buildings under discussion."

Of second-place entry, Elaine's essay on "Is Greatness Out of Date?" the judges declared:

"This is a really impressive piece of writing, based on wide reading and expressing the conclusions of the writer clearly and with conviction."

Ken Harker's fifth-place winner was on "Active Passivity: A Comparative Study by a Christian." The judges described it as a "scholarly piece of work."

The following week another *Times* article presented an analysis of Mrs. Steiger's teaching:

Mrs. Steiger has the reputation of being a "tough" teacher. She expects each pupil to finish assignments on time and she demands scholarly work.

Those pupils who successfully complete the course know the struggle is worth it. . . .

What's the secret of her success as a teacher? Mrs. Steiger says it's not her success but her pupils'.

"I try to lead them into searching within themselves, to find their own convictions and develop their own ideas.

"When they start, they're usually sure that their own ideas aren't worth very much. I demand that they express their own ideas, not mirror mine or those of someone else," Mrs. Steiger reports.

Here's what her composition pupils face during a semester:

A daily composition expressing their views on any subject they choose. A weekly paper on a subject assigned by Mrs. Steiger. A research paper at the end of the term of about 2500 to 3000 words.

That's a tough one-class schedule for a high school pupil carrying a full load of subjects. It's a tough schedule for a teacher, who, besides reading, criticizing and grading the papers, must teach four other English classes.

Mrs. Steiger estimates it takes her about eight hours of homework each week to study the compositions alone. She points out their errors, suggests new approaches and urges the writer to try a bit harder the next time.

"I've found that teenagers want constructive criticism. They're more interested in what they learn from the critique than they are in the grade they get," she said.

Her biggest job is reading the daily journals written by the pupils.

"They cover everything imaginable. By the time a pupil has been in the class two weeks, I know him as a person. They write about everything. Their views of God, their families, other teenagers, foreign policy, science and even teachers. . . . As they begin to express themselves freely, they become aware that their ideas have value. They become more confident and they approach larger and more important subjects unafraid," Mrs. Steiger commented.

"All I do is give them the chance to tell me what they think," she said.

Then there was Henrietta Parker, of the Chemistry Department. The *News* carried an article about her on December 18, 1959:

A pioneering approach to the teaching of chemistry was underway at Shortridge High School today, one of nine high schools in the nation participating in the experiment.

"The emphasis is on the theoretical part of chemistry," teacher Henrietta Parker explained, "with particular emphasis on atomic structure and bonding.

"We have tried to keep descriptive chemistry—the memorization—down to a minimum."

Few if any answers are given the pupils.

"Our attempt is to let them discover answers," Mrs. Parker explained.

"It should make college chemistry much simpler for them." . . .

Henrietta Parker

The "chemical bond approach" at Shortridge teaches the pupils that atoms form different types of bonds. How these atoms are joined is a determining factor in the chemistry of a substance.

Armed with this knowledge, the pupil is in a position to predict (rather than memorize) how one compound may react in relation to another. He even may find himself doing some abstract thinking in chemistry. . . .

Mrs. Parker is convinced that high school chemistry pupils can—"if challenged"—learn more than may have previously been required.

"If we don't challenge them, we don't know whether they can or can't," she reasons.

Mrs. Parker was one of 18 chemistry teachers—nine college and nine high school—who gathered last summer at Reed College, Portland, Ore., to write a new approach to high school chemistry teaching. The conference was sponsored by the American Chemical Society under a grant by the National Science Foundation. . . .

Mrs. Parker was the only woman in the group, a distinction to which she long ago became accustomed in the field of chemistry, since her first contact with the science as an eighth grader in Pittsburgh. She later taught for seven years at Carnegie Institute of Technology in Pittsburgh. . . .

Others who shared Mrs. Parker's view that "if we don't challenge them, we don't know whether they can or can't" were a succession of music directors. Beginning in 1960 under Don Martin and continuing under Don Neuen and then Thomas Preble, Shortridge staged a "Choral Classic," first in Caleb Mills Hall and later in Clowes Hall. All the choral groups participated. Amy Morrison (Perry), class of 1961, remembers the A Capella Choir as her greatest Shortridge experience. "Don Neuen really knew how to get the most from us. We went to school every morning at 7:30 to rehearse. We pounded each other on the back to increase our breath control, and we worked endlessly on our vowel sounds as well as on the music. When I went to Duke, I joined the choir there, but it was nothing compared to Shortridge. We just sang. We didn't try to get any better." Don Neuen is now head of the vocal department at the Eastman School of Music in Buffalo, New York.

·   ·   ·   ·   ·

Still, in spite of all the recognition of excellence, the school was changing. For many years the student body had been fairly homogenous: the majority had been college bound. Now, however, many students were coming in without basic skills, and many of the teachers were not well equipped to teach such students. As early as 1956 Mr. Hadley suggested that Shortridge should be an academic school with some sort of entrance requirement.

Attitudes in the community created difficulties, too. Two members of the PTA board remember going to see Mr. Hadley in the fall of 1958. Near the end of their discussion with him they noticed that he was looking at his watch, and they started to leave. "No," he said,

> I have at least five more minutes. I was just thinking about the Armistice Day parade. We have always had a tradition that the top ROTC student and the vice-president of the junior class lead off, and that the second place cadet and the class secretary follow. It was bound to happen sometime. This year the two top ROTC boys are black and both girls are white. I didn't want the girls to be uncomfortable, so I called them in and asked them about it. They both thought I was being ridiculous and said so:
>
> "They're perfectly nice boys. There is absolutely no reason we shouldn't walk beside them."
>
> In exactly four minutes they're going to swing down the steps of the World War Memorial, and in exactly six minutes my phone is going to start ringing. I'm ready for them.

# The Turbulent Sixties

I N JUNE OF 1960 Mr. Hadley retired as principal of Shortridge High
School. He left a school that was still winning prizes, but that also
had many unsolved problems, as did the country as a whole. He
was replaced by Robert J. Shultz, Shortridge graduate, class of 1927,
and longtime director of the Shortridge band. The *Indianapolis Times* carried this article on September 11, 1960:

## BOB SHULTZ TACKLES JOB
## OTHERS WOULDN'T HAVE

Robert J. Shultz stands six feet, two inches tall and weighs about
220 pounds. His hair is graying and he wears glasses. He is usually
smiling.

He's a man in love with his work and he's known throughout the
Indianapolis Public Schools for his enthusiasm.

It was with this characteristic enthusiasm that he tackled a job some
of his fellow educators say they wouldn't have on a platinum platter.
He's the new principal of Shortridge High School.

The job is a tough one. . . .

The high school has been caught up in the shifting attitudes, pressures and needs of an economically changing neighborhood.

As a result Shortridge has become an educational headache.

Long a strictly academic school concentrating on high academic
standards, it has little room to expand into an all encompassing institution with vocational training facilities.

Its alumni have suggested it become the city's college prep school
for gifted pupils or that its boundaries be changed to insure its fine
academic record. Both proposals have met with opposition.

Bob Shultz walked into Shortridge this summer, succeeding Joel
W. Hadley who retired as principal.

It was really the third time he'd enrolled at Shortridge. He was graduated from the school in 1927, became a teacher there in 1931, serving 20 years. In 1951 he was made head of the school system's adult education and extended school services division. Now he's back at Shortridge.

He really became a teacher before he was graduated from Shortridge. He taught three physics classes for a short time after the head of the science department was killed in an accident. . ? .

The soft-voiced principal is an expert on Shortridge. Besides being a physics, mathematics and music instructor (he describes the combination as "odd") he has served as director of the school band and as director of productions. In this job he was in charge of the Shortridge Junior Vaudeville, long regarded as one of the country's best high school talent shows. He knows the school and he knows the faculty. . . .

Although Bob Shultz usually is smiling, there are times he is serious. And he's deadly serious about making Shortridge tick.

His "little talk" to the Shortridge faculty and his "chats" with pupils carried one theme—"we're going to produce."

His fellow teachers think it will happen. . . .

Shortridge did continue to produce even as difficulties multiplied. The greatest problem was uncertainty about the future. What did the school board and the school administration intend for the city's oldest high school? Nobody could find out, probably because nobody knew.

Shortridge parents, students, and teachers mounted a crusade on three fronts. One was an effort to demonstrate the enthusiasm and energy which were still present in the school by a display of excellence. Another was to work on human relations and to make integrated education successful. The third was to persuade the school board to adopt a districting plan that would stem the tide toward an all black school.

Prizes and honors continued to roll in—for math and Latin in the state contests, for modern languages in the Indiana University honors program, for writers in the *Atlantic Monthly* contest (a third place, a fifth place, and two honorable mentions in 1964), and for chemistry. In 1964 David Marks, Bruce Seymour, and Bob Evans placed one, two, and three in the American Chemical Society Contest.

Still, the most dramatic example of Shortridge excellence came from the Music Department. In 1960, under music director Don Martin, Shortridge put on its first Choral Classic. This was an ambitious program of classical music for which the young choir members trained rigorously. Guest soloists of high quality sang with them, and members of the Indianapolis Symphony provided accompaniment. Don Martin transferred to North Central High School the following year and was succeeded first by Don Neuen, who left to become director of music at

A Capella Choir, 1957, Don Martin directing

Ball State University, and then by Thomas Preble, each of whom was able to encourage and train the young singers to reach ever higher levels of performance.

The first Choral Classics were given in Caleb Mills Hall and were free to the public. As this concert became a recognized musical event, however, the choir began charging admission. The students found themselves able to sell a sufficient number of tickets to fill Caleb Mills Hall with paying customers for two nights running. Support also came from a list of patrons and from the proceeds of candy sales.

In 1964, the first year that Mr. Preble directed the choir, the Choral Classic took another great leap forward. The Shortridge singers became the first high school group ever to appear in Clowes Hall on the Butler University campus. For this momentous occasion they sang Mozart's C Minor Mass and Peter Mennin's Symphony #4. They gave the concert first in Caleb Mills Hall, receiving a standing ovation from the audience and ecstatic reviews from the critics.

Walter Whitworth of the *Indianapolis News* began his review saying, "The annual concert, sung by selected members of Shortridge's choruses, has become a major event in the music season, easily sharing honors with other programs of the musical year," and then went on:

> The listener remembers the age of the five score teen-agers on stage only for a moment, for his attention is immediately riveted on the startling maturity of the heedful, well-trained group, whose achievement is impressive.

This year's Choral Classic was sung, last night, in Caleb Mills Hall under the guidance of a new conductor, Thomas Preble, a young man whose ambitions and skills follow the pathway of his predecessor, Don Neuen, in devoting the slightly more than two hours of the evening to Mozart's C Minor Mass and to Peter Mennin's Symphony No. 4, subtitled "The Cycle," he let his ambitions be known, and, as the young folk sang, he let it be known further that his ambitions did not outrun his talents. . . .

His comprehension of Mozart was steady and enlightened, and his way with Mennin, was, to use . . . his own word in describing the score, exciting. . . .

Preble and his wonderful group were given a standing ovation.

Henry Butler of the *Times* was equally enthusiastic:

The choristers were phenomenally good in the Mozart, which is full of difficult florid passages. They managed expressiveness in such choruses as the "Qui tollis," remarkably Bachian in its somber beauty.

They registered visible delight in the next-to-final item in the Mass, the "Osanna in excelsis," full of life and marvelous counterpoint. . . .

The Mozart was a revelation of the Shortridge Choir's enthusiasm and solid artistic achievement. How many high schools in the United States could offer comparable choral performance?

Preble's selection of the Mennin work was exceedingly apt. It's atmospheric. . . .

Its blend of orchestral and choral contributions is fascinating. Here the choristers had a totally different role, which they performed admirably.

Their quality is superb. Their ensemble is extraordinarily good.

When the concert was repeated at Clowes Hall it was attended by the composer, Peter Mennin, president of the Juilliard School of Music. "I just called him up and told him what we were doing," reported Mr. Preble, "and said it had occurred to me that he might like to attend. He told me he was indeed interested and would check his calendar. Half an hour later he called back to say he would be there." Mr. Mennin received an ovation, along with the singers, and the Choral Parents held a reception for him after the concert.

The Choral Parents had become one of Shortridge's most enthusiastic support groups, and they worked mightily for this ambitious musical enterprise. However, the greatest contribution came from the whole structure of vocal music at Shortridge, which is described on the jacket of the phonograph record that the choir made in 1965:

When a student interested in singing enters Shortridge High School, he sees before him a great array of choral ensembles. He will find nine active organizations meeting daily for a period of forty minutes. As he enrolls in one of the beginning choirs and gradually advances up the ladder, his eyes are constantly on the A Cappella Choir. Finally after approximately two years of concentrated study of theory and correct choral technique, he is ready to audition for, and possibly become a member of the A Cappella Choir. This total set-up involves some 500 singers each day.

The A Cappella, being the "top" choir, exists in a completely different atmosphere than all the other groups. While "lighter" is sung in all other ensembles (with the exception of the Madrigal Singers) the literature for this organization is at least 75% classical in nature. The most encouraging fact is the unanimous desire of all members of the choir to sing serious music. They have made for themselves a sort of "choral society," and wish it to remain as such.

The following is a complete list of works, other than seasonal and city festival music that, by the end of this school year, will have been performed since 1960:

1. Bach: Cantata No. 79, The Lord is a Sun and Shield
2. Bach: Cantata No. 82, Come Redeemer
3. Vivaldi: Gloria
4. Haydn: Complete oratorio, The Creation
5. Haydn: The "Spring Section" from the oratorio, The Seasons
6. Schubert: Mass in G
7. Mozart: Vesperae Solemnes de Confessore
8. Rossini: Stabat Mater
9. Hanson: Song of Democracy
10. Mozart: Mass in C Minor
11. Mennin: Symphony No. 4
12. Brahms: German Requiem
13. Poulenc: Gloria

.  .  .  .  .

Shortridge was still achieving and still receiving acclaim, but it was also facing ominous difficulties. The continued existence of the *Echo* was threatened. It was losing money at the rate of ten dollars a day, because of loss of advertising and because of diminishing support from the student body.

A large percentage of the freshman class now entered Shortridge with below average reading scores. Mr. Shultz set up special study tables for them and arranged for help. Honor Society members took up tutoring as a project. Still, a number of the longtime Shortridge teachers had trouble teaching slow classes, which were now part of most of their schedules. Some of them had difficulty teaching black students and sponsoring extracurricular activities in which those students participated. A number of Shortridge teachers transferred to Arlington High School, which opened in 1962 with a student body that was all white because of its location. Racial tension was cause for concern. Fights were not as frequent as they were rumored to be, but they did occur.

The choir had integrated without any difficulty. It was a regular school class with clear cut standards of behavior as well as pride of accomplishment. The Junior Vaudeville was more difficult. Black students prepared acts for the Vaudeville which were cut. The judges said they were cut because other acts were better. The students muttered, "prejudice." In 1962 the first black act appeared in the Vaudeville. In 1964, fifteen years after the desegregation of the schools, the Vaudeville had its first integrated act. After that the Vaudeville seemed not to be a problem.

The students established a Human Relations Council under the sponsorship of history teacher Roy Aberson. Its objectives were to encourage dialogue between black and white students, to promote a successfully integrated school, and to deal with any matters which tended to interfere with that goal. They were crusaders for Shortridge. So were many of their parents.

Mrs. Lowell Thomas, mother of Steven, class of 1959, Mack, class of 1964, and Laurie, class of 1968, says in retrospect, "Those were stirring times. I felt as though we were all fighting a holy war." Mrs. Thomas has entitled the mothers who fought those battles for Shortridge "Shortridge Mothers Emeritus," and she still gets them together for an occasional morning coffee, thus continuing the tradition that all Shortridge groups have reunions.

As early as 1959 the Shortridge PTA, under Educational Standards chairman Mrs. Claude Otten, held a meeting to discuss what was becoming known as "the Shortridge problem." A huge crowd of parents filled the Shortridge gym. They decided to appoint a committee to analyze the situation and present some suggestions to the school board. The committee reported:

PROBLEM:

The percentage of Negro students at Shortridge continues to rise. Because of the high proportion of economically and culturally disadvantaged young people in this group the existence of Shortridge as a fine academic high school is threatened unless measures are taken now to preserve it.

A mass exodus of families, white and Negro, determined on adequate college preparation for their children, may be foreseen with a consequent loss of tax revenue and probable racial strife.

GOAL:

An academic, integrated Shortridge. The city's investment in Shortridge's fine physical plant and the gradual achievement of its nationwide reputation will soon be irrevocably lost unless—50 percent Negro is the crucial point. Beyond that Shortridge cannot maintain itself.

The committee's primary recommendation to the school board was to redraw school districts so that more of the student body would come from elementary schools with predominantly white enrollment.

Although the school board did not respond to the PTA directly, it did redistribute the feeder schools. Because Broad Ripple was overcrowded, School 70 graduates were pushed back into Shortridge, which helped to reduce the change in racial ratio. This was short-lived. In 1964 North Central opened its new larger high school, leaving vacancies at Broad Ripple. Shortridge again lost School 70 as a feeder school.

By the fall of 1964, the number of black students at Shortridge reached 60 percent, and too many of them were failing to meet academic standards. Black Shortridge parent, Roselyn Richardson, wife of attorney Henry J. Richardson, Jr., a Shortridge graduate, was then serving on the Committee for Merit Employment, which was concerned with more employment of minority workers. She says:

It was a full employment year, and here were all these businessmen, Chamber of Commerce and all, moaning that they didn't know how to find minority employees. I said, "Well, that's because you are not in touch with the high schools. That's where your workers will be coming from. How about if I see what I can set up between business and the schools?"

They were pleased with the idea, so I went straight from that meeting to see Mr. Shultz. It was right after the first grading period, and I found him tearing his hair out over a whole sheaf of triple F report cards. He said, "We can't go on like this. I'm calling the parents of all these students to come, with their children, to a meeting to discuss what should be done."

I told him, "That fits right in with what I came to talk to you about. What I would like to do is to get some business representatives to come talk to your meeting." He thought that was a fine idea, so we did it.

Peerless Pump, Kroger, AFNB and RCA sent their personnel directors to talk to all those failing students and their parents. The business representatives all made the same point: "Without your high school diplomas you're dead. With your diplomas, there are jobs out there waiting for you." It was very effective. The number of triple F students decreased by 50 percent. This was before the academic plan went into effect.

That was just the beginning. The next year I was asked to join the PTA board. After I had turned down the chairmanship of the telephone committee and another similar assignment, the board created a new committee on pupil motivation and offered me a chairmanship, which I could hardly wait to accept.

It was a new program. To a considerable extent the kids and I made it up as we went along, but the administration, the faculty, and the parents all cooperated. I want to make the point that Shortridge led the way. We were the first school to hold "Career Days" and we had the first "Job Fair." Shortridge spirit was as strong as ever.

Career Days permitted the students to visit businesses. Eli Lilly and Company allowed one student to visit each of its departments for half a day. So did the Indiana National Bank and the Indianapolis newspapers. Mrs. Richardson thinks it was important that the students went by themselves, and that they were required to make a report about their experiences. The businesses also reported on their visitors. She says:

It was just at the time when all the kids made a point of looking terrible. I said to them, "For this business visit, the girls have to wear a dress and the boys have to wear a coat and tie." Some of them said they didn't have a dress or they didn't have a coat and tie, so I said, "Then don't go." They all managed to come up with the required dress.

The Shortridge Motivation Committee reported in June of 1967:

This committee arranged for nine companies to send interviewers for a Job Fair in June, 1966, for non-college-bound seniors. As a result, 147 out of 187 are employed, 45 of whom are also receiving post-high-school education.

and for the following year:

The Motivation Committee arranged two auditorium programs. One was based on the TV show, *What's My Line*, using four guests with unusual "lines" and student panelists to question them. At the other auditorium program, Charles A. Gillespie, Allison Division of General Motors, and Sam Jones, Indianapolis Urban League, spoke to freshmen, juniors and seniors about the realities of the business world.

The second annual Job Fair was held May 22, 1967, for seniors looking for summer or permanent employment. Twelve Indianapolis companies sent personnel to Caleb Mills Hall to interview pupils for jobs. Also, there were counselors from public and private vocational and technical schools, a beauty school, Indiana Health Careers, Apprenticeship Information Center, State Employment Service, CAAP and the Urban League. Several members of the Motivation Committee will do follow-up work over the summer to assist seniors whose career plans are not yet resolved. . . .

· · · · ·

Increased efforts at student motivation and interaction with business were not the only Shortridge projects in 1964. Spearheaded by the Human Relations Council, a large group of black and white students undertook a march on the school board in an effort to "Save Shortridge." They worked out their agenda carefully with clear statements of purpose and procedure:

*Purpose:*

We are marching in order to demonstrate that Shortridge students are sincerely concerned with the problems facing our school. It is our hope to indicate to the School Board and to the Indianapolis community that we students actually and deeply appreciate the values of an integrated education. We believe that the school system is failing to fulfill its purpose when students graduating from high school live in hate of people of other races because they have not had the opportunity to make friends among them. Above all we feel the responsibility to defend and preserve the advantages which we have received at Shortridge.

Officers of Human Relations Council, 1968

*Time:*

Students will assemble at the Meridian Street entrance to Short-ridge at 5:00, Tuesday, September 29, 1964. We plan to leave Short-ridge at 6:00. The group will disperse about 8:00.

*Procedure:*

At Shortridge we will divide into small groups. Some of the pre-liminary organizers of the march will explain the purposes and rules to these groups. We will march down Meridian Street to the School Board building at 150 North Meridian. The student group will then form a circle around the building, using the alley on each side and the parking lot on the back. However, the majority of the group should remain in the front of the building. Several students will then enter the meeting, scheduled to begin at 7:30, and will deliver speeches explaining our point of view and our reasons for having made this march. About 8:00 the group will break up. This must be accomplished quickly in order to avoid blocking the area; extra North Meridian buses will be stationed there.

*Rules:*

The main value of our march is its sincerity. Therefore an expres-sion of solemnity and determination must be maintained throughout the demonstration. Do not forget that many people will get only one impression of the march as they pass by; we must at all times be sure that this impression is a good one. We ask adherence to the following rules:

1. We wish to avoid any trouble or violence. Return no insults and initiate no unbecoming actions.

2. Do not speak unnecessarily among yourselves. We must keep good order.

3. Singing will greatly increase our spirit and lessen the chances of excessive talking. Please join in the songs strongly and with feeling.

4. Stay in the ranks as they are arranged. Safety and order require the maintenance of assigned positions.

5. Please do not smoke and refrain from noticeable gum-chewing.

6. Refer all questions and difficulties to your small group leader.

The student marchers succeeded in conveying sincerity, and Short-ridge parents continued to press for a redistricting plan aimed at integrat-ing all the schools and thus avoiding "tipping" the racial balance toward an all-black school. The Shortridge Alumni Association took on new life. Its president, Dr. Ebner Blatt, class of 1927, sent a ringing appeal for help to the alumni on April 5, 1965:

On the threshhold of an integrated world, students are fortunate if they are educated to live in the 20th century. The "Shortridge prob-lem" is really a city problem that involves quality education for all children and that poses the overall question of what kind of city we want Indianapolis to become.

At the moment the Indianapolis Board of School Commissioners has a choice of taking steps to eliminate de facto segregation from city high schools or of hoping that inaction will solve the problem.

School Board inaction in dealing with de facto segregation can affect the future city in these ways:

1. Shortridge will be an all-Negro school within five years, the second all-Negro high school for the city, at a time when the nation is striving for integration.

2. The city will have lost a unique asset, a 100 year old school of national renown, with 15 years experience of successful integration.

3. White families with public school children will not move into the Shortridge area, and Negro families of higher income and educational brackets will seek integrated schools elsewhere.

4. The exodus to the suburbs will be accelerated.

5. Handsome neighborhoods, with tax value and beauty for the city, will deteriorate without the availability of a desirable high school.

6. Indianapolis will have moved in the direction of those cities having a poverty center, predominantly Negro, surrounded by suburbs, predominantly white.

School Board action to establish the goal of integrated high schools with priority implementation in the Shortridge area, can affect the city in these ways:

1. Integration will be extended in time to all city high schools.

2. A stabilized, integrated Shortridge will be a continuing asset educationally and culturally for future students.

3. Families that would flee a segregated school will stay in the Shortridge area and others will be attracted into the area.

4. Butler-Tarkington, Mapleton-Fall Creek, and the new Meridian-Kessler neighborhood associations can advertise the convenience of a fine school.

5. As Negroes are assigned to schools in different parts of the city, many will move there. There is hope here for many harmoniously integrated neighborhoods throughout the city.

6. Indianapolis merchants, commercial and residential realtors, midtown apartment owners, and private property owners will all benefit if we encourage an integrated, safe, and vital city that will attract all strata of people instead of just the poverty core.

Spring of 1965 is not a moment of despair but the last best time to begin a plan to integrate all high schools. Education is the key to many phases of redevelopment that our new Greater Indianapolis Progress Committee will tackle. One School Board decision cannot solve all the problems of the city, but School Board leadership is essential if all the other community efforts are to succeed.

You can help by communicating to the Indianapolis Board of School Commissioners your support for action now for Shortridge and the whole city.

The Shortridge parents, students, and alumni presented their plan for integrating the entire school system to a school board that was sympathetic to Shortridge problems. Both President Harry McGuff and Vice-president Richard Lugar were loyal Shortridge alumni, but they were also hearing from many other sections of the city. Patrons of other schools did not want to have their children's school situation tampered with in order to "save Shortridge." Neither did most of them share the view that all schools should be integrated.

In the face of all this the board fell back on a plan that had been suggested by Mr. Hadley as early as 1956. They voted on August 27, 1965, to make Shortridge an academic school and to require entrance examinations for all entering freshmen beginning in the fall of 1966. In a comprehensive article describing the plan, Don Baker, city editor of the *Times*, made a number of points:

> Shortridge today is not as good as its faculty and alumni boast, but not as bad as its critics complain. . . .
>
> "WHAT TO DO ABOUT SHORTRIDGE" has been subject of debates, demonstrations and political promises for nearly a decade. It's a story common to every major city. What once was the "select" all-white residential area has become an overcrowded tenement-laden ghetto, with whites fleeing to suburban areas.
>
> But while the whites moved, Shortridge remained in their minds and hearts. It has nagged at the conscience of the conservatives. . . .
>
> Civil rights leaders believe some old grads have been too busy pointing to the pride of past achievements to face the problems of the present. . . .
>
> Enlightened school supporters, white and Negro, heightened their insistence that the School Board take steps to preserve both integration and high academic standing at the school.
>
> A biracial neighborhood group, the Butler-Tarkington Association, set out to establish good relations with residents of both races, and to maintain Shortridge as an integrated school. To do this, they had to stop the white exodus. And, in that small area within the Shortridge district, they have succeeded.
>
> But other neighborhoods lacked the leadership of Butler-Tarkington, which was boosted by professors from nearby Butler University.
>
> School officials didn't help matters, however, when they approved transfer of about 100 whites from the Shortridge district to the new northeast school (Arlington) and permitted graduates of white P.S. 70,

traditionally a Shortridge feeder school, the option of attending either Shortridge or Broad Ripple. . . .

Brightest stars in the entire controversy have been the pupils themselves. About 200 Shortridge pupils, white and Negro, staged a 33-block march to the School Board office, carrying signs "Save our School," and urging the board at a public meeting to take decisive action.

Now the school board had taken decisive action. According to the *Times* article:

The action came as a surprise to civil rights leaders, school patrons and administrators, who had expected the board to order new district lines to solve the school racial imbalance.

But Lugar termed as "unbelievable naivete" the "hopeful wishing" . . . that redistricting to get near equal numbers of whites and Negroes enrolled could be accomplished without protests and ill will.

Neither did it prove possible to turn Shortridge into an academic school without protests and ill will. Not only was George Ostheimer, superintendent of schools, openly critical of the plan, but the resentment that other high schools had long felt towards Shortridge now came to an angry boil. If Shortridge was *the* academic school, what were they?

Students, teachers, parents, and alumni of longtime rival Broad Ripple were furious and vocal. So were patrons of many of the other high schools. The black community was divided on the question. Most wanted integration and wanted to maintain Shortridge as a quality school, but they would have greatly preferred general redistricting. Gertrude Page, the only black member of the school board, voted for the Shortridge plan. Black Shortridge parents Mr. and Mrs. Henry Richardson were pleased by it, but the faculty members at Crispus Attucks were outraged. Their school had been established by law as a totally segregated institution. Through the years they had made it into a good school. It was still segregated, although no longer by law, but now all its better students were being encouraged to go to Shortridge, while the weaker students who could not pass the entrance exams would, for the most part, be shunted into Attucks.

.    .    .    .    .

In 1965, just about the time the academic plan was approved, Jean Wells Whitcraft was made head of the English Department. Mrs. Whitcraft says of this:

The very thought of following Mildred Foster as department head was awesome. She had done such an outstanding job and was so widely respected that I trembled at the prospect, but I needn't have. She left me with a staff of twenty-eight cooperative and highly qualified teachers, all of whom were committed to a program of excellence in an academic school. For example, Rachel Schumacher, Eugenia Hayden, and Gladys Brewer structured a World Literature course for seniors which was an in-depth, college-level offering.

Mrs. Schumacher used a unique twist. She began her first class by assigning consecutive numbers to each student—daily roll call was taken that way—*not* by name. As each country's literature was introduced, the corresponding number in *that* language became applicable and the students answered the roll in French, German, Spanish, etc. They enjoyed it and considered their ability to count in five languages a bonus to their knowledge of each country's literary heritage.

Mrs. Brewer also taught the Advanced Composition class, and, as Mrs. Steiger had done in the past, she became a regular in the number of National Council of Teachers of English winners, with students whose prize writings were published for national acclaim. She required constant, daily familiarity with the written language, including several sessions each week devoted to in-class writing. I remember one of her assignments was "Analysis of a hand: what it means to me." This brought responses ranging from a physical description of that necessary appendage to the more profound "Hand of God." Class attendance was remarkable. No one wanted to miss the humor-filled, personal stimulation of a real expert.

In the late '60s, a city-wide interest in "paired" courses developed. Shortridge became involved quickly and paired English and history courses at the junior level—melding the American literature and American history curricula. Mrs. Elsie Howard of the History Department aided the English teachers in this programming. She was also sponsor for a very active History Club.

Through the expertise of Mrs. Esther Hillman, who had a master's degree in art, as well as in English, and a wealth of talent in each field, a "cored" merger of these subjects was achieved. The program was exciting, although eventually the logistics of finding adequate accommodations for the numbers of students involved proved unmanageable, and it had to be discontinued.

Shortridge also pioneered in offering Advanced Placement Tests, which were "after-class" opportunities for earned college credit. Lester Groth, Lloyd Green and I administered these tests in twenty-one areas, and we admitted students from surrounding high schools which had not yet developed criteria for administration.

In spite of opposition, the academic plan got off to a promising start. The *Christian Science Monitor* reported on August 31, 1966:

There is a special air of pride around Shortridge High School these days.

Come September, this campus will be the scene of an exciting academic experiment which could well shift the tide of racial history in Indianapolis.

For years the city's school board has wrestled with a common and thorny urban problem: how to have racially mixed schools without sending whites scurrying to the suburbs.

The Negro public-school population here now verges on 30 percent. Shortridge, which had no Negro students in 1950, recently passed the 75 percent mark.

Whites in the area, in the words of one observer, were "bailing out right and left," heading for top-flight suburban North Central High School and the like. The property tax base in the Shortridge district was dwindling fast. So was the number of achievement students.

One by one the board rejected coercion, redistricting, and other common stopgap solutions.

Finally, by a vote of 6 to 1, it endorsed an idea suggested a full decade ago by Joel Hadley, former Shortridge principal: convert Shortridge into the best college-preparatory school the city ever had. . . .

"Admittedly, it's sort of an end run around the Maginot line, and there are many who feel the decision has come too late to reverse the trend," says Richard Lugar. He's an articulate young schoolboard member who has been chief promoter of the Shortridge plan since his election to the board in 1964.

However, results so far are encouraging. Of 500 applicants for this fall's freshman class, 272 with a median IQ of 110 were selected. The Negro percentage of the new class has dropped to a more balanced 46. . . .

One realtor recently reported a sale of seven homes in the area to white parents of the new freshmen.

The *Indianapolis Sunday Star* carried an article on February 20, 1966, confirming the rise of property values in the Shortridge area, saying, in part:

Dr. Roscoe R. Polin, president of the Butler-Tarkington Neighborhood Association, said property values in that area definitely have been on the rise.

Thomas S. Osborne, general sales manager for A. H. M. Graves Inc., realtors . . . said he believes racial patterns have stabilized in the area.

"White buyers do not mind living in an integrated neighborhood if they feel they are not going to be overwhelmed," he said. "Buyers and realtors alike do not believe this is going to happen. . . ."

Although the academic plan had a favorable press, it faced serious difficulties from the beginning. Two hundred and seventy-two entering freshmen were not really enough for a school that was designed for over two thousand students. Enrollment would have to increase if the plan was to work. The hostility of the other schools was a threat. So was the lukewarm support of the school administration, which was soon followed by lack of support from the board as well.

The Indianapolis Board of School Commissioners has seven members elected for staggered terms. In the spring of 1966, at the end of the first year of the Shortridge academic plan, three of the six commissioners who had voted for that plan, President Harry McGuff, Ortho Scales, and Mrs. Ralph Coble, went off the board. Robert L. Mottern, who had voted against it, stayed on. He was joined by newly elected members Mark W. Gray, Mrs. John Alexander, and Marvin Lewallen, all of whom shared his point of view.

Richard Lugar, who, as vice-president, would normally have succeeded to the presidency of the board, heard in the afternoon before the first meeting that those four were in caucus. When the school board meeting took place, Mr. Mottern was elected president, and, as Senator Lugar now says, "From that time on I would have had trouble so much as inserting a comma in a document." He says that it was the obvious end of his usefulness as a school board member that led some leaders of the Republican party to suggest that he run for mayor of Indianapolis. He resigned from the board, ran for mayor, and was elected.

The greatest problems at Shortridge, however, did not come directly from the community but from the rise of racial turmoil in the country as a whole. The year 1966 was one of increased militancy. Black leaders Stokely Carmichael and Floyd McKissick challenged the nonviolent philosophy of Martin Luther King. "Black Power" became the slogan for much of the civil rights movement. Schools and the issues of de facto and de jure segregation were central to the controversy.

At Shortridge, both faculty and students did their best to maintain an educational atmosphere. Special efforts toward racial harmony and good student-faculty relations came from two white teachers, Roy Aberson and Thomas Preble, and three black teachers, Julian Coleman, Mary Walker, and Ernestine McCree. Many students tried hard, too. Sandy Read (Ryeberg), class of 1966, Vaudeville chairman in 1965, and member of the A Capella Choir, recalls these efforts:

> We all felt enormous pressure. The future of the school was in question, along with the future of some basic values.
> The choir was certainly the most dynamic organization in Shortridge. Tom Preble was committed to egalitarianism, but he was also a

Julian Coleman

perfectionist. He drove us to work harder and harder and to set our sights high. Some people felt he pushed too hard. Perhaps he did, but for the most part it worked. For one thing, everyone recognized that he always tried to be fair. We had a great sense of fellowship in the choir. It was almost a family.

Preble also organized a big brother/big sister program. We volunteered for it, and then we were assigned to take care of the incoming freshmen on an individual basis. Girls were assigned to girls, boys to boys, but nearly always a white student drew a black little brother or sister and a black student a white one. The upperclassman began by orienting the freshman, showing him/her where things were around school, talking about various programs, and giving hints about study habits. Each six weeks big brothers and sisters would meet again with their freshmen to discuss grades, offer help, and encourage participation in extra-curricular activities. It was pretty successful. I felt good about

A Capella Choir, 1967

my little sisters, and I probably wouldn't have known either of them otherwise.

Mr. Aberson's Human Relations Council was a smaller group than the big brothers and sisters, but it had a lot of impact. The members were able to get Whitney Young (National President of the Urban League) to come speak to the school. I remember what an impressive occasion that was.

Most important of all, we had a lot of remarkable teachers: Dorothy Otto, Allen Sutherland, Ruth Richards in biology, Tom Payne, Eugenia Hayden—her literature course was marvelous—Rachel Schumacher, Doris Elkins in journalism, Bill Gibson in math, and Sidney Pratt [Sidney Pratt, class of 1957, was a niece of Mary Pratt's—like her aunt she was active in everything that went on at Shortridge]. They all were strong in their subject areas, but they taught us a lot more than that. . . .

In the summer of 1967 the United States experienced the worst racial disturbances in its history. Riots occurred in more than one hundred cities, the most violent in Detroit and Newark. Indianapolis did not have a riot, but it had its share of racial turmoil, and Shortridge did not escape.

The year 1968 was to bring Shortridge both glory and ignominy. The choir sang again in Clowes Hall, receiving its customary rave reviews. The outstanding stars of that year, however, were on the basket-

*Dorothy Otto*

Allen Sutherland

1968 state finalists

ball team. Coach George Theofanis led his Blue Devils through the most triumphant season in Shortridge basketball history. They made it to the finals of the State Tourney (the 1933 team lost in the semifinals), and they were described by all the sportswriters as well-disciplined, well-coached, sportsmanlike players. One called them "a sweetheart of a basketball team." They were finally defeated by Gary Roosevelt, whose players were considerably taller and heavier than their Shortridge challengers.

Sports enthusiast and Shortridge booster Mayor Richard Lugar hosted a congratulatory dinner for the athletes at the Marott Hotel on April 4, 1968. Before going to the dinner Lugar had deployed all available police officers to protect the security of presidential candidate Robert Kennedy, who had come to Indianapolis to campaign in what the mayor feared might be an explosive black neighborhood. It was not Kennedy who was attacked that night, however. Martin Luther King was killed in Memphis. Mayor Lugar received word of the assassination towards the end of the dinner.

After that, black militancy rose everywhere. Shortridge had its first dramatic episode just three weeks later, April 26, 1968. It involved an ancient history textbook that had been in use for at least forty years.

Very few high schools offer a course in ancient history, but Minnie Lloyd had established one at Shortridge, and, partly because she taught it, many students considered it a high-status course. She selected the text, *Ancient Times, a History of the Early World*, by James Henry Breasted, long the director of the Oriental Institute of the University of Chicago. It was written in 1916 and revised by Breasted's son in 1935 and again in 1944. Some of those who were in school in the 1920s, 1930s, and 1940s can remember that Miss Lloyd told her classes that there were shortcomings in the book, but that they were using it because it was the best one she had been able to find.

After Miss Lloyd retired, the course was taught by Dorothy Peterson and then taken over in 1956 by Dorothy Otto. Both taught it much as Miss Lloyd had. They continued to use the same text because it still appeared to be the best available. Like Miss Lloyd, Mrs. Otto mentioned to her classes that the book had shortcomings, and she gave them lists of sources to consult during reference period to provide a balanced point of view. But times had changed.

A major civil rights complaint of the 1960s concerned the teaching of history in the United States in such a way as to suggest that black people had no history. A history text, used in a school with a majority of black students, that talked about the "Great White Race" proved to be inflammatory. The *Indianapolis Star*, April 27, 1968, elaborates:

A textbook used in a Shortridge High School ancient history course for freshmen was burned yesterday by demonstrators at Tarkington Park in protest of statements allegedly derogatory to Negroes. . . .

The book has been the target of criticism for several weeks, and the Mayor's Human Rights Commission is examining the book to document any historical inaccuracies it may contain.

A copy of the book was burned at noon before a crowd of about 100, about a dozen of them Shortridge High School pupils. A "strike" which had been urged on Shortridge pupils did not materialize. . . .

At 2 P.M., the Rev. Charles Smith, pastor of Coppin Chapel AME Church, and officials of the College Room, addressed about 100 boys and girls in front of Shortridge with book ashes in a box at his feet.

At a meeting later of Shortridge pupils and Shortridge history department chairman Thomas A. Payne, Payne told about 60 youngsters that although the book has some inadequacies, it remains the most thorough on the market for histories of Greece, Rome and other historical peoples. . . .

He said the choice of terms by Breasted "perhaps was indelicate," but noted that racial sensitivities were not high when the book was being edited.

Objections are aimed also at statements that geographically-isolated Negro peoples in Africa did not contribute to the growth of western civilization through interaction with the "Great White Race." The book specifies that Negro and Mongol peoples "occupy an important place in the modern world, but they played no part in the rise of civilization."

Mrs. Dorothy Otto, who teaches the course, said she devotes five to ten minutes to the first section of the book, in which the protested comments are made, and mentions what is inaccurate or incomplete. . . .

Mrs. Otto remembers this as one of the worst days of her life, but she found some consolation from the fact that the participating students were not from her Ancient History class.

As a college counselor, Mrs. Otto could also take satisfaction from the record of student achievement. In 1968, 138 Shortridge seniors won $307,820 in college scholarships. The school also pointed proudly to having produced eighty National Merit Scholarship finalists in seven years (including two Presidential Scholars, one of whom (white) went to Harvard and the other (black) to Yale).

George Ostheimer, superintendent of schools, had announced in February of 1968 that the Shortridge Plan (the academic plan) would continue through June of 1970, but that its future would be decided on the basis of enrollment in September, 1969. Life at Shortridge continued through the 1968–69 school year with students, teachers, and parents

Wednesday *Echo* staff, 1968–69

still fighting to get their message before the public, primarily eighth-graders and their parents, in order to preserve their school's college preparatory status. All the regular activities continued in spite of the general turbulence of the times. Patzetta Jackson (Davis), a black graduate of the class of 1969 and a member of the A Capella Choir, has spoken of her Shortridge experience in almost the same words as Sandy Read Ryeberg:

> It was a wonderful place to go to high school and the choir was the most important part of it to me. Mr. Preble made us work hard, but we saw what it meant to him, and he showed us what it means to be really professional. We experienced a lot of camaraderie—we were like a big family, and I think the final concert was a significant emotional event for all of us.
>
> Of course, there were some things that went wrong in school, but mostly we all got along. We developed strong relationships and we got a fine education. It wasn't just Mr. Preble. There were a lot of dedicated teachers. I particularly remember Mr. Aberson, Miss Richards and Miss Gaines, the gym teacher. I admired Mr. Theofanis enormously—I liked all those athletes, and I am grateful to Miss Wahl, from whom I learned that math was not for me, without suffering any undue pain.

Among the things that "went wrong in school" was an explosive incident that occurred on February 27, 1969. It resulted from an altercation between a student and the dean of boys, William Merrill, which had resulted in the arrest and expulsion of the student. This was followed by angry protest from a group of students, who circulated a petition containing a demand for reinstatement of the student. The petition was presented at a sometimes stormy meeting in Caleb Mills Hall the following day.

Mr. Shultz, the principal, was in California when this took place. All he could do was keep in touch by phone, but the vice-principals Arthur Shull and R. Lloyd Green, and the dean of boys, William Merrill, all spoke to the restless group and were joined on the platform by several parents who also spoke. According to the report in the *Indianapolis News*:

> William Crawford, secretary of the Black Coalition (a group involving many separate black organizations in the city) said, "Your basic need is for quality. We're not saying not to criticize, we only say to be positive in your criticism." Crawford also told the students they should not be ignored because of their age.

Vice-principal Arthur Shull, Principal Robert J. Shultz,
and Vice-principal R. Lloyd Green

"We're dealing with a racist society, and it not only oppresses black people, but white people also," he said. "But what we are seeing now is not so much a polarization of races, but a polarization of age." . . .

Mrs. Robert DeFrantz, wife of a School Board member and the parent of a Shortridge student, said, "I am speaking to you as a black woman, and I have experienced and still do experience sometimes the harassment you are concerned about. But I think you are missing the most important point of this whole thing because you won't listen." . . .

Mrs. William F. Lieber, president of the Shortridge PTA, expressed concern that the Shortridge academic plan would be put in further jeopardy if the matter were not handled in a responsible manner. She pledged to the students to do anything she could to open up channels of communication between them and parents, school officials and school board members. . . .

This incident was followed by another when a group of twenty black students, under the instigation of one of the militant black leaders, walked out of the auditorium during a symphony concert and stood outside the building chanting their independence and black pride. They were arrested, and the case received widespread publicity, which suggested that Shortridge students were out of control.

Fremont Power of the *Indianapolis News* provided a forum for rebuttal in his column, April 14, 1969.

A teacher who has given several years of his working life and effort and talent to a high school like Shortridge understandably would be concerned about its image now after the disruptions and arrests there Feb. 27.

This is very obviously the position of Thomas D. Preble, young head of the Shortridge music department. He is very obviously proud and defensive of the continuing efforts being made there to run a workably integrated school.

Of the whole racial problem, he writes: "What we have heard and seen in the news in the last few months would seem to point out the fact that (1) integration is not working, and (2) the blacks do not want it to work.

"This, of course, could be read into the statements of numerous blacks who stand very tall and shout separatism, white racism, etc.

"For the white who doesn't quite know how to handle all this, this becomes a comforting factor, 'Well, you see, they don't even want to integrate, so why should we?'

"What a relief! We hear a few blacks against integration and we are able to justify our own brand of racism.

"I feel this attitude by a few blacks is a 'cop-out.' In other words,

*Ball State University*

Thomas D. Preble

it's a lot easier to compete with a black group, few of whom are more than minimally educated, than to compete with the world as a whole, black and white.

"I'm not throwing out the idea of racism. There is that present. It is up to us, black and white, to fight this, but I feel it has to be done from within, rather than from the polarized viewpoint of these few.

"My point in this letter is to communicate to you the idea that though these racists, black or white, seem to garner the publicity, integration is still in fashion and will still work."

Getting to the Shortridge situation, Preble writes: "If you want to see the leaders of the school, you won't find them in court. You will find them in their classrooms. . . .

"They don't make much news, but there are 2,000 of them at Shortridge, black and white, who will succeed, not because they have accepted 'whitey's' standard, but because they know that knowledge is the answer. Racism, black and white, will be conquered by knowledge. It's as simple as that! . . .

"Do you want to see a demonstration of what I've been saying? Come see 100 black and white kids give testimony to what knowledge, discipline and love can give them. It will not be the attention-getter that 20 students earlier made, but it will show you and your public that

R. Lloyd Green

integration and the love of each other which can come from it, will prevail."

He referred to the 10th annual Shortridge choral classic at 8 p.m. Thursday and Friday in Clowes Hall, where the school's 100 voice choir will be heard in Bach's cantata, "Jesu Meine Freude," Poulenc's "Mass in G" and five contemporary numbers. . . .

On July 2, 1969, Mr. Shultz asked to be transferred from the position of Shortridge principal. He was placed in the Curriculum Division at the Central School Office of the Indianapolis Public Schools, and his place as principal of Shortridge High School was given to R. Lloyd Green, who had served as vice-principal in charge of curriculum for many years. Roy Aberson was named human relations counselor.

By the beginning of 1970, the school board was discussing a proposed phaseout for Shortridge, but by fall that plan had been dropped in favor of simply dropping the academic plan and making Shortridge a comprehensive high school again. On May 25, 1970, Thomas Preble resigned "to protest the damaging attitude to the school by IPS top administrators." He is now employed by the U.S. State Department as supervisor of music for all the schools for dependents of Americans stationed in Europe. All the hard work of parents, students, and teachers seemed to have failed—and yet. . . .

# The Last Years

ALTHOUGH SHORTRIDGE was beset by problems as it entered its last decade, it had not lost its spirit. The first *Echo* of the 1970–71 school year carried a rousing editorial:

Shortridge Ready to Start
Another Make or Break Year

It appears that this will be another do or die year for Shortridge High School. . . .

The most dramatic crisis of our recent history hit Shortridge like a bomb one Monday morning in January of last year, as the morning newspaper announced that the School Board was planning to phase-out Shortridge completely. The SOS (Save Our Shortridge) went out.

The school was saved with the unsatisfactory result of Shortridge being converted back into a comprehensive school with much the same district it had before the Shortridge academic plan.

What progress has been made in the last seven years if we are at exactly the same place we started? None, perhaps, but I choose to believe that we are better off now than we would have been had we chosen to ignore these battles. . . . During the entire struggle of the academic plan the parent groups and teachers at Shortridge went "above and beyond the call of duty" in school and community involvement. . . . Repeatedly they petitioned the School Board and the school administration for help and when the school officials failed to give any assistance they went ahead and did it themselves. . . .

It is a steep hill to climb. What can you say? "Here we go again, so get ready!"

Margie Sanderson, Editor

Shortridge "got ready," but, nonetheless, it experienced a particularly difficult few years, as did urban public schools nationwide. The school was caught between the need to assist those students who were entering high school inadequately prepared and the need to maintain the standards that guaranteed Shortridge graduates would continue to be qualified for college work at any institution they might choose. English Department head Jean Wells Whitcraft says of this:

> By the early 1970's the educational climate of the city was changing. There was an undercurrent of restlessness—a demand for a dynamic "explosion" in curriculum—a thrust for something "new" to attract waning interest. There was also great pressure to lower standards—specifically to give up the English VI test.

The English VI test was a grammar test which Shortridge students had long been required to pass in order to graduate. It was administered in the junior year, and those who failed were given remedial work and then required to take it again, and perhaps again, until they passed it. Shortridge was the only Indianapolis public high school which required this test. Mrs. Whitcraft describes it:

> It was a comprehensive test, which students prepared for intensively for sixteen weeks, although the grammar had been taught in previous semesters. I don't know just when it was established. I can't remember whether or not I took it as a student (class of 1940), but by the time I came back to Shortridge as a teacher in 1958, it had been required for a long time, and both the administration and the members of the English Department considered it to be extremely important. We tried to meet the demand for new curriculum without giving in to the pressure to abandon the grammar requirement. The English teachers did an extraordinary amount of "homework" and created a whole group of new elective courses which were offered to the students. A final poll then produced the subjects where there would be sufficient enrollment. Among these were "Humor in Literature," "Literature of the Bible," "Radio Script Writing," and "Word Derivation." The new courses were very popular, and I'm sure the students benefited from diversifying their programs.

When Shortridge ceased to be an "academic school" and became a comprehensive high school again, pressure to drop the English VI test mounted. Principal R. Lloyd Green and Mrs. Whitcraft resisted as long as they could because they believed the test benefited the students whether they liked it or not and because Shortridge was a school that had always taught its students to write. By 1974, however, the test was dropped as a requirement for graduation, although it continued to be used as a teaching device. Mathematics Department head William E.

Gibson says that his teachers also were pressured by the Indianapolis school administration to lower their standards, although "it was nothing compared with the furor over the English VI test."

An *Echo* article on September 24, 1970, by Karla Saperstein, describes the extent of the problems and the efforts being made to solve them as seen from a student's point of view:

> When Shortridge returned to the comprehensive program last spring, Supt. Dr. Stanley Campbell issued a challenge. . . .
>
> Campbell questioned whether Shortridge teachers could competently teach some 300 non-college bound freshmen. . . .
>
> Many incoming freshmen have not attained the learning level of their peers. Several have not passed the fourth grade in reading and/or math level. Two programs, exclusively for these students, were begun this summer and were incorporated into the fall curriculum. Both are continuations of the summer classes and are taught similarly.
>
> The courses were very informal and included more than sitting in the classroom for two hours each day. Reading students were allowed to use their creative ability in art rooms and were given tours of several interesting sites in Indianapolis.
>
> Classes were taught by Mrs. Rosemary Carpenter, now Dean of Girls. She was assisted by six Shortridge students and one alumnus. Primary class functions were speed reading (including use of flash cards), workbook exercises, enjoyment reading and oral recitation. Tours were arranged by Mrs. Edward Tyler of the PTA Motivation Committee and Mrs. William Lieber, former PTA president. The purpose was to expose students to various job opportunities and rewards for remaining in school. . . .
>
> Miss Debby Culloden [class of 1966] is teaching similar classes this fall, under the name of Remedial Reading. Miss Culloden has two student aides and again emphasizes personal contact.
>
> Miss Lucille Wahl conducted a course of the same nature in mathematics, with one exception—she had no aides. However, she still found time to meet each pupil and her findings were thought-provoking.
>
> "I was very concerned with the fact that many were coming to school hungry," she said. "Many, I called the night before to make sure they had pressed shirts or dresses to wear and they had done their work."
>
> Miss Wahl is now teaching many of the same students and others in special math classes. More than 90 pupils are enrolled in her two classes and there are more waiting. Overhead projectors, reference math books, flash cards and close personal tutoring are methods used teaching the course.
>
> Dr. Campbell issued the challenge and Shortridge teachers accepted. It appears as if they may prove him wrong.

The Shortridge PTA formed a committee of teachers' aides to help those students who were coming into high school unprepared and to offer the individual attention which teachers with full class loads could not give. The *Echo* of November 5, 1970, noted that twelve parents were scheduled to meet the next day in Mr. Green's office with Mrs. Schwab, who would instruct them in how to tutor in reading. The article also asked for more parent volunteers and reminded teachers to notify Mr. Green or Vice-principal Arthur Shull how many aides were needed what periods, what classes, and whether or not the aides were to teach in the classroom or tutor.

While the administration and the PTA were trying to help students catch up with their academic work, Mr. Aberson's Human Relations Council focused on helping both students and teachers get along with each other. According to the *Echo* for October 29, 1970:

> The Human Relations Council will present its first series of skits concerning student-teacher relations today at 3:45 in room 209. . . .

Benjamin Johnson

Today, students will perform three skits where the pupils will take the position of the teacher in a teacher-student classroom situation. The purpose is to bring the problems to the surface and attempt to have action taken. . . .

A discussion period is planned at the termination of the presentations.

Plans have been made to have teachers perform skits in the near future to present their version of the situation.

Other changes were taking place. At the end of the first semester of the 1970–71 school year the *Echo* ceased to be a four-page daily publication and became an eight-page weekly. In January of 1972, after twenty-three years at Shortridge, eight as a math teacher, twelve as vice-principal in charge of curriculum, and three as principal, Mr. Green was reassigned to an administrative position with the Indianapolis Public Schools. He was succeeded by Robert Carnal, who had been dean of boys at Howe High School and then a vice-principal at Broad Ripple. Longtime Shortridge vice-principal in charge of business, Arthur Shull, was also reassigned to the downtown school office, and was replaced by Benjamin Johnson, former principal of School 50. When Mr. Carnal resigned in June of 1973, Mr. Johnson became principal of Shortridge and served until its closing in 1981.

. . . . .

Shortridge in the 1970s was a different place from the Shortridge that its older alumni remember. Security was a major problem; so was truancy. Still, Shortridge retained much of its vitality, and it still had its strong parent support group. Most of its students now called it "the Ridge," but they knew they were attending a school with a long tradition of achievement. They also knew that their school did its best to provide job opportunities for its graduates and that it continued to offer an excellent college preparatory education—even though its college-bound students were fewer than they had been in the past. One who took full advantage of the strong college preparatory education was black student Woodrow A. Myers, Jr. (now Dr. Myers), who graduated from Shortridge in 1970 with a scholarship to Stanford. He had been a football player at Shortridge, and he played on the Stanford team for two years before quitting football to concentrate on his medical studies. Myers went from Stanford to Harvard Medical School, and after receiving his medical degree he returned to Stanford and achieved a master's degree in business administration. He then became assistant professor of medicine at the University of California at San Francisco. In January, 1985, Dr.

Students walking down the hall, 1974

Myers decided to return to his native state to accept the appointment offered by Governor Robert D. Orr to be Indiana health commissioner.

A memo from the Shortridge PTA Board in February, 1973, entitled "SHORTRIDGE NOW" illustrates both a sense of accomplishment and feelings of frustration:

> We wish to communicate with SHS families and friends and to dispel the kinds of rumors, half-truths and untruths that surround most urban schools today. We list here a number of random FACTS about current SHS activities:
>
> SHS seniors of 1972 received over $360,000 in financial aid to attend eastern and midwestern colleges. PTA Motivation committee keeps follow-up facts on graduates.
>
> SHS is city champ in both football and basketball. . . .
>
> SHS has two foreign students at the moment: Agustin Arteaga from Mexico and Morricio Suratte Singer from Paraguay. David Ryder was SHS American Field Service representative last summer in Switzerland. Daphne Mullen will spend two weeks during March in Russia

with a special group of American high school students. Carla Spinks and Marilyn Watkins hope for France, Michelle Anderson for Germany with the I.U. Honors group.

Accelerated Math has given 5 years of math in 4 to a group of senior "accelerators." Advanced Placement tests for college credits for seniors will be given this spring in English, Math, German, French, Biology and Chemistry. Career Sampling Program sent 330 pupils out to "sample" adult jobs last semester. All students may apply for such visits.

Merit Scholar finalists are Phil Lowry, Alexis Mersky and Cathleen Walsh. On standardized tests, SHS has 7 out of top 20 in Chemistry and #1 in Math in the state of Indiana.

SHS is in its 3rd year of an artist-in-residence program. Professional dancers as well as visual artists have been in-residence this year, with help from the State Arts Commission, National Endowment for the Arts, Indianapolis Foundation, and others. . . .

Unique to Shortridge: the study of Russian; art apprenticeships for serious students with local professional artists; college credits to be earned within the SHS building by a special arrangement with IUPUI in Trigonometry, Calculus, Advanced Chemistry and Advanced Biology classes.

Not mentioned in this article but important to Shortridge students was the large number of awards and scholarships. In addition to those that were given in each of the Indianapolis high schools, such as the

The Charity Dye Library, 1976

Snow Award for the student with the highest scholastic average, the Riley Medal for the second on the honor roll, the Phi Beta Kappa award, and the Gold Star Scholarship, there were special Shortridge awards that reflected Shortridge history: the George Buck Scholarship, the Faculty Memorial Scholarship, the Shortridge Trust Scholarship, the Steve Wright Scholarship (Steve Wright was a Shortridge student who died shortly after graduation), the Dads' Club Scholarship, the Joel W. Hadley Scholarship, the PTA Scholarship Awards, the Elizabeth Nolan Scholarship, the Frank B. Wade Award, the Al J. Kettler Award, the Donald G. Klopp Award, and the Class of 1929 Awards.

In spite of all that had been said about "tipping points," Shortridge never became an all-black school. After the abandonment of the academic plan in 1970, the ratio of black students to white went up as high as eighty-nine percent to eleven percent, but by the end of 1981 it was down seventy-five percent to twenty-five percent. (Enrollment was also down to 1,432 students.) The white students who attended did so mostly by their own choice, and they speak well of their experience.

All through the decade of the 1970s, there was constant question as to whether Shortridge was to continue as an Indianapolis high school. The building was in serious need of renovation but was allowed to deteriorate because of its uncertain future. In the spring of 1977, the school board voted to keep Shortridge open and to make it a magnet school for the performing arts. In 1978 the board committed itself to a remodeling program, to bring the plant up to current safety and health building codes and to erect separate new structures for physical education and the performing arts. Later the board reneged on the commitment for repair and maintenance of the main buildings and voted only to build a new physical education facility and to remodel the portion of the building dedicated to performing arts. The Shortridge School of Performing Arts opened in 1978.

In 1979 the Shortridge PTA sponsored an essay contest among the students to write on "What Shortridge Means to Me." Three hundred and forty students responded, and their essays were printed in a pamphlet entitled *Shortridge Speaks*. One girl wrote bleakly, "Shortridge means to me what any other school would mean—nothing," but most responded positively. Here are a few of the things that some of them said:

Julia Wegner, freshman—

What Shortridge means to me? That's tough! It means so many things. It means dragging myself out of bed at 6:00 A.M. to get here. It means worrying about the test I just stayed up most of the night study-

ing for. . . . It means feeling like a criminal if I don't have a hall pass.
. . . That is Shortridge the way I see it almost every day.

Then, of course, there are times when I look down a hall or sit in a
room and I think "who else did this very thing 50 years ago?" There are
times I look at the walls and instead of seeing plain old chipped paint
and plaster, I see deep scars made by the dull blow of time. I see
memories and secrets locked up in lockers, the combinations long forgotten. I can hear the footsteps of people leaving never to return and
soon even the echoes of their voices just fade out altogether. Sometimes
when I get these feelings, a strange loyalty surges. I feel secure when I
think of all the years Shortridge has stood tall and strong, weathering
the blows and remaining good and solid as ever. I hope the feeling lasts
a long time for everyone.

## Mike Selby, freshman—

I am proud of this old school. Everyday as I walk through her
grand halls and wonder at her history, I feel a feeling of great pride.
Not only have I learned, but I have experienced the opportunities given
by Shortridge. . . .

I feel protected within her walls but not just the building itself—
the wonderful teachers it houses.

The warmth radiated from the walls of Shortridge develop within
me a strong spirit of loyalty and devotion.

I feel that Shortridge has enriched me as a person. When the day
comes, I will be able to give my contributions to society and be proud,
very proud, of my Alma Mater. . . .

## Brian Reichel, freshman—

To me Shortridge is a raggedy old high school full of beautiful
people. Shortridge is dearly in need of physical remodeling, but the
people, students and faculty alike, are far from needing remodeling.
. . . If my first year has been an example of things to come, I feel my
next three years will be the best of my life.

## Gary Berry, senior—

When a visitor enters the halls of Shortridge, he enters a spectrum
of sights and sounds, students of all races, colors and creeds working
together in a system of self-help and cooperation. . . . We at Shortridge
may be ragged and at times funny; it seems the School Board won't
give us any money. We've traveled so long, singing this song; yet we're
not tired. The tune is familiar, the words still the same; yet, as I look
ahead, we'll hear them again. Dear Shortridge with all your cracks and
weeds, you give an education and that's all a student needs.

Alphonso Bailey, senior—

> SHS has really helped me in a lot of ways. . . . The school has helped me so much that now I just feel like running around it shouting, "Thank you 'ridge for four great years!"

Finally, Marina Ashanin, senior, on the difficulties of conveying the Shortridge message to the community—

> As editor of the 1979 yearbook and chairperson of the fifth annual French Club dinner, I have been in many situations in which I have had to "Sell Shortridge." I have had to present a positive image of Shortridge High School on paper, to the news media, to parents, to advertisers, to prospective students, and to school board members. It was not easy. Even though there are many impressive things about Shortridge, people still have trouble accepting the fact that Shortridge *can* be and *is* a credit to the Indianapolis Public School system.
>
> When faced with the aforementioned problems, I found the support of fellow students, staff, faculty and parents tremendous. These people cared about the fate of Shortridge and joined together to help gain ground for the school.
>
> This type of unity and cooperation has helped me to grow a great deal. I have not only learned how to get along with many different types of people, but I have also seen the rewards for hard work and determination. . . . Shortridge has a great spirit and is willing and able to fight for what it stands for.

In this series of essays the Shortridge faculty as a whole received an excellent press. Almost all the students of the 1970s, however, place particular emphasis on the contributions of three people: veteran teacher Roy Aberson, human relations counselor and member of the Social Studies Department; Allen Sutherland, teacher of both French and English and after 1977 head of the Language Department (both English and foreign language); and Benjamin Johnson, Shortridge's last principal.

An article written by Tom Keating of the *Indianapolis Star* shortly after the school board had finally voted on February 25, 1981, to close Shortridge, describes Johnson's role:

> We often have an interesting attitude about teachers and school administrators.
>
> We pay them peanuts yet expect them to mold and develop what we value most—our children.
>
> If pupils at a school behave badly it is convenient to say the teachers and administrators have lost control.
>
> If pupils at a school distinguish themselves by their maturity and good sense, we like to point to good training in the home.

Sometimes it might be the other way around.

In recent weeks, the pupils at Shortridge High School were operating in a situation laced with emotion and strong feelings.

They were told their school wouldn't close, then it would, then maybe it wouldn't and then finally that it definitely was not going to exist past this June.

The student body gathered at rallies, marched downtown, had candlelight vigils, put together petitions, made fiery speeches and presented articulate, logical arguments.

They did about everything they could in a losing cause—everything except act irrationally or take advantage of the moment to cause havoc.

Part of the reason for this undoubtedly lies in some sort of innate common sense but part of the reason also may lie in the tone set by a low-key man named Benjamin Johnson, the Shortridge principal, and the faculty he has assembled.

Johnson, 50, is a former Butler University fullback who while in the United States Army starred on an all-service championship football team at Brooke Army Medical Center.

He has been principal at Shortridge 10 years and for some time has been in a difficult position.

"I guess I've felt like I was walking on a tight rope," Johnson admitted. "I'm an employee, an administrator for the Indianapolis Public Schools and as such I'm expected to follow orders. I feel strongly that I must do that to give example to the things I tell the kids.

"On the other hand, I love Shortridge. I've loved every day I worked here and everyone of the kids has meant something to me. They never let me down. Not once. I hate to see this school close."

Throughout the often confusing deliberations of the Indianapolis School Board, Johnson maintained a quiet dignity and managed not to voice criticism while leaving no doubt with the pupils that he was behind them 100 percent.

One teacher at the school used this analogy:

"How many times have you seen a basketball coach lose control of himself and then wonder why his team takes the cue and does the same thing? Johnson was like a calm coach on the bench and to their credit, the kids acted mature and reasonable.

"Not many people know this but the night the school board met and finally closed Shortridge, Johnson was scheduled to receive an award from the Center for Leadership Development at the convention center. It was a big award. He was named Man of the Year. He didn't say anything but simply skipped the banquet and spent all evening with his kids at the school board meeting."

Johnson dismissed this kind of talk by changing the subject to what would happen to the underclassmen at Shortridge.

"We have 12 more weeks of school and we're trying to keep everything as normal as possible," Johnson said. "As far as I know, the juniors will be given a choice as to what school they attend next year.

"Of our 1,500 underclassmen, about 500 will go to Broad Ripple and the other 1,000 will divide among maybe Northwest, Attucks, Howe and Marshall. . . .

"We're meeting with representatives of Broad Ripple within the week to talk about how we can have a smooth transition for those 500 pupils. . . . We're also going to discuss sending certain things from our school to their school in order to keep the Shortridge name alive."

The image of the calm coach in control of his team held good through graduation night. Alan Nolan, president of the class of 1941, and father of Jack Nolan, graduation speaker for the class of 1981, described that event:

> Emotions were awfully high. There was a lot of anger in the Butler Theatron that night, and it wouldn't have taken much to cause it to explode, but the school board was wise enough not to send one of their members to give out diplomas as they usually do. Ben Johnson handled the whole thing. He gave the diplomas to the graduates, and he made it a dignified occasion.

A few lines from Jack Nolan's address to his classmates serve as Shortridge's final valediction:

> You can close a building, but you cannot kill a feeling, a spirit. We should—and will—keep alive the feeling for this school. We are the last, but not the least, of a great tradition. We hold our heads high as we move into the future. . . .

# List of
# Contributors

Finney, Joan Dearmin, 1943
 In memory of Nancy Dearmin Tyson,
  sister, 1947
Fisher, Dr. John (Jack), 1936
Fledderjohn, Karl, 1952, and Mary Ann
 Hilligoss, 1953
Forshaw, William S., 1930
Fox, R. Michael, 1961, and Janet
 Wupper, 1961
Fox, Stephen G., 1965, and Donna Ros,
 1965
 In memory of Evelyn Pier Ros,
  mother, 1927
Fuller, Samuel Ashby, 1941
Gehrlein, William C., 1939
George, Nancy Elizabeth Clark, 1958
 In memory of Ruth S. Clark, teacher
 In honor of John R. Thomson, teacher
Gilliom, Richard L., 1939, and Marion
 F. Thompson, 1940
Gloin, James A., 1919
Grubb, Jean, 1920
Grubbs, Robert I., 1951
Gruen, Virginia Fosler, 1930
Grummann, Carl A., 1932
Grumme, Fred J., 1933
Gutknecht, Joan Casey, 1936
 In memory of Dorothy Naughton
  Brown, 1936
Harger, Dr. and Mrs. Robert W., 1938
 In memory of William J. Kitzmiller,
  1935
Harrison, Dorothy Belle Foster, 1932
Harter, Margaret Randall, 1932
 In memory of Arthur J. Randall,
  father, 1895
Hauck, Kenneth E., 1943
Helm, Elizabeth Matthews, 1918
 In memory of
  William Horn Sr., cousin, 1914
  William Horn Jr., cousin, 1943
  Robert Horn, cousin, 1919
Hendrickson, Thomas A., 1945, and
 Sandra Bly Shepard, 1949
Holden, Charles J. (Haug), 1934
Holeman, Mark M., 1938
Hollett, Byron P., 1932
Hunter, Jack A., 1933
Huse, Stephen M., 1961, and Ann
 Tanner, 1962
Isley, Paul E., 1936, and William L.,
 1936

Jennings, Robert K., 1929
 In memory of
  William Silver Jennings, father,
   teacher
  Frank B. Wade, teacher
Johnson, Bruce H., 1929
Johnson, Linda Walker Arvin, 1954
 In memory of Kent Stephen Arvin,
  late husband, 1953
Jones, Jack A., 1949
Kettler, Jean Richardson, 1923, and
 David Kettler, 1958
 In memory of Al J. Kettler, husband,
  father, teacher
King, J. B., 1947
Kingsbury, Virginia, 1914
Klein, Robert B., 1945, and Lillian
 Fletcher, 1944
Knox, Roland F., 1936, and Maizie Ruth
 Tyner, 1938
Laird, Barbara Masters, 1940
Lasbury, Charles F., 1945
Link, Hugh, 1943
Lorenz, Mary Jane Steeg, 1932
Lucus, Dr. Robert D., 1958
 In memory of Gladys T. Brewer,
  teacher, 1918
Lugar, Senator Richard G., 1950
Macdonald, George, 1929, and Mildred
 Sommer, 1929
 In memory of Daniel Austen Sommer,
  father, 1800's
MacDougall, Dr. John Duncan, 1942
Manly, Marian Wilcox, 1939
Martin, Wesley P., 1936, and Lue
 McWhirter, 1936
Mawardi, Dr. Betty Hosmer, 1939
Maynard, Frederick C. Jr., 1940
McCormick, Roy C., 1936, and Ruth
 Zitzlaff, 1936
McCullough, Dr. and Mrs. Ervin, 1938
McLauchlan, James C., and Juliet Baker,
 1931
 In memory of
  Thaddeus Ream Baker, father
  Alice Day Baker, mother
McLaughlin, H. Roll, 1941
McMurray, Elizabeth Hurd, 1924
McNally, Dorothea Campbell, 1912, and
 Daniel Neil, 1948, and Alexander
 Campbell, 1952
Mead, William John (Jack), 1958

Meeker, Martha Jo Cantwell, 1939

Merrill, Robert H., 1939, and Helen
Marie Billeter, 1939

Merrill, William H., 1934, and Jane
Robinson, 1934

Messersmith, Fae Houston, 1926
In memory of Lloyd Messersmith,
husband, coach

Meyer, John R., 1944

Miller, Annalee Webb, 1927

Miner, Joseph A., 1934

Mitchell, Marvin, 1955

Moffett, Paul, 1950, and Suzanne Berry,
1951

Mooney, Joseph, 1934, and Marian
Kissel, 1933

Morris, Donald R., 1950

Morrison, Donald A. Jr., 1934, and
Mary Wynne, 1934

Most, Charles R., 1953

Moynahan, Roger T., 1940, and
Bettyjane Mitchell, 1941

Mundt, Arthur F., 1936, and Joan
Cross, 1940

Nay, Jean Pennington, 1933

Neville, Marjorie Dalman, 1935

Nicely, Philip A., 1960

Nolan, Alan T., 1941

Norris, Betty Quigley, 1935

Olcott, Joan LeBien, 1946

Otto, Dorothy Lambert, 1926
In memory of Dr. John A. Lambert,
father, 1878

Otto, Eloise Byrkit, 1930
In memory of James H. Otto, husband, 1928

Otto, William C., 1926
In memory of William N. Otto,
father, teacher

Parrish, James O., 1958
In memory of Allison Parrish
Newbold, sister, 1954

Penrose, Ann L. Cantwell, 1941

Pensinger, J. William, 1933

Peterson, John D., 1951, and Nancy
Browning, 1951

Phillips, William L. (Andy), 1949, and
Barbara Nourse, 1951

Pinder, Jane Curry, 1940
In honor of Grace Buchanan Vitz,
teacher

Pinter, John J., 1952

Pratt, Richard A., 1946

Pratt, William D., 1937

Quaintance, Lucy Ester, 1957

Reed, E. Louise Lasbury, 1945

Reel, William L., 1946

Ritchey, Lydia Jameson, 1918

Roggie, Alice Marie Woolling, 1933

Ruch, Stewart E., 1935

Rust, Betty Clemons, 1936

Sagalowsky, Dr. Howard S., 1961

Sage, Sandra K., 1958

Sawrey, Joseph A., 1946, and Marion
Thompson, 1946

Schneider, Margaret Brown, 1950

Seaman, Jean Underwood, 1929
In memory of Mrs. George V.
Underwood Sr., mother

SerVaas, Dr. Beurt, 1937

Servaas, John O., 1934

Seward, James F., 1933
In memory of Kenneth G. Peterman,
coach

Sexson, Ward E., 1951, and Lynn
Boatman, 1951
In memory of
Mr. and Mrs. C. Burl Sexson,
parents
Richard J. Boatman, father

Seymour, James H., 1961

Shelton, Kermit P., 1932, and Beatrice
O'Donnell, 1933

Shultz, Robert J., 1927, and Mildred
Lawler, 1928

Silverman, Morris (Moe), 1955

Sipe, Mary Ann Russe, 1932
In memory of Mary Pratt, teacher,
1901

Smith, Dr. Charles L., 1932, and Mary
Atwater, 1937

Smith, Joan Wall, 1925

Snider, Harrison, 1929

Snyder, Frank H., 1932, and Anna Mae
Jones, 1935

Snyder, Myrtie Bush, 1909

Sommer, John M., 1949

Sparks, Robert J., 1951

Spencer, Herbert C., 1938, and Mary
Lu Marshall, 1941

Stahl, Muriel Adams, 1928

Stauber, Gene, 1940

Stayton, Dr. and Mrs. Chester, 1937

Sternberger, Robert S., 1938

Stineman, Vern E., 1933
Taylor, Helen Taggart, 1934
    In memory of Lillian W., Atkins,
        1900, and Alex L. Taggart, 1900,
        parents
Taylor, Joseph K., 1929, and Margaret
    Rees, 1931
Thompson, Merritt L., 1922, and
    Kathryn Hancock, 1941
    In memory of Dorothy Bowser
        Thompson, teacher, 1914
Thompson, Philip, 1932, and David
    Thompson, 1933
    In memory of
        Edna Stout Thompson, mother, 1906
        John Thompson, brother, 1930
Thornbrough, Gayle, 1932
Townsend, J. Russell Jr., 1927, and
    Virginia Holt, 1928
Trent, Mary Vance, 1932
Tucker, Fred C. Jr., 1935
Underwood, Gen. (Ret.) George V. Jr.,
    1931

    In memory of Dr. George V.
        Underwood Sr., father
Van Tassel, Dr. Charles, 1940, and
    Marge Little, 1939
Vickery, Betty Jane Ball, 1937
    In memory of George E. Vickery,
        husband, 1935
    In honor of the Class of 1937
Voyles, Col. (Ret.) James H., 1934, and
    Margaret Ober, 1936
Wade, Lucille W., 1927
Wakefield, Dan, 1950
Walker, Charles L. Jr., 1947
Walker, Irma Roller, 1924
Walton, William, 1967
Weaver, Bonnie Jean McKechnie, 1934
Westfall, Russell E., 1932
Whitcraft, Sara Jean Wells, 1940
White, Howard L., 1937
Wilcox, Howard S., 1938
Wilson, Dr. Hobson L., 1956, and
    Nancy Leffel, 1956
Zaklan, Harry F., 1933

## SPONSORS

Abels, Caroline Rehm, 1934
Adney, Mary Alice Claycombe, 1938
Alpert, Dr. Arnold L., 1953
Althaus, Alice Miller, 1926
Ballentine, Dorothy Dauner, 1930
Bamberger, Julian, 1922
    In memory of Laura Miller
        Bamberger
Barrett, Patricia Wilson, 1949
Batchelder, William H., 1958
Baum, Martha Rose Scott, 1931
Beasley, John Byron, 1935, and Mary
    Anna Butz, 1935
Beckman, Robert, 1932, and Louise
    Brown, 1933
Beggs, Robert J., 1953, and Katharine
    Ferriday, 1953
Berns, Herman E., 1931
Best, John (Jack) W., 1954
Betley, Kathryn Gloin, 1960
Billings, Thomas M., 1935, and Eleanor
    Coldwell, 1935
Black, Anne Richardt, 1945
Blatt, Berenice and Joseph, 1966, and
    David, 1969
    In memory of Dr. A. Ebner Blatt,
        husband, father, 1927

Bolton, Linda Keehn, 1957
    In memory of Genevieve B. Keehn,
        mother, teacher
Brandt, Alfred W. Jr., 1933
Breunig, LeRoy C., 1932
Broun, Christiana Lohrmann, 1923
    In memory of Dr. Henry Lohrmann,
        father, 1887
Brown, Robert E., 1927, and Ruth
    Hickman, 1933
Buckles, Alice W. Auerback, 1931
Buddenbaum, Gerald, 1960, and Jan
    Cox, 1960
Burich, William J., 1932
Burns, David V., 1929, and Jessie
    Strickland, 1929
Callis, Theodore, 1926
Campbell, Ron, 1953, and Carolyn
    Turner, 1954
Caplin, Dr. James A., 1960
Caplin, Dr. Richard L., 1959
Cardarelli, Victor A., 1942
Cavins, Dr. A. W., 1917
Clark, Dr. George A., 1946
Clark, Jan L., 1967
Cline, Charles R., 1935, and Marylou
    Growe, 1935

Clise, W. Kent, 1959
Collins, Charles E., 1929
Compton, Robert H., 1932
Conover, Mary K. Schwab, 1930
Cook, Gene Gentry, 1931
Cooley, James B., 1944
Copeland, James L., 1957, and Roberta
Demlow, 1957
Cramer, Betty F., 1939
Cree, Ann Burkert, 1924
Cruickshank, Betty Higbee, 1936
Daily, William A., 1931
Daily, Wilson S., 1923
In memory of Lenora Bernloehr Daily,
deceased wife, 1919
Davenport, Benner E. Jr., 1961
Davenport, Flora Walters, 1927
Davis, William F., 1931, and Barbara
Holt, 1933
Davis, Dr. William W., 1928
In memory of Frank B. Wade, teacher
Dean, Noble Jr., 1935
Demlow, Charles E., 1961
In memory of James E. Demlow,
brother, 1946
DeVoe, Mary Ochsner, 1955
Dirks, David M., 1959
Duckwall, Christopher K., 1963
Duke, Dr. Richard H., 1929, and
Patricia Tucker, 1937
Dyar, Dr. Robert W., 1952
Dyer, Mr. and Mrs. William A. Jr.
Dyer, William E., 1956, and Judith
Cutler, 1958
Efroymson, Dan, 1959
Efroymson, Mr. and Mrs. Robert A.
Evans, Elizabeth F., 1923
Evans, Thomas W., 1921
Failey, Robert B. Jr., 1933
Fay, Jane Strohm Patten, 1941
In memory of Margaret Nordyke
Strohm, mother, 1913
Fehsenfeld, Frank B., 1931
Fenstermaker, Ward (Bud), 1935, and
Maude N. Balke, 1935
Fernandes, Alvin C. Jr., 1935
Ferree, Dr. H. Lane, 1955
Fink, Mary Lapinska, 1933
Fisher, George A. Jr., 1929, and Norma
Jo Davidson, 1926
Fleck, Richard R., 1949
Fobes, Sheila Brown, 1931
Garns, Mildred L., 1920

Garrett, Dr. Robert A., 1936
In memory of Rousseau McClellan,
teacher
Goldsmith, Dr. Jerrold K., 1953
Grimmer, John E., 1948
Grosskoff, George, 1944
Haggard, Dr. David B., 1946
Hahn, Florence Moffett Milford, 1913
Hall, Christine Schrader, 1938
Hall, Gordon E., 1932
Hanika, Tim, 1942
Hargitt, Edwin Forry, 1952
Harshman, Mavourneen, 1941
Heard, Charlene E., 1931
Hemingway, Susan Gray Shedd, 1926
In memory of Carolyn S. Ashbrook,
aunt, teacher
Henry, Joanne Landers, 1944
Hibbs, Nancy Socwell, 1934
Hixon, C. Edward, 1934, and Luella
Johnson, 1936
Hollowell, Cynthia Hendricks, 1945
In memory of Thomas A. Hendricks,
father, 1910
Hough, Barbara Kiger, 1941
Houghton, Norris, 1927
Howell, Lorinda Cottingham, 1924
Hume, Jessica Vestal, 1963
Irwin, H. William, 1938
Jinks, Dr. James C., 1951
Johnston, R. Cameron, 1946
Jones, Nicholas L., 1953
In memory of Joe G. Hughes, 1953
Julian, Frances Bloch, 1941
Kappes, Peter, 1951
Kasle, Dennis A., 1961
Katz, Isadore H., 1935
Kellum, Robert W., 1918
Kerbox, William E., 1942
Kershner, Frederick Doyle Jr., 1933
Kincannon, Louis E., 1948
King, Margaret Zapf, 1938
Kingsbury, Virginia Ann, 1950
Kiser, Julian A., 1933
Kizer, Gretchen Keehn, 1954
In memory of Genevieve B. Keehn,
mother, teacher
Klineman, James M., 1955, and Elaine
Efroymson, 1957
Kothe, Shubrick T., 1936
In memory of those members of the
Class of 1936 killed in World War II
Krahulik, Irene Duncan, 1962

Krieg, Virginia Ballweg, 1926

Lacy, Richard C., 1948

Landers, Octavia Greene, 1922

Lane, Martin S., 1926, and Margaret
  Hair, 1929

Larsen, Earl C., 1959, and Barbara H.

Leahy, Harriette Thompson, 1927
  In memory of Mrs. John William
    (Hortense) Thompson, mother

Lentz, Kathryn Heath, 1930

LeSaulnier, Jeannette, 1929

Lewis, Helen Arzet, 1929

Lieber, William, 1943, and Sally
  Stewart, 1943

Linn, Matilda Daugherty, 1922

MacDougall, Beulah S. Ward, 1913

Martin, Jane Ebner, 1953

McCauley, George A., 1967

McDonald, Rev. Wallace I., 1928, and
  Martha Clinehens, 1928

McKinney, E. Kirk, 1941, and Alice
  Green, 1943

McKinney, Mr. and Mrs. Robert H., 1943

McVey, Jack P., 1948

Mead, Franklin B., 1955

Meeker, Howard R. (Bob) Jr., 1941

Mendenhall, Kiefer, 1958

Merritt, James W., 1951

Metcalf, Catherine Hoffman, 1920
  In memory of
    Harold B. Metcalf, husband, 1920
    Clyde Hoffman, brother, 1926
    William Hoffman, brother, 1929

Miers, Lois LeSaulnier, 1936

Modrall, Emily Dorgan, 1930

Morrison, Dr. Lewis E., 1936

Murray, Marjorie Anne Geupel, 1940

Myers, Joseph N., 1932, and Ruth
  Sumner, 1941

Newsom, Karen L. Tyner, 1965

Nie, William L., 1963, and Elizabeth
  Kenney, 1964

Nigh, Robert D., 1941

Otten, Lois (PTA)

Otto, W. David, 1958
  In memory of William N. Otto,
    grandfather, teacher

Owen, Kent and Suzann, 1957

Parrish, Mary Ann Ogden, 1926

Patrick, William D., 1928

Patterson, Ivalue Robinson, 1961, and
  Lucia Robinson Wellington, 1965

Peet, Dr. William E., 1946, and Carolyn
  Metzger, 1946

Perkins, Samuel Elliott IV, 1927

Perry, Douglas R., 1961

Ponder, Phyllis Harting, 1948
  In memory of Mary Ruth Fox
    Harting, mother, 1917

Price, Catherine Fyfe, 1932

Raffensperger, Alberta Alexander, 1927

Ramey, William S., 1930, and Louise
  Ellen Trimble, 1936

Redding, Bloor, 1948, and Molly
  Kuerhmann, 1950

Reilly, Thomas E. Jr., 1957

Reinken, Paul E., 1936

Ricos, Nick G., 1944

Roesener, Elizabeth A., 1934

Rose, Helen Thompson, 1920
  In memory
    Margaret Thompson, sister, 1925
    John William Thompson, brother,
      1936

Rosenberg, Dr. Gabriel S., 1950

Ross, Caroline Hendricks, 1944

Ross, Maxine Jett, 1965

Sando, Briant, 1936
  In honor of Robert L. Nipper, coach

Saunders, Lucretia Ann, 1937

Schahet, Gary N., 1960

Scheidker, Carl E., 1933

Schoch, Marie, 1928, and Marjorie, 1933
  In memory of John T. Fritsche, uncle,
    1906

Schuster, Dr. Dwight W., 1934

Shearer, Warren W., 1932

Shiffler, Judith K. Mendenhall, 1962

Short, Louise Edwards, 1934
  In memory of Mr. and Mrs. Walter
    H. Edwards Sr., parents

Smith, Robert M., 1932

Snyder, Parker William, 1946, and Zoe
  Fuller, 1945

Spaid, Gwendolyn Dorey, 1920

Stalcup, Betty Harger, 1936

Stalker, Frances, 1931

Stark, Maribel Snider, 1934

Steeg, Ted, 1948

Stewart, Allegra, 1917

Stewart, Helen Gearen, 1930
  In memory of James Stewart,
    husband, 1930

Stuart, James A. Jr., 1930, and Kathryn
  Fitchey, 1930

Summers, Lynn N., 1934, and Mary
  Jane Shafer, 1934

Sutherlin, John Robert, 1931

Thompson, James G., 1952, and Judy Ross, 1953

Thornbrough, Emma Lou, 1930

Tompkins, Stewart D., 1944, and Charlene Lammers, 1947

Trimpe, Earl C., 1945

Trout, Mary Frances Litten, 1930

Troyer, John C., 1922, and Isabelle Layman, 1925

VanRiper, Guernsey Jr., 1925

Vonnegut, Walter G., 1944

Waltermire, William N., 1933, and Katherine, 1932

Wampler, Mary E. Bowland, 1934
In memory of Edna E. Watts, sister

Wann, Vickie Hays, 1965

Ward, JoAnn Stedfeld, 1932

Watson, Alice Kelly, 1932

Webb, Dr. William M., 1929, and Maxine Ballweg, 1929

Welland, Mei Chen, 1955

Westcott, Frances E., 1923
In memory of Ferne Orr Westcott, mother, 1903

Williams, Monica Lennox, 1948
In memory of Eleanor King Lennox, mother, 1921

Withers, Anne, 1926

Wood, Elizabeth Lupton, 1930

Woolling, Dr. Kenneth R., 1935

Worth, Harold M. and Alene McComb, 1930
In memory of Roy Edward Worth, son, 1964

Wright, J. Harold, 1927, and Jane Kaylor, 1931

Wright, Virginia Carson, 1934
In memory of Howard F. Wright, husband, teacher

Yates, Byron, 1937, and Harriett Kinnaman, 1938

Yosha, Louis (Buddy), 1956

Zerfas, Dr. Charles P.
In memory of Helen L. Lesh Zerfas, mother

Zink, Mr. and Mrs. James E., 1935

Zuckerberg, Joe, 1955, and Charlotte Tamler, 1955

## OTHER CONTRIBUTORS

Anonymous

Abell, Joan, 1953

Alig, Leona Tobey, 1930

Anderson, Jack M., 1938, and Barbara L. Price, 1945

Andrews, Martha Usher, 1965

Atkinson, Robert P., 1929, and Patricia Moorman, 1932
In memory of Mabel A. Null Moorman, mother, 1899

Babcock, Charles D., 1953, and Janet York, 1954

Baldwin, Jeanette Waughtell, 1927

Batchelor, Mary Glossbrenner, 1940

Bates, Miriam Weir, 1919

Batista, Kathryn McLaughlin, 1919

Bauer, Rea D., 1922

Beitman, Floyd R., 1944

Bell, Richard N., 1965

Bingham, James E. Jr., 1955

Birthright, Mary Lee Richter, 1934

Blackwell, Charles E., 1932

Borchers, Mary B. Lennon, 1934

Bowen, Veronica H., 1943

Boyd, Alan W., 1914

Brafford, Ralph, 1932, and Betty Lutz, 1933

Brandt, Mariamelia Schmidt, 1930

Brethauer, Ellen Miller, 1965

Brewer, Helen Lambert, 1912
In memory of Dr. John A. Lambert, father, 1878

Brown, Evelyn Bentley, 1929

Bruce, Robert G., 1952

Bruyn, Nelleke A., 1965

Burton, Alpha Bassett, 1925, and Jerry M. Burton, 1950

Buschmann, Margaret Kayser, 1937

Byrne, Robert W. Jr., 1956, and Nancy Otto, 1956
In memory of William N. Otto, grandfather, teacher

Capron, Phillip L., 1939, and Marcia Matthews, 1947

Carr, Dr. Jack D., 1932

Carr, Marjory Hennis, 1933

Carr, Sarah Wills, 1931

Cave, Thomas A., 1949

Chambers, Robert W., 1931

Chandler, Marshall R., 1926

Cintora, Donna Rae Faro, 1962

Clay, Barbara Ballinger, 1933

Clay, Helen Root, 1935

Cole, R. Michael, 1961

Cook, Alice Dimmick, 1923
Crawford, Margaret Paul, 1934
Davis, Ruth Fifer, 1919
de Blumenthal, Helen Langston, 1929
Dee, Kathryn Bowlby, 1923
Diener, Nancy Hurt, 1938
Digman, Betty Humphreys, 1932
Dill, Lois Axline, 1929
Dix, Elaine Van Nest, 1956
Dodson, Lois LaFara Richardson, 1935
   In memory of
      Thad Richardson, 1934
      Howard O. Dodson, 1929
Driggs, Doris R., 1932
Duckwall, Helen Briggs, 1929
Edwards, Walter, H. Jr., 1931, and
   Lucy Beasley, 1931
Egan, Martha Hedrick, 1930
Eldridge, Lt. Col. (Ret.) George Brooks,
   1930
Elrod, Thomas J., 1935
Ewbank, John R., 1934
Falender, Herbert D., 1934
Faro, Rev. Randy, 1963, and Betsy
   Otto, 1962
   In memory of William N. Otto,
     grandfather, teacher
Fauvre, Henry S., 1934, and Marynette
   Hiatt, 1934
Fernkas, Margaret Cheesman, 1958
Flickinger, Dan E., 1937
Foster, Carol Hansen, 1972
Foust, Virginia Burford, 1935
Fuller, John L. H., 1913
Funderburk, Charlotte Schmidt, 1932
Gaines, Caryl, 1934
Gallagher, Mary Vyverberg, 1954
Gerow, Noni Allerdice, 1965
Gibson, William R., 1940, and Hazel
   Alfke, 1942
Glenn, Mary Jane Davie, 1935
Godfrey, Louise Strickland, 1920
Goode, Emma Gossett, 1938
Goodman, Morris, 1914
Gralia, Dr. Mars J. II, 1960
Greist, Dr. Thomas H., 1965
Groves, Roberta (Bobbie) Baldwin, 1963
Grueninger, Othmar, and Libby Jones,
   1950
Haerle, Rudolph, 1920
Hancock, Richard L., 1950, and Arlene
   Clifton, 1951
Harakas, Marion Peter, 1932

Harcourt, Marion Goldthwaite, 1946
Hatfield, Helen Schlesinger, 1931
   In memory of Dr. Nicholas W.
     Hatfield, husband, 1927
Hathaway, Ruth Harry, 1937
Hays, Herbert G., 1931
Heathco, Rosalie Schell, 1926
Heitman, Sara Hilligoss, 1960
Herr, Donald W., 1934
Heseman, Dottie Gaskins, 1952
Hole, Agnes Calvert, 1929
Hollis, Nancy Manning, 1953
Hoskins, Walter, 1929, and Barbara
   Barrett, 1930
Howell, Robert C., 1957
Hudgins, Thomas F., 1932
Huey, Evelyn Lloyd, 1934
Jessup, Florence Redding, 1952
Johnson, Diane E. Grosvenor, 1959
Johnson, Herbert H., 1933, and
   Bettyann Jones, 1934
Johnson, Louise Manning Dickson, 1934
Jonson, Addie Axline, 1926
Jordan, Mary Jane Clippinger, 1932
   In memory of Gilbert B. Clippinger,
     father, 1905
Kaplan, Susan Stuart, 1956
Kappes, Philip S., 1943
Kaufman, James, 1955, and Jane Mess,
   1957
Keener, Patricia Fowler, 1960
Kelly, Jean Rau, 1934
Kett, Gilbert F., 1949
King, Janet Crowder, 1950
Kingdon, Bettie Lichtenberg, 1935
Knight, Sandra Kingdon, 1957
Kwitny, Jonathan, 1958
Laatz, Mary Jane, 1934
Lacy, Mr. and Mrs. Andre B., 1957
Leer, Dr. Jack R., 1948
Light, Richard, D., 1944, and Betty Jane
   Thompson, 1944
Little, Donald W., 1933, and Jean
   McElwaine, 1933
Loer, James E. Jr., 1955
Long, Mary Alice Planque, 1925
Lueckenbach, Virginia Small, 1924
Lydon, Martha Adams, 1929
   In memory of Valentia Meng
     Cartwright, 1927
Mann, Mary Louise, 1919
Matchett, Margaret Stump, 1934
Mathers, Elsie Thiesing, 1925

Matthews, Joseph C., 1919, and
  Katharine Lennox, 1921
McCormick, Gene E., 1942
McKinstray, John M., 1932
Mess, Robert, 1955
Messenger, Dorothy Morris, 1930
Miller, John R., 1934
Miller, Van J., 1927
Mills, Sylvia Baldwin, 1953
Morehouse, Grace E. Moore, 1931
Morris, Tobe, 1952
Morse, Daniel P., 1933
Murray, Willard A., 1935, and Helen
  Boyer, 1935
Mutter, Sharon Crockett, 1960
Needler, Edna Mae Leonard, 1931
Nelson, Jeanne Spiegel, 1932
Noble, Helen J., 1924
Norman, Florence Pyle, 1932
O'Haver, Marian Johnson, 1933
Patterson, Eunice Brenner, 1936
Pickett, Frances Walters, 1922
Pierce, George O., 1919
Pierson, Margaret B., 1917
Plaut, Katherine Armstrong, 1942
Plimpton, Judith Black, 1955
  In memory of Enoch D. Burton,
    teacher
Prescott, James H., 1931
Preston Barbara Wildhack, 1950
Preston, Lucy Ashjian, 1923
Price, Lawrence, 1927
Price, M. Katherine, 1925
Pritchard, Thomas, 1960, and Donna
  Moore, 1960
Pruyn, Mary Louise Colvin, 1933
Purdy, Gail Raymond, 1956
Randall, Ann M., 1965
Rawlings, Mary Ann, 1955
Rawson, Bertha L. Drane, 1931
  In honor of Barbara L. Nelson,
    daughter, 1952
Raynor, Elise Schmidt, 1929
Robinson, Samuel S., 1933
Rubin, Barbara Blatt, 1926
Sabens, Margaret L. Schucker, 1953
Sahm, Albert W., 1933
Sawyer, Ruth Rehm, 1936
Schellenberg, Walter and Dorathy F.
  Glenn, 1935
Schnabel, Lois Kennedy, 1926
  In memory of Nell Merrick Thomas,
    teacher

Schoch, Mona Jane Wilson, teacher
Schrader, Jean Hackerd, 1938
Senn, Mary Stone, 1941
  In memory of Mary Frances Greene
Sharp, Ann E. Brown, 1932
Shaw, Carol Otto, 1954
  In memory of William N. Otto,
    grandfather, teacher
Shirley, John W., 1928
Shirley, Walter L. Jr., 1943, and Marian
  Osborn, 1944
Silver, David M., 1937
Simmons, James L., 1936
Smith, G. Vance Jr., 1948
Smith, Mary Catherine McLain, 1931
Smith, Richard L., 1949
Smitherman, Mary K. Stohler, 1951
Snyder, Evelyn Henschen, 1927
Snively, Allen B., 1957
Sommer, George, 1942, and Margaret
  Sigler, 1941
Sordean, Hattie Bridgford, 1932
Sputh, Dr. Carl B., 1933
Stadler, Doris Goldsmith, 1935
Stalions, Helen M. Jensen, 1933
Stansifer, June Wier, 1926
  In memory of
    Elizabeth Rawls, teacher, 1904
    Nettie May Hisey Wier, mother,
      1893
Steele, Betty Kalleen, 1932
Stefanic, Linda Lohmann, 1961
Stewart, Burton R., 1944
Stilwell, Ruth Bertsch, 1936
Stokely, Jeanette Tarkington, 1937
Stout, Richard, 1949, and Barbara
  Redding, 1949
Strickland, Jack A., 1932
Teetor, Mary Ann Compton, 1946
Thomas, Laurel Jean, 1967
Traubman, Libby Linn, 1959
Trent, Madeline, 1934
Troyer, Tom, 1954
Trumbo, Barry W., 1962
Tussing, Jean Benham, 1937
Tyner, Mary Zell, 1932
Udell, Jerry G., 1958
Ulen, Thomas S., 1964
Vandivier, Dr. James M., 1952, and
  Julie Webster, 1959
Vonnegut, Kurt, 1940
Vonnegut, Ralph C., 1914
Wacker, Jane Pfeiffer, 1934

Wakefield, Lynn Hansen, 1970
Walter, Florence Berrie, 1931
Washburn, Mary Lucille Moore, 1933
Webster, Mary E., 1932
Weigel, William R., 1959, and Anne
Temple, 1959
White, J. Russel, 1933
Wieck, Elizabeth Lambert, 1916
In memory of Dr. John A. Lambert,
father, 1878
Wilcox, Marie Sangernebo, 1920

Wildhack, Margaret Jameson, 1939
Wiles, Margaret Jones, 1929
Wilks, Eleanor Pangborn, 1932
Wolfe, Dana Hackerd, 1940
Wood, James W., 1955, and Sandra
McDermond, 1957
Wood, R. Stewart Jr., 1952
Young, Clarice Townsend, 1939
Zendt, Esther Hoover, 1932
Ziegner, Edward H., 1938

# Project Organization

Senator Richard G. Lugar '50, *Honorary Chairman*
Alex M. Clark '33, *Chairman*

## *Acknowledgments*

The service and expertise contributed by the following persons are gratefully acknowledged.

Nancy Barney '52
Janet Fahey
Alice Johnston
Alan T. Nolan '41
Arthur S. Overbay Jr. '41

Frank Personett
Joan Saba
John T. Sutton '34
Howard S. Wilcox '38
Class representatives

Assistance provided by many others
on behalf of the project also is appreciated.

# Index

Page numbers of illustrations for subject entries are designated by italics.

The typeface used in this book is Janson, an excellent example of the influential and sturdy Dutch printing types that prevailed in England in the seventeenth and early eighteenth centuries.

The book is printed on 70-pound Warren Olde Style which is a well established, distinctive wove-finish paper noted for its refinement and pleasing texture. An important feature of Olde Style is its built-in non-acid permanence.

Book design by Frank Personett

Typography by Typoservice Corporation
Printed by Pioneer Printing Services